DESCARTES
AGAINST
THE
SKEPTICS

DESCARTES
AGAINST
THE
SKEPTICS

E. M. CURLEY

BASIL BLACKWELL

OXFORD

1978

First published in the United Kingdom by
Basil Blackwell, Oxford 1978

British Library Cataloguing in Publication Data

Curley, E M
    Descartes against the skeptics.

        1. Descartes, René
    I. Title   194   B1875
    ISBN 0–631–19010–4

Printed in the United States of America

To my parents

PREFACE

THIS book had its origins in a survey of recent work on seventeenth-century Continental philosophy, a survey undertaken in 1968 for the *American Philosophical Quarterly* and ultimately published in 1974. I found a great deal to be enthusiastic about in that work, particularly in the recent work on Descartes. I found it often very insightful and felt we were finally coming to a better understanding of Descartes.

Perhaps it will seem strange to suggest that we have not yet properly understood a figure as influential as Descartes. Philosophy since Descartes has been so largely a reaction to his work that it is disturbing to think subsequent developments could be based on misconceptions. But philosophy is a hard subject, and understanding a philosopher of Descartes' originality and genius is one of its hardest tasks. Too often, I fear, people with the philosophical ability and imagination to understand a Descartes have not been willing to submit themselves to the discipline a properly historical approach requires: attention to texts, familiarity with the whole body of the philosopher's writings and the languages in which he wrote, knowledge of the intellectual climate in which he worked, and acquaintance with a large body of often dull scholarly work.

For all the enthusiasm I felt, I could not for very long remain satisfied even with the best of recent work. A writer would begin promisingly, then take a wrong turn and reach incredible conclusions. Or he would, at some stage, accept too easily a common interpretation or criticism. Or he would just not ask the questions he should ask. Soon I found myself with more to say than I could hope to crowd into an article. The material did not seem even to lend itself to a series of articles; with a systematic philosopher like Descartes, it is very difficult to treat one problem in isolation from others; the solution of one problem (for example, Is Descartes' knowledge of the self intuitive or inferential? or Is the central argument of the *Meditations* circular?) may require the solution of a great many other problems (What, precisely, were his views on inference? What was his philosophy of science?).

Because of the systematic character of the work with which it deals, this book has a very definite structure. Each chapter is intended to make some contribution to those that follow, and each of the later chapters depends in some way on those that preceded. And although I should hope that this structure would be evident to the attentive reader, it may be useful to make some general comments on the relationship of the several parts to the whole.

The first two chapters deal with Descartes' early scientific and methodological work and the historical context in which that work was done. Chapter 1 sounds certain themes that will recur in later chapters: that Descartes was an active participant in the scientific revolution, highly optimistic about the possibility of constructing a universal science, but also deeply disturbed by the critique of human reason offered in writers like Montaigne. There are no great novelties in any of this. Scholars working in the area will find the themes familiar enough, though some of the detail may be unfamiliar. Still, even scholars who know perfectly well that the encounter with skeptical authors was important in Descartes' development do not always put that knowledge to good use. They may be temperamentally unable to take skepticism as seriously as Descartes did, or they may have too abstract a conception of the skeptical opponent.

Chapter 2 finds this ambivalence toward reason reflected in the different methods recommended by Descartes' two treatises on method: the early *Regulae*, directed primarily against scholastic Aristotelianism, yet sharing many of the defects of Aristotelianism; and the later *Discourse*, concerned with more fundamental problems of first principles which the *Regulae* had ignored, and directed more against skepticism than against scholasticism. I feel that one great weakness in recent Anglo-Saxon work on Descartes has been its failure to attend to the difficulties of Descartes' earliest methodological work. A proper understanding of the *Meditations* requires a devaluation of the *Regulae*.

The key feature of Descartes' mature method is its attempt to justify first principles by turning the skeptic's own weapons against him and showing that some propositions are immune to any reasonable doubt. One of the central concerns of this book is to make explicit just what the criteria of reasonable doubt are, and Chapter 3 begins this process by analyzing in detail Descartes' version of one of the most familiar skeptical arguments, the one from dreaming. That argument is defended against a variety of twentieth-century criticisms, and suggestions are made about the epistemic requirements of the skeptical arguments deployed by the method of doubt. Those requirements are justified in Chapter 4, where I analyze Descartes' use of the method of doubt to establish his own existence. In Chapter 5 I undertake to show how, given this conception of the method of doubt, Descartes' attempt to found certainty on the existence of a nondeceiving God escapes the common charge of circularity. Throughout the book I argue that much criticism of Descartes stems from a failure to see his work in the context of the late Renaissance skepticism against which it is so largely directed.

Having found that there is no difficulty in principle with Descartes' procedure, I move on in Chapter 6, to the substantive question of the soundness of Descartes' arguments for the existence of God. After a lengthy discussion, I find all of them wanting, though I contend that Descartes' version of the ontological argument has considerable plausibility. In Chapter 7 I turn to the question of whether any of Descartes' other central claims in the *Meditations* can be saved from the wreckage of his system. I discuss two dualistic theses, defending one by an application of the method of Chapter 4 and rejecting Descartes' main argument for the other. In the final chapter I ask, "How much of Descartes' physics is hidden beneath the surface of the *Meditations*?"—and argue that there is a good deal more than might be apparent.

It will be seen from this account that my book is partly concerned with understanding what Descartes said and partly concerned with whether what Descartes said is true. I think the his-

PREFACE

torian of philosophy must have this double concern with truth. He must take considerable pains to discover what his author's views and arguments really were. The difficulty of this task should not be underestimated. Sometimes the work of previous historians is illuminating; but sometimes it makes it hard to see the past as it really was; often a subsequent philosopher, more concerned with philosophic truth than with historical truth, will introduce (or articulate especially persuasively) a misinterpretation that becomes deeply entrenched in the secondary literature. I am thinking particularly here of Bayle on Spinoza, Berkeley on Locke, Ryle on Descartes. Freeing himself from the spell of received interpretations requires hard work, patience, and a healthy strain of skepticism.

Nevertheless, he may hope for compensation, not just in a better understanding of a philosopher no longer living, but in a better understanding of philosophy. One of the legacies of logical positivism was a contemptuous attitude toward the history of philosophy. The great philosophers of the past were seen to be a confused lot, whose mistakes could easily be detected even by comparatively undistinguished twentieth-century philosophers. After all, philosophy is progressive discipline. If we were unable to clarify the problems with which philosophy deals, would our trouble still be worthwhile?

Although philosophy is a progressive discipline, it does not make progress rapidly or smoothly. Not everything Descartes says is true, or even clearly thought out. Nevertheless, he is an exceptionally interesting philosopher, some of whose intuitions and arguments are still sound. And even in our own day there are not so many good philosophers about that we can afford to neglect a Descartes just because he has been dead long enough to belong to the history of philosophy. Sometimes making progress may require taking a step back and starting again.

I have been working at this book for some time now, and many people have given me the benefit of their comments, too many for all of them to be mentioned here. I should like particularly to express my gratitude to Harry Frankfurt, Anthony Kenny, Martial Gueroult, Margaret Wilson, Hiram Caton, John Passmore, Maurice

x

Mandelbaum, Stephen Voss, Philip Davis, Peter Sheehan, W. H. Walsh, and the reader for the Harvard University Press. I am also very grateful to the Australian National University for providing splendid working conditions and to Jean Norman, Anna van der Vliet, and my wife, Ruth, for all the help they gave in preparing the work for publication.

CONTENTS

BIBLIOGRAPHICAL NOTE

I. Editions of Descartes' Works. The standard edition of Descartes' works is still:

> (1) *Oeuvres de Descartes*. Vols. I–XII, ed. C. Adam and P. Tannery. Paris: Leopold Cerf, 1897–1913. cited as: AT.

Unless otherwise indicated, translations of Descartes will be my own and will come from (1) or from:

> (2) *Oeuvres philosophiques de Descartes*. Vols. I–III, ed. F. Alquié. Paris: Garnier, 1963–1973. Cited as: Alquié, *Oeuvres*.

There is much to be said in favor of using the Alquié edition for most purposes. It contains virtually everything one would want, in careful French translations, and, as a bonus, has a better Latin text of the *Meditations* than AT. It is chronologically arranged, very well annotated, gives the AT pagination for longer works, and incorporates many important results of scholarly work done since AT. Its principal disadvantage is an inevitable one in an edition so compact and handy: it does not give the Latin text of any work other than the *Meditations*. Since the Latin versions of works written originally in Latin seem to me often to have more authority than their contemporary French translations (cf. footnote 13 in Chapter 2), AT remains an essential tool. But when a French translation diverges notably from the Latin, Alquié frequently indicates the fact. Variations in the Latin and French versions will be indicated by LV and FV, respectively.

There is one interesting work which Alquié does not include, on the perfectly correct ground that it is not a work by Descartes, namely, Burman's record of his interview with Descartes in 1648. Though it must be regarded with some suspicion, I have frequently cited it, with a reference both to the Latin text in AT and to the French translation in:

> (3) *Descartes, oeuvres et lettres*. Ed. A. Bridoux. Paris: Gallimard, 1937, Bibliothèque de la Pléiade. Cited as: Bridoux.

The main advantage of the Bridoux edition is that it offers a great deal of text in a very compact one-volume edition.

BIBLIOGRAPHICAL NOTES

My practice generally is to give two references for each quote: one to an edition in the original language and one to an English-language translation, if one exists. The most commonly used and comprehensive English edition of Descartes' works is still:

(4) *Descartes, Philosophical Writings.* Vols. I–II, ed. E. S. Haldane and G. R. T. Ross. Cambridge: Cambridge University Press, 1911–1912. Also available in a Dover reprint. Cited as: HR.

This is the English-language edition I cite in preference to any other, but I do not regard it as very satisfactory. It gives little editorial assistance. It omits much that is of great interest. Its translations are (inevitably, I suppose) often doubtful or just inaccurate. And for works extant in two versions, it does not systematically indicate whether it follows the Latin or the French (though frequently it shows an unwarranted preference for the French).

Until it is replaced by something more satisfactory, HR must remain the standard English-language edition. In the meantime students who cannot read Latin or French can remedy some of HR's defects by consulting:

(5) *Descartes' Philosophical Writings.* Ed. N. K. Smith. London: Macmillan, 1952. Cited as: KS. Also available in Modern Library.

(6) *Descartes, Philosophical Writings.* Ed. E. Anscombe and P. Geach. London: Nelson, 1954. Cited as: AG.

(7) *Discourse on Method, Optics, Geometry and Meteorology.* Ed. P. Olscamp. Indianapolis: Bobbs-Merrill, 1965. Cited as: Olscamp.

(8) *Treatise of Man.* Ed. T. S. Hall. Cambridge, Mass.: Harvard University Press, 1972. Cited as: Hall.

(9) *Descartes, Philosophical Letters.* Ed. A. Kenny. Oxford: Clarendon Press, 1970. Cited as: *Philosophical Letters.*

As will be clear from this list, the translation situation has been improving in recent years—gradually and piecemeal. But until we have something in English comparable to the Alquié edition, serious students (those in graduate seminars, say) will be well advised to learn French thoroughly enough to use it. As this book goes to press, I know of no complete published English translation of *The Principles of Philosophy* or *Le monde.* Originally I had added the interview with Burman, but this is now available in *Descartes' Conversation with Burman,* translated with an introduction and commentary by John Cottingham (Oxford: Clarendon Press, 1976).

II. Other Works. The following is a list of commentaries, general works on the period, and other works which I have found I wished to cite frequently:

(1) Alquié, F., *La découverte métaphysique de l'homme chez Descartes*. Paris: Presses Universitaires de France, 1950. Cited as: Alquié, *Découverte*.

(2) Beck, L. J. *The Method of Descartes, a Study of the Regulae*. Oxford: Clarendon Press, 1952. Cited as: Beck, *Method*.

(3) —— *The Metaphysics of Descartes, a Study of the Meditations*. Oxford: Clarendon Press, 1965. Cited as: Beck, *Metaphysics*.

(4) Blake, R. M., C. J. Ducasse, and E. H. Madden, eds. *Theories of Scientific Method, the Renaissance through the Nineteenth Century*. Seattle: University of Washington Press, 1960. Cited as: Blake, Ducasse, and Madden.

(5) Caton, H. *The Origin of Subjectivity, an Essay on Descartes*. New Haven: Yale University Press, 1973. Cited as: Caton.

(6) Doney, W., ed. *Descartes, a Collection of Critical Essays*. Garden City, N.Y.: Doubleday/Anchor, 1967. Cited as: Doney.

(7) Frankfurt, H. *Demons, Dreamers and Madmen*. Indianapolis: Bobbs-Merrill, 1970. Cited as: Frankfurt.

(8) Gilson, E. *Discours de la méthode, texte et commentaire*. Paris: J. Vrin, 1947. Cited as: Gilson.

(9) —— *Nouvelles réflexions sur la preuve ontologique de Descartes*. Paris: J. Vrin, 1955. Cited as: Gueroult, *Réflexions*.

(10) Gueroult, M. *Descartes selon l'ordre des raisons*. 2 vols. Paris: Aubier, 1953. Cited as: Gueroult, *Ordre*.

(11) Kenny, A. *Descartes*. New York: Random House, 1968. Cited as: Kenny.

(12) Montaigne, Michel de. *The Complete Essays*, trans. D. Frame. Stanford: Stanford University Press, 1957. Cited as: Montaigne.

(13) Popkin, R. *The History of Scepticism from Erasmus to Descartes*, rev. ed. New York: Harper and Row, 1964. Cited as: Popkin.

(14) Ryle, G. *The Concept of Mind*. London: Hutchinson's University Library, 1949. Cited as: Ryle.

(15) Smith, N. K. *New Studies in the Philosophy of Descartes*. London: Macmillan, 1952. Cited as: Kemp Smith.

Items (5) and (6) contain useful bibliographies of recent work on Descartes. For still more recent work, students may consult *The Philosopher's Index*, a computerized guide to current philosophical research in general, and the *Archives de philosophie*, which offers a running bibliography of work on Descartes.

Translations of twentieth-century commentaries are my own.

DESCARTES
AGAINST
THE
SKEPTICS

Another error is an impatience of doubt, and haste to assertion without due and mature suspension of judgment . . . if a man will begin with certainties, he shall end in doubts; but if he will be content to begin with doubts, he shall end in certainties.

—Bacon, *The Advancement of Learning.*

1

THE PROBLEM

Philosophy may be born in wonder, but it is kept alive by dissatisfaction, by the feeling that our predecessors and contemporaries have not got things straight, and that some better answer can be found to the questions which perplex us. To understand a philosopher it is essential to find out what his questions were and why he was dissatisfied with existing answers to them.

Descartes' fundamental question is this: is it possible to work out a scientific account of the nature of things which will be perfectly general, intelligible to anyone, and absolutely certain? The answer he wants to give, and hopes to be able to defend, is "yes." Thus the original title of his first published work, now familiar to us as the *Discourse on Method*, was to have been: "The Project of a Universal Science Which Could Raise Our Nature to Its Highest Degree of Perfection."[1] Expressions of this optimism about man's capacity for knowledge go back to the earliest writings we have from Descartes:

> The sciences are now masked. If the masks were lifted, they would appear in all their beauty. To someone who sees completely the chain of the sciences, it will seem no more difficult to retain them in his mind than to retain the series of numbers. (Alquié, *Oeuvres* I, 46)

Note that we have here both hope for the future and a condemnation of the present. *Now* the sciences are masked.

The early years of the seventeenth century were indeed a time

1. Letter to Mersenne, March 1636, Alquié, *Oeuvres* I, 516; *Philosophical Letters*, 28.

when an intelligent observer might view the existing state of science with mixed feelings. The medieval world picture, with its blend of Aristotelian physics and Ptolemaic astronomy, was crumbling. The Newtonian system which was ultimately to replace it was yet to be formulated. Some of the elements which were to make up the Newtonian system were already available. As early as 1543 Copernicus had formulated a heliocentric astronomy. During the years in which Descartes was being schooled by the Jesuits at La Flèche, Kepler was working out his laws of planetary motion, and Galileo was making, with his new telescope, the discoveries Descartes was to write so enthusiastically about in the opening lines of his *Dioptrique*:

> The whole conduct of our life depends on our senses, among which sight is the most comprehensive and noble; there is no doubt that the inventions which serve to increase its power are the most useful there can be. And it is difficult to find any invention which increases the power of sight more than do those marvelous telescopes, which have revealed, in the short time they have been in use, more new stars in the heavens . . . than have ever been seen there before. (AT VI, 80–81; Olscamp, 65)

Nevertheless, Descartes recognized that much work remained to be done. That admirable instrument had been stumbled on by chance, not invented by following a proper scientific method. And so long as its construction lay in the hands of men who did not understand the principles of optics, it would remain imperfect. So it was necessary to study optics. But it is characteristic of Descartes that he conceived this study very broadly. It was concerned not only with the behavior of light rays but also with the laws of mechanics which explain that behavior, and with the physiology of vision.

This passion for a system, for a unified science, is one of the features which distinguishes Descartes' scientific work. And it did respond to a need in the science of his day. Recent work by historians of science, like T. S. Kuhn, has emphasized that acceptance of the new ideas was, properly, very gradual, that many problems remained unsolved, and that the new astronomy could not triumph until it was fitted into a satisfactory general theory, which included a new mechanics.

It was part of Descartes' ambition to provide that general

theory, and it is a mark of his genius that by his death in 1650, he had, in some measure, succeeded. In the mid-seventeenth century, Cartesian science did present itself as a very real alternative to Aristotelian science. And arguably, it made an important contribution to the developing Newtonian scheme.[2]

Were it not for the Inquisition, the first work Descartes published would have been a critique of scholastic physics and a sketch of the mechanistic physics he hoped to establish in its place, *Le monde*. He was at work on this in the early 1630s, and was very near publishing it, when he learned that Galileo had been condemned for holding that the earth moves. The same doctrine was integral to Descartes' own treatise, as he indicated in a letter to Mersenne (November 1633):

> If this is false, all the foundations of my philosophy are false also, for they demonstrate it very clearly. And it is so connected with all the parts of my treatise, that I would not know how to eliminate it without great harm to the rest. (Alquié, *Oeuvres* I, 488)

So the publication of *Le monde* had to wait until 1664, many years after Descartes' death. Though left unfinished, it provides a very good introduction to Cartesian science.

To the modern reader the beginning of *Le monde* is apt to seem somewhat odd for a scientific treatise. Descartes starts out by distinguishing sharply between our ideas and those features of the physical world which produce them. But this is symptomatic of a radically revised picture of the physical world. Superficially, the Cartesian theory of matter may not seem greatly different from the Aristotelian theory. As in the Aristotelian account, there is a division of bodies into elementary ones, composed simply of one element, and mixed bodies, composed of more than one element. Like the Aristotelians, Descartes rejects the notion of a void. Though he reduces the number of elements from four (earth, air, fire, and water) to three (corresponding roughly to earth, air, and fire), this may seem a comparatively minor economy.

If we examine the character of these elements, however, we find a marked difference. Where the Aristotelian elements are distin-

2. See Brian Ellis, "The Origin and Nature of Newton's Laws of Motion," in *Beyond the Edge of Certainty*, ed. Robert Colodny (Englewood Cliffs, N.J.: Prentice-Hall, 1965), pp. 29–68.

guished from one another by such qualities as heat or cold, dryness or moisture, the Cartesian elements are composed of fundamentally the same kind of matter—particles of one element being distinguished from those of another only by geometric and kinematic properties. The first element, analogous to the fire of traditional theory, is composed of the smallest, fastest moving particles, which are so flexible that they can not be said to have any determinate shape. The second element, comparable to the air of traditional theory, is composed of larger particles, round in shape and moving rapidly. The third element, analogous to the earth of traditional theory, is composed of the largest, slowest moving particles.

Many qualities that existing physical theory takes as fundamental, Descartes thinks he can explain in terms of these geometric and kinematic properties:

> If you find it strange that, to explain these elements, I do not use the qualities they call heat, cold, moisture and dryness, as the philosophers do, I shall tell you that these qualities seem to me to stand in need of explanation themselves. Unless I am deceived, not only these four qualities, but also all the others, and even all the forms of inanimate bodies, can be explained, without there being any need to suppose, for this effect, anything else in their matter except the motion, size, shape and arrangement of its parts. (AT XI, 25–26)

Here Descartes is not merely rejecting a particular theory. He is setting himself in opposition to a whole style of explanation, a style for which Aristotle himself cannot be held directly responsible, but which his medieval followers deployed very widely:

> For medieval and later peripatetic scientists, whatever caused sense perception was assumed to be a form or quality. Heat, color, solidity, fluidity, taste, odor, volatility, corrosiveness and a host of other properties were perceptible because the body under observation possessed, more or less completely, certain forms. The classic example is that of heat; when fire was applied to a body, it grew hot by acquiring temporarily from the fire the "form of heat"; if it received this form imperfectly, the body cooled upon removal from the fire; if it were capable of receiving the form perfectly, it caught fire and would then communicate the form to other bodies.[3]

3. M. Boas, "The Establishment of the Mechanical Philosophy," *Osiris*, 10 (1952), 415–416.

For Descartes this manner of explaining a phenomenon was simply too easy. Anything could be explained in this way, and so nothing was really explained. By contrast the mechanical explanations of Cartesian science were peculiarly intelligible. So Descartes wrote to Plempius (3 October 1637):

> If my philosophy seems too crass to [Fromondus], because, like mechanics, it considers shapes, sizes and motions, he condemns what I think is above all worthy of praise, and what I principally prefer in my system . . . namely, that in my manner of philosophizing no reason is admitted which is not mathematical or evident, and no conclusions which are not confirmed by very certain experiments. (Alquié, *Oeuvres* I, 792)

So powerful did this new style of explanation seem that by the latter part of the seventeenth century the doctrine of substantial forms was little more than a subject for ridicule on the popular stage.

Similarly, Descartes rejects explanations which attribute to non-human nature anything which appears to involve the distinctively mental attribute of thought:

> When the wine which is in a barrel does not run through the opening in the bottom because the top is closed, they speak improperly who say, as is ordinarily done, that this happens because of fear of the void. They know perfectly well that the wine does not have a mind with which it could fear anything; and even if it did, I know of no reason why it should fear the void, which is, in fact, only a chimera. (AT XI, 20)

The correct explanation of the phenomenon, in Cartesian terms, is that since matter is to be identified with extension, there is and can be no empty space. A vacuum is a contradiction in terms. Hence, the world is a plenum, in which all motion must be in a closed curve. Body A can only move if it pushes body B out of its way, B must in turn push C, and sooner or later we must get back to A. The wine stays in the barrel because the top of the barrel prevents the "circle of moving bodies" from being formed.

Now so far we do not have very much that is distinctively Cartesian. The rejection of substantial forms and of teleological explanations of the behavior of inanimate objects is common property among a number of Descartes' contemporaries, as is the insistence on mechanical explanations. Galileo, Bacon, Gassendi, Hobbes, and many lesser figures were all arguing, independently, for much the same sort of antischolastic program. The rejection of the void does set Descartes apart from most of the other new philosophers, but is a point of similarity with scholastic Aristotelianism.

What is most interesting and novel in *Le monde* is the way Descartes carries out his program. After setting out his theory of matter he lays down various laws of nature which are supposed to govern the operation of these material bodies. He assumes, of course, a creationist point of view. God has created the material world and has endowed bodies with a certain initial quantity of motion. But subsequent changes in the world are due not to divine action directly but to the operation of one body on another, according to laws God has established. Created things are entirely dependent on God for their continued existence. Unless he conserves a body from one moment to the next, it will cease to exist. But God is immutable. Hence he will conserve it as it is. Any change it undergoes must therefore be due to an encounter with some other body. (See *Le monde*, chapter vii.)

Here we have a metaphysical or, perhaps more accurately, a theological approach to physics which is distinctively Cartesian. One consequence of this approach is that we find in Descartes one of the earliest correct statements of the principle of inertia, and the origin of the principle of the conservation of momentum. If any change a body undergoes is due to interaction with some other body, then a body which is at rest and not acted on by any other body will remain at rest. A body which is in motion and not acted on by any other body will continue in motion in a straight line. The only way bodies can interact, on this theory, is for them to collide, and the laws of impact are governed by the fundamental principle that in any collision the total quantity of motion is preserved. Anything else would be incompatible with God's nature as an immutable being.

Descartes proceeds from this foundation of the laws of mechanics in the divine nature to give an account of what he considers to be the principal phenomena of the physical world. We get a heliocentric description of the solar system, mechanical explanations of planetary motion, of the rotation of the moon around the earth and of the earth on its axis, an explanation of gravity, of the tides, of light and its main properties—and finally, a detailed examination of the human body, complete with mechanical explanations of its chief functions, such as the circulation of the blood, respiration, digestion, perception, and even, insofar as they have a physiological basis, imagination and memory.[4]

It is, literally, an incredible story, and we cannot follow Descartes into all its details. As a piece of purely scientific work, it had both great strengths and great weaknesses. In 1644 Descartes succeeded in revising his system in such a way that its Copernican character was concealed and it could be published. Of this version one historian of science has written that it was

a triumph of fantastic imagination which . . . never once . . . hit upon a correct explanation. Yet it was also a work full of creative ideas, if only because Descartes had observed faithfully the tenets of his own—and the seventeenth century's—mechanical philosophy. . . . The particular mechanisms described by Descartes were absurd, but the ambition to know them and the form he adopted for them were not. For this reason Cartesian science was taken seriously for a hundred years, and one can fairly describe such a scientist as Christian Huygens as a Cartesian, though he by no means subscribed to all the Cartesian explanations. Huygens looked at the world in the same manner as Descartes and expected to find the same kind of mechanisms in it, including the aether and the vortices. Indeed, it is impossible to open any book on physical science written between 1650 and 1720, not excepting Newton's *Principia*, without coming across the problems that Descartes had tried to solve in the mechanical way, without recognising his shadow.[5]

It is, of course, an exaggeration—if one is speaking of Descartes' scientific work as a whole—to say that he never hit on a correct explanation. To take only one example, Descartes' treatment of the rainbow "made a decided advance on previous accounts," precisely

4. The *Traité de l'homme*, though traditionally treated as a separate work, is in fact only a part of *Le monde*. Cf. Alquié, *Oeuvres* I, 307.

5. A. R. Hall, *From Galileo to Newton: 1630–1720* (New York: Harper and Row, 1963), pp. 120–121.

because it did explain certain features of the rainbow which had not been explained before.[6] But if it would be equally an understatement to say that Descartes' reach exceeded his grasp, that is at least partly because his reach was so ambitious.

Le monde is Descartes' first substantial attempt to realize his program of a universal science and it illustrates the close connection which Descartes insisted on between philosophy and science. Descartes would not distinguish them in the way we are accustomed to and his interest in science is not merely in what we now call philosophy of science. In the *Principles* he writes that

> the whole of philosophy is like a tree, whose roots are metaphysics, whose trunk is physics and whose branches are all the other sciences, which may be reduced to three principal sciences: medicine, mechanics and morals. (Alquié, *Oeuvres* III, 779; HR I, 211)

It was a tree, we must add, which Descartes, like Bacon, wished to cultivate, not for its own sake alone but also for the sake of the fruit which might be gathered from its branches, for the mastery of nature which a more accurate understanding of nature would yield. (AT VI, 61; HR I, 119)

Such, in general, is the nature of Cartesian science. But Descartes' project called for a system of knowledge which was not only comprehensive and intelligible but also absolutely certain. After the fundamental features of Cartesian science have been worked out in *Le monde*, it is the problem of certainty and associated problems of methodology which preoccupy Descartes in much of his later work. Reflection on the character of the period in which he wrote can help us to understand this preoccupation.

The system of explanation inherited by the medieval philosophers from Aristotle and Ptolemy had been an extraordinarily

6. Such as the appearance of the colored circles at the observed angles and the appearance of the secondary bow. Cf. A. I. Sabra, *Theories of Light from Descartes to Newton* (London: Oldbourne, 1967), pp. 61–68. Descartes also appears to have discovered the law of the specific energy of the nerves before Muller and Snell's law independently of Snell. Cf. Alquié, *Oeuvres*, I, 700–701, 673, 563–564. He also appears to have known of the circulation of the blood before he knew of Harvey's proofs of it. Cf. Hall, xl. On the significance of this discovery, see J. A. Passmore, "William Harvey and the Philosophy of Science," *Australasian Journal of Philosophy*, 36 (1958), 85–94.

stable one—it had lasted over a thousand years with wide support and relatively few modifications. Then, within a period of a hundred years, it was successfully attacked and changed in a great many fundamental respects. It was not just that the movements of the heavenly bodies were explained differently—scientists were working toward a new way of looking at all motion, and in the process they were even changing their conception of the sort of thing that would count as an explanation. Explanations in terms of purposes, so-called final causes, were replaced by explanations in terms of mathematical laws. The new explanations were seen to be more satisfying intellectually. Progress was being made after what looked in retrospect to have been a long period of stagnation.

It is not surprising, then, that the "new" philosophers of the seventeenth century were much interested in scientific method and wrote books with titles like *Discourse on the Method of Rightly Conducting One's Reason and Searching for Truth in the Sciences* or *Rules for the Direction of the Mind* or *Treatise on the Correction of the Intellect* or *The Advancement of Learning*. Philosophers like Descartes, Bacon, and Spinoza wanted to analyze the causes of error, to understand why science had failed for so long to progress, and to work out a methodology which would insure that the progress newly begun would continue.

It is also not surprising that someone like Descartes should be concerned with the problem of certainty. For the scientific revolution provided, or seemed to provide, a perfect illustration of the central thesis of skepticism. It may be paradoxical that a period of tremendous advance in scientific knowledge should be favorable to the view that nothing can be known; but what looks in retrospect like a century and a half of continuous scientific advance did not—and could not—so appear to the view of the latter half of the sixteenth and the early years of the seventeenth centuries. The resistance to the new theories of the heavens and of the motions of bodies was not solely the result of an irrational intellectual conservatism. In addition to the theological objections to the new science there were persuasive scientific objections as well, and such scientific advantages as the new theories possessed were neither decisive nor such as could be appreciated by any but skilled scientists.[7] Those who did perceive that the Copernican hypothesis represented the most fruitful path of development for science are rightly regarded as geniuses. And they were often motivated in part by considerations that were not purely scientific—as Kepler, with his number mysticism and sun worship, illustrates. To the average intelligent nonscientist, accustomed, as nonscientists generally are, to being guided by the consensus of the learned, the destruction of a scientific world view which had had nearly universal acceptance for over a thousand years was deeply disturbing. It seemed to illustrate nothing so well as the skeptical position that for any given proposition counterarguments can be found as forceful as any of the arguments in its favor.

Again, the proponents of the new science were often in the position of denying propositions which had come to seem part of common sense. So, for example, Descartes writes in the first paragraph of *Le monde* that "everyone is commonly persuaded that the ideas we have in our thought are entirely like the objects from which they proceed" (AT XI, 3); but it is part of his project to cast doubt on this. And though the so-called rationalist is as likely as any empiricist to appeal to experience in support of his doubts—and does appeal to experience in the passage cited—the tendency of his argument is to emphasize the great difference between the world we experience and the world as it is in itself. Moreover, one implication of his work on the physiology of perception was that our perceptions were the result of a complex process and that the same perception might be produced in a variety of ways. So the scientific study of perception had an embarrassing tendency to undermine its own foundation.

Developments in religion had a similarly disturbing effect; for this was the era of the Reformation and the Counter Reformation.[8] Luther, in challenging the authority of the Catholic Church, rejected a criterion of religious truth which had been accepted for

7. See, e.g., T. S. Kuhn, *The Copernican Revolution* (Cambridge, Mass.: Harvard University Press, 1957).

8. See Popkin's *History of Scepticism* and his article, "The Sceptical Origins of the Modern Problem of Knowledge," in *Perception and Personal Identity*, ed. N. Care and R. Grimm (Cleveland: Case Western Reserve University Press, 1969).

over a thousand years. The new criterion, which held that what conscience is compelled to believe on reading Scripture is true, was an invitation to anarchy. A wide diversity of new sects arose, representing, apparently, all possible varieties of religious position, agreeing with Luther in maintaining that Scripture was the test of truth, but disagreeing with his interpretation of Scripture in nearly every important respect.

If the use of Luther's criterion led quickly to disruption, the challenge to the Catholic criterion gave prominence to a fundamental and ancient philosophical problem, the problem of the criterion. To say that what is true in religion is what conscience is compelled to believe after a careful reading of Scripture is evidently to put forward a thesis in religion. Now we want to know whether or not this thesis is true. But plainly, if we defend this criterion of religious truth by maintaining that it is what we are compelled to believe after a careful reading of Scripture, we lay ourselves open to the accusation of reasoning in a circle, just as much as the Catholic does if he defends the right of the Church, through its councils and papal decrees, to determine religious truth, on the basis of the Church's own pronouncement that it is the final authority in matters of religion.

To determine the truth in matters of religion, we need a criterion of truth. We are faced with competing candidates for the office. Not wishing to make the choice arbitrarily, we require a proof of the validity of whatever criterion we accept. But to judge the soundness of the proof, we require a criterion of truth, which is what we were looking for to begin with. Either we opt arbitrarily and irrationally for one criterion rather than another, or we reason in a circle, or we are off on an infinite regress of proofs which need to be supported by further proofs. So the standard skeptical dialectic ran.

The intellectual atmosphere in the latter half of the sixteenth century and the early years of the seventeenth century was a turbulent one, with radically opposed points of view widely held and persuasively argued for by their adherents. To these trends in science and religion we must add the effect of the discoveries made by travelers to the new world. The European imagination was fired with stories of new races of people, with different opinions, customs, and laws. By the end of the sixteenth century, circumstances could hardly have been more propitious for the rediscovery of the manuscripts of Sextus Empiricus. Sextus' manuals of ancient skeptical arguments quickly came to the attention of intelligent Europeans, and his influence was a profound one.[9]

Sextus distinguishes between two varieties of skepticism: the academic and the pyrrhonian. The academic holds that nothing can be known with certainty except this one thing—that nothing can be known. It allows, however, that some opinions are more probable than others, and proposes probability as the guide of life. Pyrrhonian skepticism is a more radical position. It holds that the academics are dogmatic even to affirm the impossibility of certain knowledge and denies that propositions differ in their probability. A judgment of probability can be made only by someone who possesses a standard of knowledge and truth. But the existence of such a standard is just what the pyrrhonians question. Since probability cannot guide our choices, they propose to follow custom.

In the late sixteenth century the pyrrhonian variety of skepticism was the most important and influential, particularly in the form in which it was stated by Montaigne. For our purposes, Montaigne's principal work was his "Apology for Raymond Sebond." Sebond was a theologian, the author of a book entitled *Natural Theology*, which was designed to prove all the articles of the Christian faith by human reason. Montaigne's first venture into print had been a translation of Sebond into French, undertaken at the bidding of his father. But some years later, in the second book of his essays, he returned to the subject of Sebond again, purportedly to defend Sebond against certain accusations that had been made against him.

The first of these accusations was that Christians do wrong to try to support their beliefs by human reason, that Christian belief is properly founded only on a faith inspired by divine grace. Montaigne replies by substantially conceding the truth of the charge—"it is faith and faith alone which embraces the high mysteries of our religion." Nevertheless, he maintains, we do not

9. Latin translations of the *Outlines of Pyrrhonism* and of Sextus' complete works were published in 1562 and 1569, respectively. For details on the revival of Greek skepticism, see Popkin, chap. II.

properly serve God unless we devote all of our activities to his honor. To do this we must accompany our faith with all the reason we possess.[10]

The second accusation to be met was that Sebond's arguments were not very good. This Montaigne counters by mounting a general attack on human reason. Sebond's arguments may well be weak—Montaigne does nothing to defend any of them directly— still, with all their faults, they are no worse than any other arguments.

The themes Montaigne employs in his attack on reason are familiar ones. Traditional philosophy had emphasized the central position of man in God's plan; man was supposed to be raised above the lower animals by his possession of reason and language. So Montaigne begins with an extended comparison of man and beast, all to the detriment of man. No human virtue can be found, either intellectual or moral or physical, which cannot be duplicated or surpassed in some animal, and Montaigne has a hundred illustrations from fabulous natural history to prove it, all designed to remind man of his weakness and to subdue his pride in his own abilities.[11]

The argument is reinforced by a variety of considerations: that philosophical, religious, and moral beliefs vary from one age and one country to another, that what a person believes tends to depend on irrational factors such as emotion, will, and childhood training—and most important, perhaps, that, insofar as our beliefs have any rational foundation at all, that foundation lies in the unreliable testimony of our senses.

If it were possible to have knowledge, that knowledge would have to come through the senses. So Montaigne is, in a way, an empiricist. But he is, of course, profoundly dubious of the testimony of the senses. This is not merely because they sometimes deceive us, or because what they tell us seems to depend as much

10. Cf. Descartes, "I think that all those to whom God has given the use of . . . reason are obligated to use it principally to try to know him and to know themselves." Letter to Mersenne, 15 April 1630, Alquié, Oeuvres I, 258; Philosophical Letters, 10.

11. For an interesting discussion of Montaigne's views on animals, see Descartes' letter to the Marquess of Newcastle, 23 November 1646, Alquié, Oeuvres III, 693–696; Philosophical Letters, 206–208.

on the state of the perceiver—on his health, sanity, mood, degree of alertness, and so on—as it does on the nature of the thing perceived and the external conditions of perception. Montaigne is also bothered by difficulties about the senses which are not so obvious.

Consider the possibility of our lacking certain senses we might have had. We are all aware that many of the animals seem to lack senses we are provided with. Some live their entire life without sight or hearing, a misfortune which happens to humans as well. We know that a human being born blind will have a very imperfect idea of the nature of the world around him—of distances, shapes, sizes, colors, and so on. Now suppose that there are some animals possessed naturally of senses humans lack. There seems to be no reason why there could not be such senses, and it may be that if we had senses in addition to our present five we would perceive characteristics of the world now mysterious to us, occult properties like magnetism.[12] It seems that it would be impossible for us to know that we lacked such a sense, or even to conceive very clearly what it might be that we lacked, but the hypothesis is not an empty one. Montaigne suggests that many features of the behavior of lower animals—their instinctive awareness of various things— might be owing to their having senses we lack.

The possibility, once suggested, is difficult to dismiss. You may be inclined to say that if Montaigne were right, the most this would do would be to show that we are invincibly ignorant of things we might have been able to know had we been differently constituted. But the point goes deeper than that. Since we often employ one sense to correct the defects of another, the possibility of our lacking information from senses we do not have gives further ground for suspecting error in the judgments we make on the information we have.

And again the problem of the criterion raises its head. If different men in different conditions judge differently the qualities of some object which is presented to their senses, with what right do we say that this man is correct and those men are in error? "Who," Montaigne asks,

12. Interesting in this context is Descartes' discussion of magnetism in the *Regulae* (AT X, 427; HR I, 47).

14

shall be fit to judge these differences? As we say in disputes about religion, that we must have a judge not attached to either party and free from preference and passion, which is impossible among Christians, so it is in this. For if he is old, he cannot judge the sense perception of old age, being himself a party in this dispute; if he is young, likewise, healthy, likewise; likewise, sick, asleep or awake. We would need someone exempt from all these qualities, so that with an unprejudiced judgment he might judge of these propositions as of things indifferent to him, and by that score we need a judge that never was.

To judge the appearances we receive of objects we would need a judicatory instrument, to verify this instrument, we need a demonstration, and to verify the demonstration, an instrument: there we are in a circle.[13]

The moral of the story for Montaigne is clear. Given the morass in which man finds himself whenever he tries to learn the truth—in religion, in morals, even in everyday 'common sense' judgments about the world around him—the only sensible course is to abstain from judgment, to make no claim to real knowledge of the nature of things. We may, of course, pronounce on appearances, but we should make no pretense of knowing whether or not the appearances correspond with reality.

Montaigne's attack on human reason found many adherents in the latter part of the sixteenth and in the early part of the seventeenth centuries. Some deployed his arguments in much the way Montaigne seems to have intended them to, in the aid of a Christian belief based on faith rather than reason. For others this fideistic position appears to have been a cover for a complete lack of orthodox religious conviction and a way of attacking orthodoxy by indirection. Still others, such as Gassendi and Mersenne, accepted a part of what Montaigne said, agreeing with him that we could have no genuine knowledge of the real nature of things, but arguing that a knowledge of appearances was sufficient for all practical purposes. What is important to us is not how things really are, but how they seem. So long as we can develop a science of appearances and a knowledge of what experiences may be expected to follow a given set of experiences, this is all we require.

13. Montaigne, *The Complete Essays*, trans. Donald Frame (Stanford: Stanford University Press, 1957), p. 454.

To judge from the *Discourse on Method,* Descartes was deeply impressed with the strength of the skeptic's case against human reason. One lesson he seems to have learned very well in the college at La Flèche was that he knew nothing: "I found myself embarrassed with so many doubts and errors that it seemed to me that the effort to instruct myself had no effect other than the increasing discovery of my own ignorance."[14] The themes of the skeptical dialectic echo again and again in the early chapters of the *Discourse.* Montaigne had written that presumption was "our natural and original malady" (Montaigne, 330); Descartes writes:

> I shall say nothing about philosophy, except that, seeing that it has been cultivated for many centuries by the best minds, and that nevertheless there is still nothing in it which is not disputed and therefore nothing which is not doubtful, I did not have enough presumption to hope to succeed where others had failed. (AT VI, 8; HR I, 85–86)

Like Montaigne, Descartes quotes Cicero's dictum that there is nothing so absurd that it has not been maintained by some philosopher.[15] He excuses himself from discussing theology, on the ground that the solution of its difficulties requires supernatural aid. One must be more than a man to succeed there.[16]

And though he recognizes that custom and the example of others are irrational determinants of belief,[17] he nonetheless adopts, as the first rule of his provisional morality, the classic pyrrhonian solution to the problem of deciding how, in spite of our invincible ignorance, we should act, when action is necessary. "My first maxim," he writes,

> was to obey the laws and customs of my country, retaining firmly the religion in which, by God's grace, I was instructed since my childhood. (AT VI, 23; HR I, 95)

But neither Montaigne nor Descartes can rest comfortably in this position. What greater presumption could there be than to suppose that God has specially favored the sect into which one happens to

14. AT VI, 4; HR I, 83. Cf. Montaigne on the wisdom of Socrates, Montaigne, 368.
15. AT VI, 16; HR I, 90. Cf. Montaigne, 408.
16. AT VI, 8; HR I, 85. Cf. Montaigne, 232–234, 321.
17. AT VI, 10; HR I, 87. Cf. Montaigne, I, xxiii, xxxi, xlix.

have been born by revealing the true religion to it alone? And the practical implications of the pyrrhonian solution were not always welcome. So Montaigne writes:

> What will philosophy tell us in our need? To follow the laws of our country—that is to say, the undulating sea of the opinions of a people or a prince . . . I cannot have my judgment so flexible. (Montaigne, 437; cf. p. 374)

Accused of encouraging infidels to remain in the religion of their parents, Descartes insisted that the maxim was, after all, only a provisional one and that he hoped, in the end, to arrive at the truth by using his God-given faculty of discerning the truth, not being content to accept the opinions of others for a moment.[18] One often feels that Descartes is a Protestant in spite of himself and that it was, perhaps, inevitable that his works would find a place on the Index.

The influence of Montaigne is not, however, restricted to the repetition of common skeptical themes. It shows itself in the most surprising places, where Descartes seems most himself. Consider, for example, the famous opening sentence of the *Discourse*. "Good sense is the most equitably distributed thing in the world." What could be more Cartesian? The ground given for saying this may be ironic—"everyone thinks himself so well provided with it that even those who are most difficult to satisfy in every other matter do not usually wish for more than they have" (AT VI, 2; HR I, 81)—but the claim is sincere, and Descartes was convinced of the fundamental rationality of his fellow men.[19] The differences of opinion which played such a prominent role in the skeptical critique of reason do not result from an innate difference in men's capacity to distinguish the true from the false; they stem, rather, from differences in temperament and education, from the habit we have, in

18. Letter to Mersenne, dated 27 April 1637 by AT, end of May 1637 by Alquié. See Alquié, *Oeuvres* I, 535. The accusation has in view the first maxim (AT VI, 23; HR I, 95). Descartes' reply refers his opponents to a passage later in Part III (AT VI, 27; HR I, 98).

19. In this I agree with Alquié (*Oeuvres* I, 568n) and evidently differ from Caton, *The Origin of Subjectivity* (New Haven: Yale University Press, 1973), pp. 97–99. In support of my view I would cite AT V, 175; Bridoux, 1397; AT VIII-2, 12; HR I, 210. Here again, the letter to the Marquess of Newcastle, cited above, is relevant.

different degrees, of judging rashly and of accepting the authority of others. It was this conviction which prompted Descartes to appeal over the heads of the learned to the general public in popular works like the *Discourse* and the *Search after Truth*.

And yet this pre-eminently Cartesian view has as close a parallel in Montaigne as any of the themes previously mentioned:

> It is commonly said that the fairest division of her favors Nature has given us is that of sense; for there is no one who is not content with the share of it that she has allotted him. Is that not reasonable? If anyone saw beyond, he would see beyond his sight.[20]

We may more easily call into question Montaigne's sincerity in arguing thus for man's rationality. After all, the "fair division" is introduced simply as a common opinion, and elsewhere Montaigne seems to undercut the reasoning accepted here.

> He who remembers having been mistaken so many, many times in his own judgment, is he not a fool if he does not distrust it forever after? When I find myself convicted of a false opinion by another man's reasoning, I do not so much learn that new thing he has told me and this particular bit of ignorance—that would be small gain–as I learn my weakness in general, and the treachery of my understanding. . . . To learn that we have said or done a foolish thing, that is nothing, we must learn that we are nothing but fools, a far broader and more important lesson. (Montaigne, 822)

And yet the earlier passage is more fundamental. Montaigne wants to use the diversity of opinions as a way of chastening our presumption in thinking that we have knowledge. He assumes that each differing opinion is equal in value to every other opinion. If one of the parties to a dispute had knowledge, rather than mere opinion, he would be able to convince the others, and there would no longer be a dispute.[21] The dispute goes on, so no one has knowledge. Without this assumption of common rationality, the

20. Montaigne, 499. Montaigne identifies his *sens* with a capacity for "sifting the truth." Analogously, Descartes identifies his *bon sens* or *raison* with a capacity to "judge well and distinguish the true from the false." This parallel is discussed in L. Brunschvicg, *Descartes et Pascal, Lecteurs de Montaigne* (New York: Brentano's, 1944), and Gilson, p. 83.

21. Cf. Descartes (AT X, 363; HR I, 3). The same assumption is also made in the *Discourse* (AT VI, 8; HR I, 86): "There is nothing which is not disputed, and *consequently*, which is not doubtful" (my emphasis).

diversity of opinion would be a phenomenon of no philosophic interest at all.

To find parallel thoughts in Descartes and Montaigne can never, of course, prove that Montaigne influenced Descartes. It will always remain possible that the view in question had some other source, or that Descartes arrived at it quite independently. But Descartes does sometimes refer to Montaigne explicitly, in a way which indicates a familiarity with his writing,[22] and it is rare for him to name an opponent. Moreover, some of the parallels are very striking indeed. I close this chapter with one further example—not the last we shall encounter.

One of the features which distinguishes Descartes' thought from that of his scholastic predecessors is the emphasis he places on self. Whereas scholasticism characteristically proceeds from knowledge of the world to knowledge of God, via the cosmological and teleological arguments, Descartes begins with God and the self and moves from knowledge of them to knowledge of the world. As he writes in one of his earliest letters to Mersenne (15 April 1630):

> I think that all those to whom God has given the use of . . . reason are obliged to use it mainly to try to know him and to know themselves. It is in this way that I have tried to begin my studies, and I will tell you that I would never have been able to find the foundations of physics if I had not searched for them in this way. (Alquié, *Oeuvres* I, 258–259; *Philosophical Letters*, 10)

So the constructive portions of the *Meditations* begin with the existence of the human mind, arguing that it is better known than the body, proceed from the existence of the mind to the existence of God, and only then go on to establish the existence of material things.

There is much in this movement of thought that would be quite impossible for Montaigne. The whole machinery of proofs of God's existence, with its battery of scholastic-sounding causal maxims, is certainly not in his spirit. It is, rather, a reminder that no pupil of the Jesuits wholly escapes their influence. But the primacy which is put on the self is another matter. It was Montaigne who wrote:

22. See n. 11 above.

19

I study myself more than any other subject. That is my metaphysics, that is my physics. (Montaigne, 821)

And with good reason:

These people who perch astride the epicycle of Mercury, who see so far into the heavens, yank out my teeth. For in the study I am making, the subject of which is man, when I find such an extreme variety of judgments, so deep a labyrinth of difficulties one on top of the other, so much diversity and uncertainty in the very school of wisdom, you may well wonder—since these people have not been able to come to an agreement in the knowledge of themselves and their own state which is ever present before their eyes, which is in them, since they do not know the motion of what they move themselves . . . how should I believe them about the cause of the ebb and flow of the river Nile? (Montaigne, 481)

Descartes would certainly agree with Montaigne that knowledge of the self comes first. But he would also insist that we can, without presumption, pass beyond knowledge of the self to knowledge of the world.

Descartes is not Montaigne. He is too much a child of the scientific revolution for that, too much an optimist about the possibility of knowledge and of progress in knowledge:

Our age seemed to me as flourishing and as fertile in good minds as any of its predecessors. (AT VI, 5; HR I, 83)

Descartes' age also had one good mind who had happened upon a uniquely promising method:

I have already reaped such fruits from my method that, though I always try to lean toward diffidence rather than presumption in the judgments I make of myself . . . nevertheless I cannot but feel an extreme satisfaction at the progress I think I have already made in the search for truth, and entertain such hopes for the future that, if there is any purely human occupation which has solid worth and importance, I am bold enough to believe it is the one I have chosen. (AT VI, 3; HR I, 82)

There is great hope for the future. But no one who had absorbed as many of Montaigne's ideas as had Descartes could take the possibility of knowledge for granted.

2

THE METHODS

IF MEN have the power to distinguish the true from the false, knowledge is possible. But it will not be actual unless they exercise that power critically and self-consciously. "It is not enough to have a good mind—the principal thing is to apply it well" (AT VI, 2; HR I, 82). That is what Descartes' first published work, *The Discourse on Method*, professes to teach us—how to use our reason well, how to exercise properly our faculty for distinguishing truth from falsity. That is also what Descartes' first major unpublished work professes to teach us. For the unfinished *Regulae* (*Rules For the Direction of the Mind*), undertaken sometime during the 1620s, is also a treatise on method, with the same apparent aim.

Suppose, now, that we ask whether the doctrine of these two treatises on method is the same, and which of the two is preferable as a source for the study of Descartes' thoughts on method. One might imagine that there would be a presumption in favor of the work Descartes finished and published over a work he neither finished nor published. But most recent Anglo-Saxon scholarship has preferred the *Regulae* to the *Discourse*. So we have L. J. Beck, for example, writing a book called *The Method of Descartes*, which is, in fact, a commentary on the *Regulae*.

This preference for the *Regulae* is not without reason. It is widely held that "the fundamental doctrine of the *Regulae* and the *Discourse* is the same."[1] And, indeed, each of the four rules of

1. L. Roth, *Descartes' "Discourse on Method"* (Oxford: Clarendon Press, 1937), p. 64. Beck agrees, *Method*, 1–8.

method given in Part II of the *Discourse* can be paralleled by sections of the *Regulae*. The first rule has its analogue in *Regula* 2: "We have decided that nothing is to be believed except what is known perfectly and what cannot be doubted" (AT X, 362; HR I, 3); the second and third, in *Regula* 5: "We shall follow this [method] exactly if we gradually reduce involved and obscure propositions to simpler ones, and then, from an intuition of the simplest of all, try to ascend by the same degrees to the knowledge of all the others" (AT X, 379; HR I, 14); and the fourth, in *Regula* 7: "To achieve science, we must run through all of the things which pertain to our purpose, one by one, with a movement of thought which is continuous and nowhere interrupted, and we must include all these things in a sufficient and orderly enumeration" (AT X, 387; HR I, 19).

Since the discussion in the *Regulae* is more detailed, and gives examples of how the method is to be used, it is, on anyone's view of the matter, an important supplement to the later work. As Descartes himself says, his design was not to teach the whole of his method in the *Discourse*. Even the essays which accompanied it do not, on the whole (an exception is made for the chapter on the rainbow in the *Meteors*), show how to use the method, but what can be achieved through its use. (Alquié, *Oeuvres* II, 25–26; *Philosophical Letters*, 45)

So we have to look for help where we can find it, and often we find it in the *Regulae*. We need always to keep in mind that, in the *Discourse* and later works, Descartes was writing for an audience which would not, as we do, have access to the *Regulae* to gloss difficult passages. But there is still reason to pay close attention to the *Regulae*. Even a commentator like Kemp Smith, who does not think the doctrine of the two works is the same, will justifiably devote much of his space to the *Regulae*.

Nevertheless, my contention will be that the differences between the *Regulae* and the *Discourse* are much more important and interesting than the similarities, that the method of the *Discourse*, and of Descartes' published writings generally, makes a significant advance over the first thoughts of the *Regulae*, an advance which has not been adequately analyzed by Descartes' commentators.[2] So our understanding of Descartes' method will be very imperfect if we focus our attention too much on the *Regulae* and its characteristic themes. And insofar as the method lies at the heart of Descartes' philosophy, our understanding of the whole system will suffer.

I

LET US begin with the *Regulae* and with the elements of continuity in Descartes' methodology. One of the most striking things about the opening pages of the *Regulae* is the emphasis Descartes there places on certainty. He identifies science with certain knowledge and rejects all merely probable knowledge. "We must occupy ourselves only with objects concerning which our mind seems capable of attaining a certain and indubitable knowledge" (AT X, 362; HR I, 3). If, at present, the only sciences which have achieved this ideal of certainty are arithmetic and geometry, it does not follow that arithmetic and geometry are the only sciences to be studied. The other sciences can be developed in such a way that we will be as certain about them as we now are about the mathematical sciences. The chief reason that the nonmathematical sciences are not now certain is that men have been content to introduce merely probable conjectures into them. What is required is to imitate the method of the mathematical sciences in the nonmathematical ones.

Arithmetic and geometry are more certain than the other sciences because they deal with objects "so pure and simple that they do not admit anything which experience has rendered uncertain" and because they "consist entirely in drawing consequences by way of rational deduction" (AT X, 365; HR I, 5). Their first principles

2. Kemp Smith, whose account of the method does recognize a development in Descartes' views, does not seem to me to appreciate fully the extent of that development. Gilson sometimes expresses views congenial to my own, but the apparent agreement seems superficial. See below, pp. 41–42, and cf. Gilson, 196: "As far as its essentials are concerned, the method has been from the beginning what it always had to remain." Alquié offers a better exception to the strictures of the text, though I agree with Beck (*Metaphysics*, 9–14) that he exaggerates the importance of the differences between the *Discourse* and the *Meditations*.

are known by intuition, defined as "the conception of a pure and attentive mind, a conception so easy and distinct that no doubt remains about what we understand" (AT X, 368; HR I, 7). The consequences of these first principles are known by deduction, that is, by a "necessary inference from other things known with certainty" (AT X, 369; HR I, 8). If we restrict ourselves to what we can know by intuition and deduction, we will never have to be content with less than certainty.

But even if we so restrict ourselves, we will not necessarily arrive at knowledge in every area where we are capable of having knowledge. Part of the reason why people have relied on conjecture in the nonmathematical sciences is that in complicated matters the right intuitions are not always easy to come by. The principal secret of the method consists in ordering the objects of our thought so that we can reduce the complex and obscure propositions which we cannot intuit to simple ones which we can intuit (AT X, 379–381; HR I, 14–15). Once we have reached the right simples, we will be able to work our way back, through a combination of intuition and deduction, to a certain knowledge of the complex proposition we were initially concerned with.

So far we have been summarizing the first six of the *Rules* and, apart from some terminological differences, we have nothing that would sound very strange to a reader of the *Discourse*. Intuition is a very important technical concept in the *Regulae*, though it is not even mentioned in the *Discourse*, but it is arguable that some such notion is at least implied by the *Discourse's* first rule: Never receive anything as true which you do not know evidently to be true. This, it may be claimed, is just a compendious way of saying: accept nothing unless you perceive it intuitively or can deduce it by intuitively evident steps from things you can intuit. And certainly the prominent role the *Regulae* gives to mathematics as a model for the nonmathematical sciences is reminiscent of the famous passage in the *Discourse* in which Descartes writes that:

> Those long chains of reasons, all simple and easy, which the geometers customarily use to arrive at their most difficult demonstrations, gave me reason to think that everything which man can know is connected in the same way, and that—provided only that we abstain from accepting anything as true which isn't true and al-

ways keep the order which is needed to deduce one thing from another—there can be nothing so remote but what we can reach it, nothing so hidden but what we can discover it. (AT VI, 19; HR I, 92)

In the *Discourse,* as in the *Regulae,* mathematics has achieved its certainty and become a model for the other sciences by beginning with the simple and proceeding from there to the complex. And so far, "it has been the mathematicians alone who have been able to succeed in finding any demonstrations" (AT VI, 19; HR I, 93).

If the *Discourse* says nothing explicit about intuition, it says little that is useful about deduction. This is one respect in which the *Regulae* provides a valuable supplement to the *Discourse.* It is evident enough in the *Discourse* that though Descartes places great importance on deduction, he is hostile to the traditional logic of Aristotle, as interpreted by the scholastics. Still, the grounds of this hostility are not at all clear in the *Discourse.* To understand them we must turn to the *Regulae.*

The initial formulation of the Cartesian requirements for deduction in the *Regulae* makes them sound very like the Aristotelian requirements for demonstration in the *Posterior Analytics.* For both the Cartesian deduction and the Aristotelian demonstration, there must be a necessary inference from premises known with certainty.[3] And for both the Cartesian deduction and the Aristotelian demonstration, the ultimate premises seem to be known by intuition.[4] The most important difference between them, on the face of it, is that Descartes would reject the requirement that the

3. Cf. AT X, 369, HR I, 8, with *Posterior Analytics* I, 2, 71b8–33. The similarities have not escaped Aristotelian scholars, as Beck notes (*Method,* 110, n2). He quotes Joachim as saying, "Aristotle's conception of *apodeixis,* looked at from this point of view, is in principle identical with Descartes' conception of 'deductio' "; and Mure as saying, "The *Regulae* of Descartes offers a theory of demonstration which entails much the same difficulties as Aristotle's."

4. This is clear enough in the case of Descartes. Cf. *Regula* 3. In Aristotle the supplement to deduction seems sometimes to be induction (cf. *Nicomachean Ethics* VI, 3) and sometimes intuition (cf. *Nicomachean Ethics* VI, 6). But presumably induction is here not so much a form of argument as a process by which we come to have an intuition. (Cf. *Posterior Analytics* II, 19, 99b20–100b18, and W. D. Ross, *Aristotle* (London: Methuen, 1966), pp. 54–55).

inference which is to lead to scientific knowledge be syllogistic in form.

Why does Descartes reject the syllogism? There seem to be two lines of reasoning, each of which is problematic, though one, I think, is better than the other.

In the *Discourse* Descartes complains that while syllogisms may be useful in explaining to others what one already knows, or in talking without judgment about the things one does not know, no one will ever learn anything from them which he does not already know (AT VI, 17; HR I, 91). Syllogistic reasoning does not lead to new knowledge. But why does Descartes think that is so? The answer seems to be that Descartes accepts a criticism of the syllogism of the sort that we tend to associate with John Stuart Mill, though it has a much longer history than that. In the *Regulae* Descartes explains that syllogistic reasoning

> makes absolutely no contribution to knowledge of the truth, since the dialecticians cannot construct by their rules any syllogism which has a true conclusion unless they already possess its matter, that is, unless they already know in advance the very truth they are deducing in that syllogism. (AT X, 406; HR I, 32)

Descartes does not make his point very clearly here. It sounds as though he may think that a valid syllogism (one constructed according to the rules of the syllogism) cannot have a true conclusion unless the premises are true.[5] And if he does think that, he is certainly confused about the distinction between validity and soundness.

I think it unlikely, however, that he is confused about that. That a true conclusion can follow from false premises was a standard point in discussions of the hypothetical method, and one Descartes himself makes elsewhere.[6] I take Descartes to mean simply that the validity of the argument is not sufficient in itself to establish the truth of the conclusion. A true conclusion may follow from false premises, but so also may a false conclusion. If the argument

5. As suggested by J. A. Passmore in "Descartes, the British Empiricists and Formal Logic," *Philosophical Review*, 62 (1953), 543–553.

6. Cf. AT VI, 83; Olscamp, 66–67; and Blake's "The Theory of Hypothesis Among Renaissance Astronomers," in Blake, Ducasse, and Madden.

is to be a demonstration of the truth of its conclusion, its premises must be both true and known to be true. And the difficulty about the syllogism is that in a syllogism the premises cannot be known to be true unless the conclusion is known first, so that the argument will be circular.

Descartes does not present any argument for the charge of circularity; but I suppose that he was familiar with the following argument, which is found in Sextus Empiricus and in many of the Renaissance skeptics.[7] Probably he presumed that his readers would also know it. We are asked to consider the following syllogism:

All men are animals.
Socrates is a man.
Therefore, Socrates is an animal.

If this argument is to be a demonstration of its conclusion, the premises must be known to be true. So the question is asked, "How do we know that the premises are true?" And in particular, "How do we know that the universal, major premise is true?" It seems that the only possible answer is "by induction." And then the question is "By a perfect induction or by an imperfect one?" If we know the major premise by a perfect induction, one generalizing from a knowledge of all instances, then clearly we must first know that Socrates, who is a man, is an animal. The argument will be circular and therefore not demonstrative. If we know the major premise by an imperfect induction, which generalizes from an incomplete sample, then we do not have certain knowledge of the major premise, and so again demonstration escapes us.

This is more convincing if we use, as Mill does, an argument with a contingent major premise as an example. To use an argument with a necessary major premise, as Sextus does, is to invite a reply invoking the Aristotelian notion of intuitive induction, which may conclude to a certain conclusion from a limited sample. But Sextus has other grounds for rejecting those arguments, as we shall see.

One difficulty about this critique of the syllogism is that there

7. Cf. *Outlines of Pyrrhonism* II, 195–197, and 204. See also Popkin, *passim.*

does not seem to be any good reason for restricting it to the syllogism. The problem is that (1) a valid syllogism cannot establish the truth of its conclusion unless the premises are known to be true, and that (2) since, in a valid syllogism, the truth of the conclusion is a necessary condition of the truth of the premises, knowing the truth of the conclusion appears to be a necessary condition of knowing the truth of the premises. At any rate, the principle

If p entails q, then (a knows that p) entails
(a knows that q)

is a very tempting one, in cases where the inference from p to q is obvious.[8] What is crucial here is not that the argument is syllogistic, but that it is valid, that the premises are sufficient for the conclusion, or to put it differently, that it is not possible that the premises should be true unless the conclusion is true. Wherever that is the case, the way will be open for the skeptic to question our knowledge of the premises. So the skeptical criticism of syllogistic reasoning as circular will be just as damaging to Cartesian deductions as it is to Aristotelian demonstrations. For surely the premises of Cartesian deductions are meant to be sufficient for their conclusions, and they are also meant to be known to be true.

That is one train of thought in Descartes' rejection of formalism, and one piece of the skeptical dialectic Descartes should have been chary about accepting. It is not really an objection to formalism, but an objection to any deduction which is put forward as a demonstration.

But there is also another point which I think Descartes wants to make about reasoning. And this one may contain something worth rescuing. Descartes maintains, in the *Regulae*, that an intuition is required not only for our knowledge of the ultimate premises of deductions but also for any discursive reasoning whatever (AT X, 369; HR I, 7). He illustrates this with the following example. To see by deduction that

(c) $2 + 2 = 3 + 1$

8. See Fred Dretske, "Epistemic Operators," *Journal of Philosophy*, 67 (1970), 1007–1023.

by inferring it from the premises

(a) $2 + 2 = 4$

and

(b) $3 + 1 = 4$

I must see, not only that the premises, (a) and (b), are true but also that the conclusion, (c), is a necessary consequence of these two propositions.

Now someone might say: this is not a demonstration. For it is not in proper syllogistic form. It is, rather, an enthymene. There is a suppressed major premise to the effect that

(a')   Things equal to the same thing are equal to each other.

The minor premise should be:

(b') $2 + 2$ and $3 + 1$ are equal to the same thing, namely, 4.

And the conclusion will be as before. Once you put the argument in this form, then you can determine its validity without any reference to intuition, for you can see without relying on an intuition that it is an instance of a valid form.

I take it that Descartes would reject this, and the question is, "Why?" After all, later in the *Regulae*, when Descartes is discussing his common notions (AT X, 419; HR I, 41), he cites as an example the maxim that things that are the same as a third thing are the same as one another. He says there, of his common notions, that they are like chains binding the other simple natures together, and that "whatever we infer by reasoning rests on their evidence." So he would admit, in the *Regulae*, that a knowledge of the universal proposition, (a'), is, in some sense, necessary for the inference. But he would deny that it should be a premise and that we should view the original inference as enthymematic.

One way of resolving this paradox, a way very natural for a twentieth-century philosopher, is to say that Descartes views his common notions as rules of inference, rather than statements. That is why they never appear as premises, though they are admitted to be prior to inferences. And I think that this resolution is fundamentally right, though it needs some arguing. As before, I will suggest that Descartes' views on inference can best be understood by placing them against the background of the classic skeptical critique of logic.

The Aristotelian theory of the categorical syllogism did not exhaust the ingenuity of ancient logicians. The logic of propositions was also studied, systematically and with considerable sophistication, by the Stoics.[9] The Stoics were primarily concerned with the identification of valid propositional inference schemata and with the derivation of the inference schemata they recognized as valid from certain basic patterns they regarded as "indemonstrable," that is, primitive. They concluded that five primitive inference schemata were both necessary and sufficient for generating all other valid propositional schemata. Among these five were such familiar principles as *modus ponens* and *modus tollens*.

The Stoics also had what we should regard as very strict views about validity. If we can trust the reports given us by Sextus—and Stoic logic is known to us mainly through its skeptical critics— they thought the inclusion of redundant or superfluous premises in an argument was not merely an inelegance, but a logical fault, sufficient to destroy the validity of the argument. (*Outlines of Pyrrhonism* II, 146.) So, for example, the argument

> If it is day, it is light.
> But in fact it is day, and also Dion is walking.
> Therefore, it is light.

was put on a par with the fallacy of affirming the consequent. If this seems an eccentric notion of validity, it may be salutary to remember that the insistence on relevance between the premises and conclusion of an argument has sometimes led modern logicians into similar views.[10]

The requirement that a valid argument not have redundant

9. For details, see W. & M. Kneale, *The Development of Logic* (Oxford: Clarendon Press, 1962), and B. Mates, *Stoic Logic* (Berkeley: University of California Press, 1953).

10. Cf. E. Nelson, "Intensional Relations," *Mind*, 39 (1930), 440–453: "I can see no reason for saying that p and q entail p, when p alone does and q is irrelevant, and hence does not function as a premise in the entailing" (p. 447). The Stoics also seem to have rejected "p and q entail p," but this may have been partly because they thought that any inference from just one premise is necessarily question-begging. Cf. the Kneales, *The Development of Logic*, p. 163.

premises provided an opening for the skeptics. They attacked each of the Stoics' five indemonstrable inference schemata in the same way, so we may as well take *modus ponens* as our example. Suppose we have an argument of the form

If p, then q
But p
So, q.

The question the skeptic raised concerns the status of the conditional premise. Is it evident or not? If it is not evident, then the argument fails to demonstrate its conclusion because it has a premise which is not known to be true. On the other hand, if the conditional is evident, then it is also unnecessary to have it as a premise and the argument fails to demonstrate its conclusion because it is redundant and hence invalid. The same criticism was also directed against each of the other four indemonstrable schemata in propositional logic and against the categorical syllogism. (Cf. *Outlines of Pyrrhonism* II, 159–166.)

This is surely taking the notion of redundance more broadly than the Stoics intended it to be taken. For even if the conditional premise of an argument in *modus ponens* is unnecessary for the validity of the argument (as it might be), it is surely not irrelevant in the way that "Dion is walking" is irrelevant to the argument in which it appeared above.

Sometimes Descartes appears to take a similar line. For example, he writes in the *Regulae* that:

> Because . . . the syllogistic forms are of no aid in perceiving the truth of things, the reader will do well to reject them altogether and to conceive that all knowledge whatsoever, except that which consists in the simple and pure intuition of an isolated thing, is a matter of the comparison of two or more things with each other. And nearly the whole work of human reason consists in preparing for this operation. For when it is open and simple, we need no assistance from art, to intuit the truth; we need only the light of nature. (AT X, 439–440; HR I, 55)

I understand Descartes' point here to be this. When a formal logician puts in logical form an inference which he regards as enthymematic, he characteristically adds a conditional or universal

31

premise. Now either we see clearly that the added premise is true or we do not. If we do not, then all we have accomplished is to burden ourselves with a premise in need of proof. But if we do see clearly that the premise is true, then we didn't really require the premise in the first place. For the original stock of premises must, then, have already been sufficient for the conclusion. Descartes does not, as the skeptics and Stoics did, say that an argument with superfluous premises is ipso facto invalid. What he claims is that nothing is gained by the shift to a formally valid argument.

This view of inference seems to require an analysis of general and hypothetical 'statements' according to which they are not statements at all, but material rules of inference which just happen to have the grammatical form of statements, that is, an analysis like that argued for by Ryle.[11] And in some places Descartes does sound very Rylean. For instance, replying to Gassendi, who thought the *cogito* should be cast in the form of a categorical syllogism, he says:

> This author supposes that the knowledge of particular propositions must always be deduced from universal ones, following the order of syllogisms in the dialectic. In that he shows how little he knows the proper order for investigating the truth. For it is certain that to find the truth one must always begin with particular notions, in order to come, afterwards, to the general ones—though having found the general notions, one can also, reciprocally, deduce other particulars from them. Thus when one teaches a child the elements of geometry, one will not make him understand in general that *when equals are subtracted from equals the remainders are equal*, or that *the whole is greater than its parts*, unless one shows him examples in particular cases. (AT IX, 205–206; HR II, 127)

Descartes is not claiming here that such general propositions are known by Baconian induction. What he does claim is that it is a necessary condition of teaching a child the meaning of a general truth of mathematics that we show him what inferences are valid in particular cases. And if seeing that those inferences are valid in particular cases is also a sufficient condition of understanding the

---

11. Ryle, however, is also moved to his antiformalism partly by worries about a vicious regress. Cf. " 'If,' 'So,' and 'Because,' " *Philosophical Analysis*, ed. M. Black (Ithaca: Cornell University Press, 1950): "The principle of an inference cannot be one of its premisses or part of its premiss" (p. 328).

general truth, then we may say that understanding the general truth just *is* seeing that certain sorts of inferences are valid.[12]

But I am not sure that Descartes would go so far as Ryle does. Ryle puts forward his analysis as applying to all conditionals. And he regards a conditional as inherently modal. "The differences between modal and hypothetical statements are in fact purely stylistic" (Ryle, " 'If,' 'So,' and 'Because,' " p. 335). The only correct way to negate a conditional is to say that it is possible that the antecedent be true and the consequent false. I suppose that a similar analysis would be offered of general statements.

It is not clear, however, that Descartes would want to make that general a claim about universal and hypothetical statements. It is true that no qualifications are expressed either in the reply to Gassendi just quoted, or in the similar and better known passage from the Second Replies (AT VII, 140–141; HR II, 38). In both of these passages, and in the *Regulae* (AT X, 369; HR I, 7), the examples Descartes is concerned with are all ones where the major premise in question is a proposition of a very special type. The majors are what Descartes calls common notions, or eternal truths (AT X, 369; HR I, 7), or what we would call necessary truths.[13]

12. See Ryle, " 'If,' 'So,' and 'Because,' " p. 330: "What we have learned, when we have learned it [i.e., if *p*, then *q*], and what we have taught, when we have taught it, is, in the first instance, to argue "*p*, so *q*" . . . and to accept such arguments from others."

13. See AT VIII–1, 22–23; HR I, 238–239. The identification of common notions with eternal truths has been challenged by some writers, but I find the arguments unconvincing. Cf. John Morris, "Cartesian Certainty," *Australasian Journal of Philosophy*, 47 (1969), 161–168. Morris notes the passage cited from the *Principles*, but thinks it a mistake made in the Latin version and corrected in the French version. But the identification *is* also present in the French version (AT IX–2, 46) and is repeated in the conversation with Burman (AT V, 167). Morris has, as many Cartesian scholars do, a preference for the French version of Descartes' works. See his "A Plea for the French Descartes," *Dialogue*, 6 (1967–1968), 236–239. But though Descartes read and approved the contemporary French translations and sometimes used them to make revisions, we need to exercise caution in deciding what variations are significant. Cf. Adam's judgment on Picot, the translator of the *Principles*, AT IX–2, vii–x. After expressing the wish that Descartes had been more exacting in his revision of the translation, he remarks that "sometimes, in fact, the version is so careless that it becomes incorrect." He cites particularly "a prejudice on the part of the translator in favor of avoiding technical terms," sometimes by simply suppressing them. Gueroult's view (*Ordre* I, 34, n4) is surely correct:

And it is important to recognize that a syllogism with a necessary major premise is a very special sort of syllogism. (We may note in passing that Ryle's typical example of an inference is also one whose major would be a necessary truth, namely, "Today is Monday, so tomorrow is Tuesday.")

First of all, familiar doctrines about the existential import of universal propositions have awkward consequences when applied to necessary universal propositions. If we hold that "All A's are B's" entails that there are A's, then we will be obliged to admit large numbers of necessary existential propositions. For it is an uncontroversial truth of modal logic that if p is necessary and p entails q, q is necessary. This might provide a reason for treating necessary universal truths as expressing material rules of inference rather than statements. It might also help to explain Descartes' insistence that knowledge of eternal truths does not give us knowledge of any existing thing (AT VIII-1, 8; HR I, 222). Descartes does not, of course, explicitly deploy the concept of a rule of inference. But the simile he uses is very suggestive. The common notions, which are the basis of all reasoning, are "like chains," binding things together (AT X, 419; HR I, 41).

Moreover it is at least a widely held view that if a valid argument contains a premise which is necessarily true, that premise can be eliminated, *salva validitate*. That is, if p and q entail r, and p is necessary, then q alone entails r. So if an argument which is not, as it stands, formally valid, were to be rendered formally valid by the addition of a premise which is necessarily true, Descartes would be right to think the exercise an empty one. If the original argument requires only the addition of a necessarily true premise to achieve formal validity, then the original argument was already valid. This is one strand in Descartes' antiformalism which seems to me defensible.[14]

---

where we have a Latin original and a translation approved by Descartes, we must consult both versions and use discretion in deciding which is more precise.

14. The modal principle appealed to here is controversial, though it is a theorem in any standard system of modal logic, i.e., any of the Lewis systems. However it is connected with the "paradoxes of strict implication," and hence is rejected by relevance-oriented logicians like Alan Anderson and Nuel Belnap (cf. their article, "Enthymemes," *Journal of Philosophy*, 58 (1961), 713–

II

So FAR I have concentrated on methodological themes which the *Regulae* and the *Discourse* have in common: the stress on certainty, the modeling of the nonmathematical sciences on mathematics, and the hostility toward formal logic. I have not given grounds for supposing that the method of the *Discourse* is, in any fundamental way, different from the method of the *Regulae*. But in spite of the similarities, it clearly is a different method.

The *Regulae* was written sometime between 1619 and 1628.[15] In the *Discourse* Descartes tells us that in the nine years between 1619 and 1628 he had not taken any part in the disputes of learned men and had not begun to look for the foundation of any philosophy more certain than the vulgar (AT VI, 30; HR I, 100), that is, any philosophy more certain than the scholastic Aristotelianism of his day.

I read this as a critical comment on the *Regulae*. In the *Regulae* the main object of criticism, the alternative to Cartesianism which needs to be rebutted, is scholasticism. Nevertheless, the method of the *Regulae* shares important assumptions with scholasticism. Like scholasticism, the *Regulae* takes the certainty of mathematics as paradigmatic and unproblematic. It relies heavily on a faculty of intuition to supply not only the ultimate premises of its deductions but also the principles of inference themselves. And it does not even consider the possibility that someone might question this reliance. The *Regulae* differs from scholasticism principally in its rejection of formalism and its hope that we can achieve in the nonmathematical sciences the absolute certainty which has hitherto been the privilege of mathematics. Like scholasticism, it is vulner-

---

723). A restricted version of the principle—viz., that if *p* and *q* entail *r*, and *p* is necessary, and *q* and *r* are contingent, then *q* entails *r*—was accepted by Peter Geach in his article, "Entailment," *Aristotelian Society Proceedings*, suppl. vol. 32 (1958), pp. 157–172. I have defended the paradoxes of strict implication in "Lewis and Entailment," *Philosophical Studies*, 23 (1972), 198–204.

15. The most recent study, Weber's *La constitution du texte des "Regulae"* (Paris: Société d'éditions d'enseignement supérieur, 1964), treats it as having been worked on over the full nine-year period, and as having many different strata.

able to any skeptical attack which can shake our confidence in mathematics, or raise effectively the problem of first principles.

In Descartes' later writings mathematics does not provide an unproblematic paradigm of certainty. As early as 1630 we find him writing to Mersenne that he thinks he has discovered how to demonstrate metaphysical truths in "a way which is more evident than the demonstrations of geometry" (15 April 1630, Alquié, *Oeuvres* I, 259; *Philosophical Letters*, 19). So the certainty of mathematics can be surpassed and Descartes thinks he can do it. But how? What is wrong with mathematics? Descartes does not tell us, except indirectly, by claiming that he would not have discovered the foundations of his physics if he had not first exercised his reason in trying to know God and himself. This is the first hint we have in Descartes of an attempt to approach certainty via arguments for the existence of God. We are not told much about the attempt, but later correspondence suggests that an early version of the *Meditations* was written about 1629.[16]

In the *Discourse* and the *Meditations* we find Descartes questioning the certainty of mathematical truths in a way which has no parallel in the *Regulae*. The *Discourse* is very vague about the grounds for doubting the truths of mathematics, saying simply that

> because there are men who deceive themselves in their reasoning and fall into paralogisms, even concerning the simplest matters in geometry, and judging that I was as subject to error as was any other, I rejected as false all the reasons formerly accepted by me as demonstrations. (AT VI, 32; HR I, 101)

No explanation is offered for the fact that men should err even in simple matters of mathematics. But the mere recognition of the occurrence of error is a striking contrast to the complacency of the *Regulae*.

16. Cf. the letters to Mersenne of 25 November 1630, Alquié, *Oeuvres* I, 287; *Philosophical Letters*, 19; and 27 February 1637(?), Alquié, *Oeuvres* I, 522; *Philosophical Letters*, 30–31. Alquié (*Découverte*, 81–83) has questioned whether this early treatise on metaphysics can be regarded as containing the Cartesian metaphysic which was to appear in 1641. But it seems to me that, although it would be extravagant to claim a complete exposition of the *Meditations*, the correspondence is sufficiently explicit to show that the broad outlines of the work were the same.

The *Meditations* will appeal not so much to the fact of error as to the possibility of deception by a superior being, even in those things which seem most evident. Our ancient belief in God becomes a ground for doubting everything, so long as we do not know that God is not a deceiver. And this, as Descartes notes in the *Principles*, is the most important ground for doubting the truths of mathematics (AT VIII-1, 6; HR I, 220).

So both the *Discourse* and the *Meditations* pose a problem which is just not present in the *Regulae*, the problem of justifying our belief in the things that seem most evident to us. Both works offer, as part of the solution to that problem, a criterion of truth which is nowhere present in the *Regulae*—that all our clear and distinct ideas are true. Indeed the phrase "clear and distinct" occurs only rarely in the *Regulae* and then not in the statement of a criterion of truth.[17] Both the *Discourse* and the *Meditations* appear to assume, as viable, the project of showing that this criterion of truth is reliable by proving the existence of a god who is not a deceiver. And both works thereby lay themselves open to a charge of circularity. For it is not easy to see how Descartes can prove God's existence and veracity without assuming the validity of the criterion of truth which he says he needs a knowledge of God's existence and veracity to validate. There is no Cartesian circle in the *Regulae* because the *Regulae* does not even have a criterion of truth to validate. Why is there this difference?

I suggest that sometime around 1628 Descartes became con-

---

17. At AT X, 407, cf. Kemp Smith, 55, n3. This is not the only important terminological difference between the *Regulae* and the later works. As Kemp Smith notes (p. 60, n2), Descartes also ceases to employ, in his published works, such key technical terms from the *Regulae* as "intuition" and "simple natures." However, I think Kemp Smith is wrong to try to connect the concept of clarity and distinctness with that of simplicity (cf. pp. 55–60). It is not true that only simple natures are capable of being known both clearly and distinctly. The piece of wax (AT VII, 31; HR I, 155) is known both clearly and distinctly, though complex. Indeed it appears from the Second Meditation that we acquire a clear and distinct idea of the wax by attending to "the things which are in it and of which it is composed" (FV, AT IX–1, 25). Also dubious is Kemp Smith's view (apparently shared by Haldane and Ross, cf. HR I, 155) that the *inspectio mentis* of the *Meditations* is simply a substitute for the *intuitio* of the *Regulae*. For our *inspectio mentis* of the piece of wax is, in the beginning, imperfect and confused, which could not be said of an intuition, as that term is understood in the *Regulae*.

vinced that the *Regulae*, though still valid at one level, did not go deeply enough into the problem of knowledge. I suggest that sometime around 1628 Descartes came to feel that pyrrhonian skepticism was a more dangerous enemy than scholasticism, and came to feel the force of skeptical arguments which cut against both his own position in the *Regulae* and that of the scholastics.

One motivation for this may have been provided by critical reflection on his own position. For as we have seen, Descartes was already disposed, in the *Regulae*, to accept skeptical criticisms of Aristotelian demonstrations which were equally valid against his own conception of reasoning. But this would, at best, provide grounds for skepticism about deduction. What about intuition?

Here again we may look to Montaigne. For there is more in Montaigne than a mere critique of empiricism. Montaigne is also a possible source for the hypothesis of a deceiving God, presented in the First Meditation as a ground for doubting even those things most evident to us.[18] Montaigne writes:

> Reason has taught me that to condemn a thing . . . dogmatically as false and impossible, is to assume the advantage of knowing the bounds and limits of God's will and the power of our Mother Nature, and that there is no more notable folly in the world than to reduce these things to the measure of our capacity and competence. If we call prodigies and miracles whatever our reason cannot reach, how many of these appear continually to our eyes! (Montaigne, 132)

and again

> Of all the ancient human opinions concerning religion, that one, it seems to me, was most probable and most excusable which recognized God as an incomprehensible power, origin and preserver of all things. (Montaigne, 380)

We do not explicitly have here the Cartesian voluntarist doctrine of the creation of the eternal truths. Montaigne does not speak here about mathematical truths and he does not say that mathe-

---

18. As Popkin notes (p. 181, n2), Pascal seems to have thought that Montaigne was the source of the hypothesis. See his "Entretien de Pascal avec Saci sur Epictète et Montaigne," in his *Oeuvres*, ed. L. Brunschvicg, P. Boutroux, and F. Gazier (Paris, Hachette, 1914), vol. IV, p. 43. Neither Popkin nor Pascal identifies any specific passages in Montaigne to support the suggestion.

matical and other eternal truths are true because God has willed that they be true.

He does, however, here maintain a position which, in Descartes, is associated with the doctrine of the creation of eternal truths, namely, that it is presumptuous for us to say that something is impossible simply because it seems impossible to us, that to say this is to limit God's power illegitimately. And that is what is of primary epistemological importance in the doctrine of the creation of eternal truths. So Descartes writes to Mersenne, in the letter (15 April 1630) in which he first announces that doctrine, that God's power

> is incomprehensible; we can indeed assert that God can do every-thing which we can comprehend, but we cannot assert that he cannot do what we cannot comprehend; for it would be temerity to think that our imagination has as great an extent as his power. (Alquié, *Oeuvres* I, 261; *Philosophical Letters*, 12)

It is no accident that the letter in which Descartes first states the doctrine of the creation of the eternal truths is also the letter in which he first claims to be able to attain a certainty greater than the certainty of mathematics by seeking knowledge of God and the self. The doctrine that God's power is incomprehensible has given him a reason for questioning the certainty of the things that seem most evident to us.

Note also that in some places Montaigne uses the incomprehensibility of God's power to suggest doubts about principles which Descartes will subsequently call eternal truths or common notions:

> We prescribe limits to God, we hold his power besieged by our reasons . . . we want to enslave him to the vain and feeble approximations of our understanding, him who has made both us and our knowledge. "Because nothing is made of nothing, God cannot have built the world without material." What! Has God placed in our hands the keys and ultimate springs of his power? Has he pledged himself not to overstep the bounds of our knowledge? (Montaigne, 389)

and

> It has always seemed to me that for a Christian this sort of talk is full of indiscretion and irreverence: "God cannot die, God cannot go back on his word, God cannot do this or that." I do not think

it is good to confine the divine power thus under the laws of our speech. (Montaigne, 392)

The principles that "nothing is made of nothing" and that "God cannot deceive" will both play very important roles in Descartes' proof, in the *Meditations*, that all our clear and distinct ideas are true. But they are also principles which can—at least in certain circumstances—be doubted, and doubted on grounds which are not merely frivolous.

Perhaps the most explicit anticipation of the extreme Cartesian doctrine of omnipotence occurs in the passage in which Montaigne criticizes "that ancient scoffer," Pliny the Elder, for having held that "God cannot do everything . . . he cannot . . . arrange that the man who has lived shall not have lived, or that the man who has had honors shall not have had them; he has no other power over the past than that of oblivion. And . . . he cannot make two times ten not be twenty" (Montaigne, 393). Here Montaigne is not merely making a claim about the limits of our knowledge, namely, the claim that, for all we know, what seems impossible may not be impossible. Rather the claim is that God's omnipotence entails the possibility of his bringing about the opposite of *any* state of affairs, including the most patently necessary ones. The examples are not only mathematical but include other principles Descartes will class as eternal truths, such as that what has been done cannot be undone (AT VII, 36; HR I, 159). And the reason for rejecting Pliny's view is the same one Descartes will offer: that view represents a human attempt to bring God down to man's measure.

Here, incidentally, we must take issue with Gueroult, who has argued (Gueroult, *Ordre* I, 42–49) that the hypothesis of a deceiving God does not, even in part, have its root in doctrines Descartes would accept, that it is an artifice quite alien to the truths of Cartesian philosophy. This puts the position too strongly. That God may deceive us, even in things that seem most evident to us, is an inference—natural, though illegitimate—from God's omnipotence. In that sense it does have its roots in Cartesian doctrine. But Gueroult is right to stress that, according to Descartes, once we understand what is really implied by God's omnipotence, we will see that not only does it not entail the possibility of God's deceiving us, in fact it excludes that possibility. So God's omnipotence, not merely his goodness, will, in the end, be what is incompatible with deception.

Now of course the difference we have emphasized between the *Regulae* and the later works is obvious to any intelligent, attentive reader. So it has not escaped the notice of those who think that the fundamental doctrine of the *Regulae* and the *Discourse* is the same. They believe the doctrine to be the same despite these differences. So Beck writes that, in the *Discourse* and the *Meditations*,

> Descartes is concerned with the principle of methodical doubt: *de omnibus dubitandum*. In the *Discours* the doubt itself does not turn on the actual intuition of the mathematical datum or on the subsequent demonstration but on our memory of the chains of reasoning which would otherwise have seemed completely demonstrative. It is in the *Meditationes* alone that the hypothesis of the "malignant demon" is used to make it possible to doubt the very intuitions on which all mathematical reasoning is and must be based. Since he cannot find a reason, Descartes must make a reason for doubting. (*Method*, 40–41)

The ground offered for doubting intuitions in the *Meditations* is, in Descartes' own words, a very "slight" and "metaphysical" one. So it is not really a reason for doubting at all. The doubt of the *Meditations* is "due to our volitional activity" and does not "correspond on our part to any real psychological experience of a cognitive nature" (*Method*, 42).

Beck is not the only scholar to read the *Discourse* in this way. Gilson provides another example. In his commentary on the *Discourse* he writes that

> in extending the doubt thus . . . Descartes generalizes in a remarkable manner the critical principles used in the *Regulae*. . . . From the point of view he had adopted in the latter work, the certainty of mathematics seemed beyond all suspicion; henceforth, on the other hand . . . he seeks a foundation for the certainty of mathematics itself. (Gilson, 290)

So far, so good. Unfortunately Gilson undoes this good work by adding that

> the doubt does not bear here on the present intuition of mathematical demonstrations, but on the memory of the reasons which

formerly seemed demonstrative to us. In fact, it is memory, not intuition, which Descartes judges it necessary to guarantee. (Gilson, 290)

But though there may be passages in some of Descartes' other writings which suggest this, there are none in the *Discourse*.

Memory is not even mentioned in the passage in question. And while the doubt is said to be a doubt about reasoning, it is a doubt about our reasoning concerning "even the simplest matters of geometry."[19] So the reasoning need not involve a long and complex argument. And if it does not, the doubt must be a doubt about our intuition, either of the premises or of the principles of inference. If people have made mistakes in simple matters of mathematics, that must be because, as Descartes says in the *Principles*, they have treated something false as if it were most certain and known per se (AT VIII-1, 6; HR I, 220).

In the *Meditations*, on the other hand, it is not the hypothesis of a "malignant demon" which alone makes possible doubt about our intuitions.[20] The demon, who is a deliberate "invention," is introduced only after Descartes has arrived at the conclusion that there is no proposition among those he formerly believed which he cannot now doubt—and doubt "not through want of thought or levity, but for valid and carefully considered reasons" (AT VII, 21; AT IX-1, 17; HR I, 147–148). Those valid reasons are found—not invented—in an opinion which has long been fixed in his mind, the opinion that there is a God who can do everything. It is true that the ground of doubt Descartes here characterizes as "valid and carefully considered" he will later (AT VII, 36; HR I, 159) call "slight and metaphysical." This is puzzling and will require ex-

19. Cf. the *Regulae*, where it is held that "deduction, i.e., the pure inference of one thing from another, can be omitted, if it is not seen, but can never be done badly by an intellect in the least degree rational" (AT X, 365; HR I, 4–5).
20. Indeed, as Richard Kennington points out, Descartes does not explicitly include deception about mathematical truths among the things the existence of the demon is supposed to put in doubt. See his "The 'Teaching of Nature' in Descartes' Soul Doctrine," *Review of Metaphysics*, 26 (1972), 86–117. The relation between God and the demon has been the subject of much scholarly controversy. In general I find myself in agreement with Kenny's position (Kenny, 34–36).

planation when we come to consider the problem of the circle. But though the doubt may be "due to our volitional activity," it is a complete misunderstanding of Descartes' theory of judgment to suppose that it does not involve "any real psychological experience of a cognitive nature." If the suspense of judgment is to be anything more than an empty subvocal utterance, it must involve a genuine perception: that our grounds for belief are not fully adequate. That is why Descartes looks for reasons for doubting, and why he treats the First Meditation, in Gilson's happy phrase, "not as a theory to understand, but as an exercise to practice."[21] If the reader has practiced his exercise well, he should feel as Descartes does at the beginning of the Second Meditation—like someone who has suddenly fallen into very deep water and is so disconcerted that he can neither fix his feet on the bottom, nor swim to the surface (AT VII, 23–24; HR I, 149).

The *Discourse* and the *Meditations* have a problem the *Regulae* does not have, the problem of justifying our belief in the things that seem most evident to us. And they have a solution to that problem which the *Regulae* does not have. They establish a criterion of truth by means of the method of doubt. It is worth noting that the passage just cited from Beck is one of the few in his commentary on the *Regulae* in which the method of doubt is even mentioned. The reason for this is simple. A commentary on the *Regulae* need not discuss the method of doubt, because the method of doubt is not present in the *Regulae*. So Kemp Smith does not go far enough when he writes that "the method of doubt recommended in the *Regulae* is not the hyperbolical doubt of the *Discourse* and the *Meditations*" (p. 80). The method of doubt simply is not recommended in the *Regulae*.

This is not obvious. After all, the *Regulae* does tell us to "reject all merely probable knowledge" and to "believe only what is perfectly known and cannot be doubted" (AT X, 362; HR I, 3). This

---

21. *Etudes sur le rôle de la pensée médiévale dans la formation du système cartésien* (Paris: Vrin, 1951), p. 186. It is curious that Beck should have missed this, since he was later (*Metaphysics*, 28–38) to show himself quite sensitive to the affinities between the *Meditations* and Loyola's *Spiritual Exercises*.

injunction, which is the *Regulae*'s analogue of the first rule of the *Discourse*, might easily be thought to summarize the method of doubt. But it does not. The method of doubt, properly understood, involves not merely a resolution to accept only what cannot be doubted but also a resolution to attempt to doubt all previous beliefs by searching for grounds of doubt:

> As regards all the opinions which up to this time I had accepted, I thought I could not do better than to undertake, once and for all, to rid myself of them, in order to replace them afterwards—either with other, better opinions, or else with the same ones, when I had made them square with the standards of reason. (AT VI, 13; HR I, 89)

It is this project, the project of systematically reviewing one's past beliefs and casting out those which do not conform to the highest standards of rationality, which defines Descartes' mature work. It is first announced in the *Discourse*,[22] where it is carried out only sketchily. It is repeated again at the beginning both of the *Meditations* and of the *Principles*, where it is said to be a project which everyone should undertake once in his life. But it has no real analogue in the *Regulae*. And it could not have a true—that is, conscious and considered—analogue in the *Regulae* since it presupposes a doctrine of judgment which the Descartes of the *Regulae* had not yet worked out, the doctrine that judgment is an act of the will which we may forbear whenever the proposition in question is not perceived clearly and distinctly.[23]

Descartes does, in the *Regulae*, discuss a project which he thinks that everyone who has the slightest regard for truth should under-

22. Kemp Smith (pp. 15–17) ascribes a decision to review all previous beliefs to the days of crisis in 1619, but there is no sign of this in any of the pre-1628 writings. His evidence is the *Discourse on Method*. But this is precisely the kind of point on which the *Discourse* cannot be accepted as history. Descartes is too much inclined to project his mature ideas into his youth and conceive his life as a unity. Alquié's introduction to the *Discourse* contains an admirable discussion of the problem of its historical accuracy (*Oeuvres* I, 555–561).

23. I have dealt with Descartes' doctrine of judgment in "Descartes, Spinoza and the Ethics of Belief," in M. Mandelbaum and E. Freeman, *Spinoza: Essays in Interpretation* (La Salle, Ill.: Open Court, 1975). See also my review of A. Kenny, *The Anatomy of the Soul*, in the *Australasian Journal of Philosophy*, 54 (1976), 80–86.

take once in his life. But that project is not the one we find in the mature Descartes. It is more Lockean than Cartesian.[24] What everyone with an interest in the truth should do, once in his life, is to determine "the nature and extent of human knowledge" (AT X, 397; HR I, 26). And the reason for undertaking this project is not the same as the reason for undertaking the later one. In the *Discourse* and the later writings we seek to doubt whatever can be doubted in order to find a foundation for our beliefs which is absolutely certain (AT VI, 29, 31–32; HR I, 99, 101). The project is one which sets Descartes in opposition to the skeptics. The project of the *Regulae*, on the other hand, is motivated by a characteristically skeptical desire to avoid futile disputes about problems which human reason is incapable of solving. There could hardly be a more important difference of doctrine than that.

The Descartes of the *Regulae* is both more and less skeptical than the Descartes of the published works. If the earlier Descartes is less sensitive to the force of the skeptical dialectic, he is also more impressed by the limits of human knowledge. And the mature Descartes knows this. So he writes to Vatier, after the publication of the *Discourse*, that he knew

> that what I said I had put in my *Treatise on Light* about the creation of the Universe would be incredible; only ten years ago, if someone else had written that the human mind was able to attain such knowledge, I myself wouldn't have been willing to believe it. (22 February 1638; Alquié, *Oeuvres* II, 27; *Philosophical Letters*, 46–47)

So Descartes himself, in the period of the *Discourse*, was acutely conscious of the progress he had made since 1628; in spite of his greater appreciation of skepticism, he was more optimistic about the possibility of human knowledge.

24. This is a point of similarity between the Descartes of the *Regulae* and Locke which is commonly passed over by those students of Descartes and Locke who speculate that Locke may have known the *Regulae*. Cf. Kemp Smith, 70, n4, and R. I. Aaron, *John Locke* (Oxford: Clarendon Press, 1955), pp. 9–12, 220–227. As for the question of Locke's access to the *Regulae*, I have discussed this in my review of Krüger's *Der Begriff des Empirismus*, in the *Journal of Philosophy*, 74 (1977), 184–189.

3

DREAMING

THE METHOD of doubt which characterizes Descartes' mature doctrine requires a deliberate search for reasonable grounds for doubting all our past beliefs. The whole project is, of course, highly problematic. How can we have reasonable grounds for doubting *everything?* If we claim to have reasonable grounds for doubting one proposition, does this claim not presuppose that there are other propositions we have good reason to believe? Nevertheless, to Descartes this project was of fundamental importance. So he writes,

> Nothing is more conducive to attaining a firm knowledge of things than first becoming accustomed to doubt all things especially corporeal ones. So although I had, some time ago, seen several books on the subject, written by Academics and Skeptics, and felt some distaste at heating up that stale dish again, still I had to give it a whole Meditation. And I would wish that, before they went on, my readers would devote some months, or at least weeks, to considering the matters treated there, not just the short time required for reading it over. (AT VII, 130; HR II, 31)

In spite of this emphatic advice, and in spite of the extensive attention which has been devoted to the First Meditation in the 300 years or more since Descartes wrote, the method of doubt and its presuppositions are still widely misunderstood.

I propose to clarify the method by examining one skeptical argument in detail, the argument from dreams. I do not choose this argument because Descartes regarded it as the most important. He thought the argument from God's omnipotence more general, and hence more fundamental (cf. AT VIII-1, 6; HR I, 220). But the dream argument raises essentially the same methodological problems. Moreover, its long history shows, and Descartes recognizes, that it can be made very persuasive, that if it is fallacious, its flaw is not easy to detect. That is one good reason for discussing it. Another is that the argument is so familiar that not much care is usually given to stating it in the strongest possible form. Defenders and critics alike treat it very casually. As a result it has been the subject of much ill-considered criticism. The argument is far better than its contemporary reputation. Those who think that Moore, Wittgenstein, and Austin have disposed of it forever must be patient and look again at the argument.

The context in which the argument occurs is one in which Descartes is considering the possibility of his being deceived by his senses. He presents himself—and there can be no doubt that this is a literary device—as an empiricist, who has come to believe whatever he believes through the evidence of his senses (cf. AT V, 146; Bridoux, 1355). He notes that his senses have sometimes deceived him and remarks that it is imprudent to trust fully those who have deceived us even once. But in the First Meditation he does not present any concrete examples of (waking) deception by the senses, probably from a desire to avoid the trite. (Even so, both Hobbes and Gassendi complained that the themes of the First Meditation were too familiar to warrant the time spent on them. See AT VII, 171, 257–258; HR II, 60, 136.)

Instead Descartes immediately counters this skeptical motif by suggesting that it is only concerning very small or distant objects that the senses deceive us. There are some propositions which simply cannot—or cannot reasonably (FV)—be doubted, even though we believe them because of the evidence of the senses: that I am here now, sitting by the fire, dressed in a winter cloak, touching this paper with my hands, that my hands exist, and indeed that my whole body exists. To doubt such propositions as these would be mad.

Then Descartes reflects that he is a man, who is accustomed to sleep at night and who is sometimes deceived by experiences he has in his dreams:

How often does my nightly rest persuade me of these familiar things—that I am here, dressed, seated by the fire—when in fact I am lying unclothed in bed. But now, certainly, I see this paper with waking eyes, this head which I shake is not asleep, I reach this hand out deliberately and consciously. Things so distinct would not happen to someone who was asleep. [LV: *non tam distincta contingerent dormienti*, FV: *ce qui arrive dans le sommeil ne semble point si clair ni si distinct que tout ceci*.] But thinking about it carefully, I remember that I have often been deceived, [LV: *delusum*, FV: *trompé*] when I slept, by similar thoughts [FV: *illusions*]. Dwelling on this thought, I see so plainly that there are no certain indications by which I can clearly [*nettement*, added in FV] distinguish being awake from being asleep that I am astounded. And my astonishment is so great that it is almost capable of persuading me that I am asleep. (AT VII, 19; IX–1, 14–15; HR I, 145–146)

This is Descartes' dream argument, as he presents it. And the question is: What, shorn of its rhetoric, does the argument come to? What are its premises? What is its conclusion?

One way of stating the argument might be as follows. It proceeds from a premise about the occurrence of dreams:

(i) Sometimes we take objects to exist in reality when they exist only in our dreams;

to a subsidiary conclusion about the similarity of dream experiences and waking ones:

(ii) There is no intrinsic difference between illusory dream experiences and veridical, waking experiences;

to a final conclusion about the possibility of deception:

(iii) We may be dreaming all the time.

This is not, I think, a very satisfactory way of putting the argument. It is too crude and simple. But it has a certain currency in the literature.

One reason some philosophers do not take much care in stating this argument is that they think any variation on this theme which is recognizable as a form of the dream argument will be open to a crushing Procedural Objection: if the conclusion of Descartes' argument were true, he could not assert its premise. So if the

48

argument were correct, it would defeat itself by removing the ground we are supposed to have for accepting the conclusion. Hence it would be idle to worry too much about the precise statement of the argument.

This line of objection has, it seems to me, been more popular than it deserves to be. Forms of it can be found in many different authors,[1] and so long as it is not examined too closely, it can seem very appealing. If we were called on to defend a premise like (i), we would contrast what we take to have been dream experiences with what we take to have been nondream experiences. And surely it is paradoxical to begin by saying that *some* experiences *are not* dream experiences and end by saying that perhaps *all* experiences *are* dream experiences.

Nevertheless, if the procedural objector presupposes *this* form of the dream argument, he makes things much too easy for himself. The reply may fairly be made on Descartes' behalf[2] that, when he is stating the dream argument at its best, he does not draw so extreme a conclusion as (iii), that instead he concludes merely

(iii') We may be dreaming at any time.

This weaker conclusion is sufficient for Descartes' skeptical purposes, but does not give the same appearance of inconsistency with the premises.

The procedural objector will not, I think, feel satisfied with this reply. He may object again that even if we substitute the more modest (iii') for (iii), there is still an incompatibility between (ii) and the assertion of (i). If (ii) is correct, then we cannot distinguish between dream experiences and waking ones. Yet (i) assumes that we can make that distinction and would make no sense if we could not.

Thus put, the Procedural Objection assumes a quite extraordinary principle of meaning, which might be formulated as follows:

1. In J. L. Austin, *Sense and Sensibilia* (New York: Oxford University Press, 1964); W. H. Walsh, *Metaphysics* (London: Hutchinson University Library, 1963); H. H. Prichard, *Knowledge and Perception* (Oxford: Clarendon Press, 1950); and G. E. Moore, "Certainty," in *Philosophical Papers* (London: Allen and Unwin, 1959, reprinted by Doney).
2. And has been made by Frankfurt, in *Demons, Dreamers and Madmen*, 51.

If it is not possible to distinguish, on the ground of intrinsic features alone, between A's and B's, then it makes no sense to say that some things are A's and others B's.

But once this assumption is stated explicitly, it does not take much reflection to see that it is false. The construction of counterexamples is left as an exercise for the reader.

Our procedural objector is a persistent fellow, and we may imagine him returning once more to the attack: "That is not what I meant at all. When I said that Descartes could not 'formulate' or 'set up' or 'state' his premise if his conclusion were true, I did not intend to lay down any principle of meaning, and certainly not the one you have just ascribed to me. What I meant was that the use of a premise like (i) implies, or presupposes, that the person using it knows it to be true, or at least believes it without question. If he does not, then he is not entitled to use it. And if (ii) is true, Descartes cannot know (i) or even believe it without question. So he cannot be entitled to use (i). Doubt requires a positive ground or basis."

Now when the Procedural Objection is put this way, we are back to the problem with which we began this chapter. But Descartes' reply is clear.

He would not accept any such requirement. The premises of the skeptical arguments of the First Meditation need not be ones Descartes knows to be true, or is certain of, or even believes without question. The dream argument may be compared on this point with the argument from God's omnipotence. The proposition that there is a being who can do everything is introduced in the First Meditation as "an opinion long established in my mind." But if it were taken to be certain or known to be true, the arguments of the Third and Fifth Meditations would be superfluous. In fact, of course, it is characterized, as late as the beginning of the Third Meditation, as a "preconceived opinion"; so it is not, at that stage, taken to be well grounded, nor even, presumably, taken to be believed without question (AT VII, 21, 36; HR I, 147, 158).

Descartes does not set high epistemic standards for the premises of his skeptical arguments. Why not? And what requirements does he set? These are questions which will occupy us in the next two chapters. For now, let me just say that the attempt to set high requirements seems quite misguided.

Suppose we found that the dream argument proceeded validly from premises we believed on reflection to be true. Why should that not be enough to give us cause for concern? What the Procedural Objection tells us, really, is that if the argument were sound, there would be some kind of difficulty about asserting or believing or knowing its premise. And that may give us a reason for looking more closely at the argument. But the objection does not tell us *what* is wrong with the argument. It does not say "This premise is false" or "That step is fallacious." And it does not seem too much to ask the objector to identify some such mistake. After all, the premise from which the argument starts out seems to be plainly true. And while it may not be obvious how the conclusion is supposed to follow from this premise, any intuitions of invalidity we have might just reflect some remediable defect in the statement of the argument, for example, the suppression of some essential but highly plausible premise. So far the most we have is some reason to feel uncertain about the premise *if* we think the argument is sound. But is the argument sound?

I

I PROPOSE, first of all, to restate the argument in a form which I think does it, and Descartes, more justice than the crude version so far considered. The reasons for some of the emendations suggested will become apparent only as we discuss possible objections:

(1) Sometimes I have very vivid experiences which, at the time, I take to be of ordinary-sized objects in my immediate vicinity, but which, subsequently, I decide were illusory experiences because they occurred while I was asleep and dreaming.

(2) Sometimes I have, in dreams, experiences which I take to be of ordinary-sized objects in my immediate vicinity and which are so like my most vivid waking experiences that they are not, in themselves, certainly distinguishable from waking experiences.

(3) If some dream experiences are so like my most vivid waking experiences that they are not, in themselves, certainly distinguishable from waking experiences, then so long as I consider only the experiences themselves, none of them, no matter how vivid, can be said with certainty to be waking and veridical, rather than sleeping and illusory.

(4) If, so long as I consider only the experiences themselves, none of my experiences can be said with certainty to be waking and veridical, then none of my beliefs about ordinary-sized objects in my immediate vicinity are certain.

(5) None of my beliefs about ordinary-sized objects in my immediate vicinity are certain.

Clearly this sequence of propositions needs some justification, if it is to be regarded as being, even for purposes of discussion, 'Descartes' argument.'

First, I have introduced a number of technical, or quasi-technical, terms ("experiences," "illusory," "veridical"), terms which are not used by Descartes and may be objected to. Descartes' dream argument is a form of 'the' argument from illusion; but as he presents it, it is relatively free of the contentious terminology Austin criticized in later versions of the argument. The use of that terminology requires explanation.

Part of the justification for framing the dream argument in this way may be brought out by considering one objection to the argument. Bourdin, the author of the Seventh Objections, contended that if the dream argument succeeded in casting doubt on propositions like "There is a fire here," then it ought also to cast doubt on mathematical propositions. Mightn't we dream that $2 + 3 = 6$? But the Descartes of the First Meditation—like the St. Augustine of the *Contra Academicos* (X, 23–XI, 25)—does not think the dream argument does cast doubt on mathematical truths.

I suggest that it is a prerequisite for any adequate presentation of the dream argument that it make clear why Descartes thought he needed a different argument to throw doubt on mathematical truths. Though not explicit in Descartes' presentation of the argument, the concept of experience is crucial to the argument. It is because dreams are the kind of experience they are that they provide a (partial) ground for skepticism. It is because mathematics is not an empirical science that its truths are not affected by the dream argument. My reconstruction of the argument is designed to bring those points out.

I use "experience" in as neutral a way as possible. For me to have an experience which I take to be of a red object is for me to be in a state in which I think I see a red object. Surely there can be no question as to whether, in this sense, experiences occur. I *am* sometimes in a state in which I think I see a red object. As I understand Descartes' argument, it involves no commitment to sense data, or any other contentious entities.

We might also note, parenthetically, that this version of the argument from illusion proceeds directly to a skeptical conclusion; it does not proceed to skepticism via the subsidiary conclusion that the immediate objects of perception are sense-data (or ideas, or what not). So we do not here run the same danger of smuggling the conclusion into the premises that some of the philosophers Austin criticizes do.

Again, as I here use the terms "illusory" and "veridical," an illusory experience is one in which what-I-think-is-the-case is not the case, a veridical experience is one in which what-I-think-is-the-case is the case. In the Latin version Descartes uses the term *delusum*. But I take it that this is only a very general term, indicating that something has gone wrong, without suggesting what has gone wrong. The French version is *trompé*. Nothing in what follows will depend on attaching any more specific meaning to the term "illusory."

One final matter of terminology. "Vivid" renders Descartes' *distincta*, which I assume is not used in its technical sense, despite the fact that the French version has both *clair* and *distinct*. This must, I think, be the translator's work. At this stage of the *Meditations*, no groundwork has been laid for the use of "clear" and "distinct" in their technical senses. There is no self-conscious use of these terms until the piece-of-wax passage in the Second Meditation,[3] and one function of that passage is to introduce them.

3. Pace Frankfurt, whose identification of an earlier use of the terms is influenced by the Haldane and Ross translation (Frankfurt, 123): "I begin to know what I am a little more clearly and distinctly than before" (cf. HR I, 153) is not an accurate rendering of either the Latin ("aliquanto melius incipio nosse quisnam sim," AT VII, 29) or the French ("je commence à connaître quel je suis, avec un peu plus de lumière et de distinction que ci-devant," AT IX, 23). The informal introduction of technical terms by way of examples is, I believe, one characteristic of the analytic mode. I have discussed the contrast between analysis and synthesis in "Spinoza as an Expositor of Descartes," in *Speculum Spinozanum*, ed. S. Hessing (London: Routledge & Kegan Paul, 1977).

By providing us with an example of clear and distinct perception, it gives us, in effect, an ostensive definition of clear and distinct perception (AT VII, 259; HR II, 212).

I turn now to matters of more substance. In saying that an experience is subsequently classed as illusory because it occurred while I was asleep and dreaming, I do not mean to subscribe to the view that "I dreamt that *p*" entails "not-*p*." It is perfectly possible that I should dream that *p* where *p* is true. I have in mind here not only cases where what is dreamed coincides with reality *per accidens* but also cases where there is some causal connection between the dream and the reality. For example, in W. Dement's and E. Wolpert's experiments in exposing sleepers to external stimuli, one stimulus used was a 100 watt light bulb, shone directly on the sleepers' faces. Sleepers so exposed subsequently reported dreams involving fire, lightning, shooting stars, and such. But one subject reported dreaming that the experimenter was flashing a light in his face.[4] Though this was indeed the case, I see no reason why we should deny that he was dreaming, so long as he satisfied the same behavioral and physiological criteria for sleep as the other subjects did.

There is not a tight, logical connection between dreaming *p* and *p*'s being false. But normally to discover that an experience is a dream experience will be to discover, inter alia, that what I thought was the case was not the case. It seems to me that I am seated by the fire, but then I find myself lying in bed. I do not recall any sequence of experiences connecting these two experiences, and the circumstances in which I find myself naturally suggest that my impression of being seated by the fire was a dream experience. Here, to decide that my experience of being seated by the fire was a dream experience is, inter alia, to decide that what I thought was the case was not the case.

The text suggests that this is the kind of case Descartes has in mind. If it is, and if it can serve as a paradigm of discovering that I have been dreaming, then in certain central cases, we become aware

4. E. Diamond, *The Science of Dreams* (London: Eyre and Spottiswoode, 1962), p. 126. The incorporation of external stimuli into dreams was known to Descartes, who also noted that such stimuli might give rise to ideas "plus remarquable et plus sensible" (AT XI, 198).

that an experience is a dream-experience only after the fact, through some other, discordant experience. Hence the temporal qualifiers ("at the time," and "subsequently,") in (1). This is also the reason for introducing the qualifiers ("in themselves," and "so long as I consider only the experiences themselves") (2), (3), and (4).

Why "ordinary-sized objects in my immediate vicinity"? Well, the context suggests that perhaps our senses deceive us only when we are concerned with forming beliefs about very small or distant objects. This suggestion will be rebutted if it can be shown that sometimes we are mistaken in experientially based beliefs which we take to be about objects neither very small nor very distant. The presumption is that if any of our beliefs about the external world are certain, these are.

With these explanations, I think we can see that Descartes does assert (something very like) my (1) and (2). (1) is a premise. I suggest, provisionally, that (2) is inferred from (1), though not deductively, that it is put forward as an explanation of (1). Descartes does not explicitly state anything very like (5), but the same considerations of context which lead me to introduce talk of "ordinary-sized objects in my immediate vicinity" require some conclusion of this sort. I offer (3) and (4) as links between (2) and (5). (2) is supposed to entail the antecedent of (3), and we are supposed to detach successively the consequents of (3) and (4) to reach (5). This may seem rather a lot of machinery, but I think it will prove an advantage to have a fairly definite argument before us.

II

So MUCH for the statement of the argument. I turn now to its assessment. Consider step (1):

> Sometimes I have very vivid experiences which, at the time, I take to be of ordinary-sized objects in my immediate vicinity, but which, subsequently, I decide were illusory experiences because they occurred while I was asleep and dreaming.

On the face of it, this is no more than an innocent statement of fact. The only remotely plausible attack on this premise that I know of comes from Norman Malcolm, who holds that it is unintelligible to suppose that experiences can occur in sleep. When I have an experience, I am in a certain psychological state. And Malcolm professes to have a "schema of proof" capable of showing the unintelligibility of supposing that any psychological state— any mental activity, like thinking, reasoning, or imagining, or any mental 'passivity,' like having an emotion, or an illusion, or a hallucination, or imagery—might occur in sleep.

What Malcolm argues, roughly, is that the criteria for sleep and the criteria for being in a psychological state are incompatible, so that if a person satisfies one set of criteria he cannot satisfy the other. From this Malcolm infers that it is impossible to verify that someone is both asleep and in a psychological state. And from that he infers that it is senseless to suppose that someone who is asleep might be thinking or having an experience.

A full treatment of this line of argument would be so long as to be inappropriate here. Suffice to say that I agree with those of Malcolm's critics who find that he is committed to an untenable form of verificationism. Malcolm uses the term "criterion" in a very strong sense, one which commits him to taking conclusive verifiability to be a necessary condition of meaningfulness. No more need be said here than that.[5]

Since bad Malcolmian arguments are the only objections I can see to step (1), I propose to turn to the second step of the argument. From (1) Descartes infers that

> (2) Sometimes I have, in dreams, experiences which I take to be of ordinary-sized objects in my immediate vicinity and which are so like my most vivid waking experiences that they are not, in themselves, certainly distinguishable from the waking experiences.

The most pertinent recent criticism of this step is Austin's in *Sense and Sensibilia*. His main targets, of course, are A. J. Ayer and H. H. Price, not Descartes. For reasons unclear to me, he finds their statements of the argument from illusion more satisfactory than Descartes'. But the claim he queries in them—that delusive and veridical experiences are not intrinsically different—is at least very

5. Verificationism dies hard, and some students of Descartes will find this rejection of Malcolm too abrupt. Cf. Kenny, 30–31. But supporting it involves a long argument, which I have offered in "Dreaming and Conceptual Revision," *Australasian Journal of Philosophy*, 53 (1975), 119–141. The definitive statement of Malcolm's argument occurs in his book, *Dreaming* (London: Routledge & Kegan Paul, 1962). An earlier version is reprinted in Doney.

like the Cartesian claim which our analysis makes step (2) of the dream argument. And some of his criticisms of Ayer and Price are therefore relevant to Descartes.

One possible line of attack on an argument like Descartes' is to query the move from (1) to (2). And in one section of *Sense and Sensibilia* this is a line Austin takes:

> Another erroneous principle which the argument here seems to rely on is this: that it *must* be the case that 'delusive and veridical experiences' are not (as such) 'qualitively' or 'intrinsically' distinguishable—for if they were distinguishable, we should never be 'deluded.' But of course, this is not so. From the fact that I am sometimes 'deluded,' mistaken, taken in through failing to distinguish A from B, it does not follow at all that A and B must be *indistinguishable*. Perhaps I should have noticed the difference if I had been more careful or attentive; perhaps I am just bad at distinguishing things of this sort (e.g. vintages); perhaps, again, I have never learned to discriminate between them, or haven't had much practice at it. . . . What sort of reception would I be likely to get from a professional tea-taster, if I were to say to him, "But there can't be any difference between the flavours of these two brands of tea, for I regularly fail to distinguish between them"? (Pp. 51–52)

Now this criticism can, I think, fairly be applied to Descartes' argument. It certainly does not *follow* from my failing to distinguish between dreams and waking experiences that they are indistinguishable. That they are indistinguishable (or at least, not distinguishable with certainty) is put forward as an explanation of my failure to distinguish them, and explanations are not, in general, entailed by the things they are meant to explain. There may, as Austin suggests, be alternative explanations.

But it does seem reasonable to require that there be *some* explanation of my being deceived. To say that perhaps I am just very bad at distinguishing between dreams and waking experiences, or that I am not, after all, a "quasi-infallible" being, "who can be taken in only where the avoidance of mistake is completely impossible," is to give no explanation at all. Here we might make to Austin the reply Descartes made to Gassendi. To say "that we err because our mind is dull, or our nature weak . . . is merely to say that we err because we are liable to error" (AT VII, 349; HR II,

205). And this does not seem a very constructive observation.

The explanation Descartes offers is at least a very natural candidate for being a correct explanation. Compare Austin's own case of the Headless Woman Illusion. The woman on stage, against a dark curtain, with her head in a black bag, looks—from where I'm sitting—*very* like a woman with no head. If there were something about the way it looks to me by which I could tell the difference, then I would not be taken in.

By contrast, some of Austin's proposed alternative explanations of error are not anywhere near so plausible when considered as explanations of a failure to distinguish between dreams and waking experiences as they are when it is a question of distinguishing vintages, or brands of tea. Last night I dreamt that there was someone at the front door. I woke from the dream in a state of some concern and went to the door to see who it might be at that hour. Could it be seriously suggested that if I had been properly trained to distinguish between dreams and waking experiences, or had had enough practice at it, I would not have been taken in?

Other alternative explanations are more promising, but not very helpful in defeating an argument for skepticism. Perhaps my dream experience was not, in fact, *very* like hearing someone at the door. Perhaps I was taken in because, being asleep, I was too groggy to be sufficiently attentive to the differences between my dream and a waking experience. This is to say, not that the experiences were indistinguishable, but that I, in that condition, was incapable of distinguishing them. But suppose this explanation were (in some or all cases) correct, and suppose we were to amend (2) by adding,

> or which are at least sufficiently like my most vivid waking experiences that I, in that condition, am not able (with certainty) to distinguish them from waking experiences.

With appropriate amendments to (3) the argument might proceed as before.[6] So it may well seem on reflection that any adequate

6. A point which seems oddly to be missed in Cicero's version of the dream argument in the *Academica*. Lucullus, attacking the skeptics, argues: "But you will say that at the time when we are experiencing them the visions we have in sleep have the same appearance as the visual presentations that we experience while awake! To begin with, there is a difference between them; but do

explanation of (1) will be close enough to (2) that the difference does not matter.

This, however, is not correct. We do not need to assume, in order to explain our being taken in by dreams, that dreams are indistinguishable (or not distinguishable by us in that condition) from *our most vivid* waking experiences. It would be sufficient to make error intelligible if we assumed merely that some dreams are very like *some* waking experiences, but not very like the most vivid ones. If we imagine our experiences graded according to vividness, we might picture a scale where some dreams are at the bottom (very vague, shadowy, and so on), some waking experiences are at the top (quite distinct), and the middle is occupied both by dreams and by waking experiences. This seems to be the sort of picture Montaigne was working with in his version of the dream argument:

> When we dream, our soul lives, acts, exercises all her faculties, neither more nor less than when she is awake; but if more loosely and obscurely, still surely not so much so that the difference is as between night and bright daylight; rather as between night and shade. There she sleeps, here she slumbers; more and less . . .
>
> Sleeping we are awake, and waking asleep. I do not see so clearly in sleep; but my wakefulness I never find pure and cloudless enough . . . (Montaigne, 451)

This picture would be sufficient to explain our sometimes being taken in. But it would not be sufficient for Descartes' skeptical purposes. For it would not yield a conclusion with the kind of generality he is after. It would give our most vivid experiences a privileged position which it is Descartes' clear intention to deny them.

So far, then, I conclude that (1) certainly does not entail (2), that at best it renders (2) more or less probable, and that it cannot even

---

not let us dwell on that, for our point is that when we are asleep we have not the same mental or sensory power and fullness of function as we have when awake" (trans. H. Rackham, Loeb Classical Library, Cambridge, Mass., Harvard University Press, 1951, p. 533). Cicero, replying on behalf of skepticism, merely reaffirms the qualitative identity of dreams and waking experiences (pp. 577–583), whereas he might have capitalized on Lucullus' concession that in sleep we are not able to distinguish what would otherwise be distinguishable.

be said to render (2) *very* probable since a weaker assumption than (2) would suffice to explain (1). However, this is not to say that (2) is false, or even shown by the objection we have considered to be at all unlikely. Nevertheless Austin does seem to think that (2) is not just wrongly inferred from (1) but also false.

To maintain the qualitative identity of illusory and veridical experiences, Austin writes, is "perfectly extraordinary":

> I may have the experience . . . of dreaming that I am being presented to the Pope. Could it be seriously suggested that having this dream is 'qualitatively indistinguishable' from *actually being presented* to the Pope? Quite obviously not. After all, we have the phrase "a dream-like quality," some waking experiences are said to have this dream-like quality, and some artists and writers occasionally try to impart it, usually with scant success, to their works. But of course, if the fact here alleged *were* a fact, the phrase would be perfectly meaningless, because applicable to everything. If dreams were not "qualitatively" different from waking experiences, then *every* waking experience would be like a dream; the dream-like quality would be, not difficult to capture, but impossible to avoid. (Pp. 48–49)

Elsewhere he claims that

> We all know that dreams are *throughout un*like waking experiences. (P. 42)

And Kenny reports that in unpublished versions of his lectures Austin maintained that there were about fifty criteria by which we could tell dreams from waking experiences (Kenny, 29).

As rhetoric this is quite effective. What is its force as argument?

Austin holds that an experience of dreaming that I am being presented to the Pope cannot seriously be said to be intrinsically indistinguishable from actually being presented to the Pope. Nothing in the context suggests that he regards this dream as a special case. Evidently he holds that *all* dreams are intrinsically distinguishable, in virtue of their 'dream-like quality,' from waking experiences. And whatever may be required for his attack on Ayer and Price, he would have to hold something as strong as this, if his criticism is to be relevant to Descartes, and if our reconstruction of Descartes' argument is correct. For (2) claims only that *some* dreams are intrinsically indistinguishable from waking experiences.

So who is it who is here making an extraordinarily sweeping claim? The only evidence Austin provides for supposing that *all* dreams are distinguishable from waking experience is that we have a use for the expression "a dream-like quality." And indeed the OED gives, for "dream-like," "like a dream: unsubstantial, vague, shadowy, or ideal, as a dream." This fact of linguistic usage presumably reflects a common belief about what dreams are like.

Descartes, however, is plainly aware of this common belief. So he writes, at one stage of the argument in the First Meditation, "things so distinct would not happen to someone who was asleep." But he rejects this. *Some* dreams, at least, are not at all indistinct. (Cf. The *Discourse*, AT VI, 38, 40; HR I, 105, 106.) Surely it would be sufficient, both for the dream argument and to account for ordinary usage, if dreams were typically, though not always, vague and shadowy.

Now let's take a different tack. Suppose we regard (2), not as something to be inferred from (1), but simply as one person's report of his impression of what some of his own dreams are like. It is not, after all, obvious from the text of the *Meditations* that this was not Descartes' own view of (2). What would be the consequences of adopting this line?

I suppose any sizable group of people will contain some whose impression of the vividness of their dreams tallies with Descartes', and who will be impatient at discussions of arguments from linguistic usage, or from the explanation of error. I can only ask those people to bear with us. Others will not clearly recall ever having had a dream as vivid as those Descartes reports. I fall in this class and so, to judge from *Sense and Sensibilia*, did Austin. If Austin's argument from the use of the term "dream-like" establishes nothing else, at least it shows the kind of impression many of us have of our dreams. For us the question may seem to be "How much weight should we give to the testimony of others?"

If that is the question, it is plainly relevant that, to judge from passages in his other works, Descartes was quite sincere in reporting very vivid dreams, which *he* found difficult to distinguish from waking experiences. For example, in the *Traité de l'homme* Descartes takes the vividness of dream experience to be a datum which an adequate physiology ought to be able to explain (AT XI, 198).

In the *Olympica* he has left us a striking account of three famous dreams which he had in 1619. Commenting on certain features of this account, Alquié remarks that, in conjunction with passages in the correspondence, they testify to a difficulty Descartes really did experience in distinguishing wake from sleep, a difficulty he used, but did not invent to suit the needs of his dialectic, in the First Meditation (Alquié, *Oeuvres* I, 54, n2).

This kind of reflection may lead to the view that *some* people, at least, do *sometimes* have extremely vivid and realistic dreams, though others do not. And that, I think, would suffice to get the dream argument under way. If some do, and some do not, have intensely realistic dreams, then it is plainly a contingent fact that those who don't don't, a fact which could be otherwise.

This view, although it may be the best we can come up with by reflection on information we all have at our disposal, and although it may be sufficient for the dream argument, seems to me to understate the case. The question "What are dreams like, as experiences?" is, on the face of it, an empirical one. It is not customary, in philosophy, to ask whether the work of empirical scientists can contribute anything to the solution of our perplexities. But in this instance I would argue that it is useful to do so.

Experimental psychologists have done a great deal of work on dreaming in the past twenty years or so. That work can be, and has been, challenged on philosophical grounds. But I have argued elsewhere that there are no *good* philosophical reasons for rejecting the findings of the experimental psychologists.[7] I shall not attempt to summarize that argument here, but shall merely present the following as facts, established by recent empirical research and having a bearing on our problem.

The first point is that dreaming is a phenomenon which occurs in conjunction with a physiological state known as the REM state. This provides us with an objective way of determining when dreams occur and how long they last. The results are surprising. Though in the morning we are normally unaware of it, the fact is that dreaming occurs periodically throughout sleep, that we each normally have several dreams during the night, and that, on the

7. In "Dreaming and Conceptual Revision," pp. 119–141.

average, about one-fifth of our total sleep time is spent in dreaming.

This is interesting partly because it supports the emphasis Descartes places on the frequency of dreaming. "How often does my nightly rest persuade me, etc." But, more important, it indicates that the conditions under which we ordinarily try to recall our dreams are not optimal. Some people never recall dreams, except when they are awakened from an REM period in a sleep laboratory. Of those who do, in normal circumstances, recall dreams, most find that they recall much more detail when they are awakened from a laboratory dream than they can when they wake in the morning at home. The experience seems to them to be much more vivid. So insofar as common beliefs about dreams are based on the impressions people have when they wake in ordinary circumstances, those beliefs are based on inadequate data. What at first appear to be individual differences in dream vividness are almost certainly individual differences in dream recall. People's ordinary waking impressions of their dreams provide poor evidence against the view that each of us, every night, has several *very* vivid dreams, without recalling them in the morning, or at least without recalling how vivid they were.

One kind of evidence which points strongly to this conclusion is the following. From a physiological point of view, REM sleep is quite distinct from non-REM sleep. Though some kind of mental activity occurs throughout sleep—the soul, as Descartes had insisted, always thinks—in REM sleep

> the physiological data describe a central nervous system that is, in fact, behaving as if it were receiving a high level of sensory input from the environment . . . its neurophysiological properties resemble those of the active waking state.[8]

Dement hypothesizes that in the REM state the central nervous system is generating 'sensory input' by itself, independently of the environment, and that, from the psychological point of view, REM mental activity is

8. W. Dement, "An Essay on Dreams," in *New Directions in Psychology*, II, ed. W. Edwards et al. (New York: Holt, Rinehart and Winston, 1965), p. 207.

not only more complex [than non-REM mental activity occurring in sleep], but presents an essentially complete perceptual field . . . just as in the waking state, all sensory modalities are ordinarily present in the dream . . . with many details in each mode.[9]

If this conjecture is correct, then it will be, not merely epistemically possible, but very probably true, that Descartes is right, and Austin wrong, about the character of dreams as experiences.

III

I SHALL pass quickly over (3). I take it to be an instance of the following schema:

If some A's are so like our paradigm B's that we cannot distinguish them with certainty from paradigm B's by any internal features, then we cannot say with certainty, on the basis of internal features alone, that something is a B rather than an A.

"Vividness" is just a label for those internal features, such as awareness of detail, which are supposed to characterize paradigmatic waking experiences. So understood, (3) seems to me to be analytic and hence beyond dispute.

So far I have argued that steps (1), (2), and (3) of our argument are all true, conceded that (2) does not follow from (1), and argued that this does not matter greatly, since we have reason to believe (2) independently of (1). I take it that (2), (3), and (4) plainly entail (5). So if we are to escape the conclusion of the dream argument, we must find some ground for rejecting

(4) If, so long as I consider only the experiences themselves, none of my experiences can be said with certainty to be waking and veridical, then none of my beliefs about ordinary-sized objects in my immediate vicinity are certain.

Now it is not, I think, easy to have clear intuitions about (4). And since its role in the argument is typically not made explicit, there is no body of existing critical discussion that we can look to for guidance. Nevertheless, I conjecture that if there is a flaw in the argument, it lies here, and not in the argument's empirical assumptions.

What, precisely, does (4) say? One way of paraphrasing it

9. Ibid, p. 205.

would be: it is a necessary condition of the certainty of our beliefs about the external world that some of our experiences possess intrinsic features which enable us to say with certainty that they are veridical rather than illusory. And this is neither an innocent statement of fact, nor a highly plausible empirical claim, nor a patently analytic truth. But then we should not expect to be able to derive interesting philosophical conclusions ex nihilo.

What might be said in favor of (4)? Someone might hold, I think, that we do have some experiences which can be said with certainty, on the basis of intrinsic features alone, to be veridical, and that it is only in virtue of our having these experiences that we can claim certainty for some of our beliefs about the external world. Whatever our contemporary dogmatists may hold—and it is often difficult to tell—the Stoic theory of *kataleptikai phantasiai* (sometimes translated "apprehensive presentations" or "graspable presentations") seems to have involved just such a doctrine.[10] This would be one form which an empiricist theory of knowledge might take, and for convenience we may refer to it as Stoic empiricism. Stoic empiricism provides one rationale for accepting (4), and if (4) is what is to be rejected in the dream argument, then Frankfurt would be right in seeing the dream argument as a reduction to absurdity of (one kind of) empiricism (Frankfurt, 50–53).

Empiricism need not take that form. An empiricist might allow that nothing about our sensory experience makes our beliefs about the external world certain. And of course an empiricist of that sort will have no reason to avoid the conclusion of the dream argument.

Or an empiricist might hold that, though the certainty of our beliefs about the external world is based on sense experience, it is only in virtue of *extrinsic* features of those experiences that some of them are certainly veridical. In particular, he might argue that it is their relation to other experiences which distinguishes certainly veridical experiences from those which are not certainly veridical. Veridical experiences are connected with other experiences in a way in which illusory ones are not.

Here I am, seated at my desk, pen in hand, paper in front of me, listening to music as I work. Not only is my present experience

10. Cf. Cicero's *Academica* I, xi, II, vi–xviii, or Sextus Empiricus, *Against the Logicians*, I, 247–260.

very vivid, in that I am aware of a great many features of my immediate environment, but there is nothing bizarre or startling about what I am presently experiencing. These are all things I recall having experienced before. They are behaving in familiar ways. I can clearly recall the experiences I was having a few minutes ago, or half an hour ago, or two hours ago. There was nothing unusual about those experiences, either in themselves or in the way they led up to my present experience. This is what I mean when I say that my present experience is connected with, or coheres with, my past experience. And this, it might be said, is what makes it certain, what entitles me to be certain, that I am not now dreaming.[11]

This view—call it coherence empiricism—has a certain initial plausibility. I think many people would say: "Yes, this is how we do distinguish our waking experience from a dream," though they might have some reservations about claiming to make that distinction with certainty on this basis. And of course there is some ground for associating Descartes himself with this view, on the strength of what he says in the Sixth Meditation, when he rebuts the dream argument:

> The hyperbolic doubts of the past few days are to be rejected as ridiculous—particularly that very general doubt concerning sleep which I was not able to distinguish from the waking state. For now I notice a great difference between them, in that dreams are never conjoined by memory with all the rest of the actions of my life, as those things are which happen to someone who is awake. If, while I was awake, someone suddenly appeared to me, and afterwards immediately disappeared, without my seeing where he had come from or gone to—as happens in sleep—then it would be

11. Cf. Hegel: "In dreams everything drifts apart, crisscrosses in the wildest disorder, objects lose all necessary objective, rational connection, and are associated only in an entirely superficial, contingent and subjective manner." He goes on, however, to qualify this with the remark that occasionally dreams do "contain something that has a tolerable connection with the real world. Especially is this so with dreams before midnight; in these the fancies can in some measure be fitted in with the real world with which we are concerned in the daytime. At midnight, as thieves well know, we sleep soundest; the soul has then withdrawn into itself away from all its interest in the outer world. After midnight dreams become more fanciful." *Hegel's Philosophy of Mind*, trans. W. Wallace and A. V. Miller (Oxford: Clarendon Press, 1971), p. 70.

reasonable for me to judge that he was a specter, or a phantom formed in my brain, rather than a true man. (AT VII, 89–90; HR I, 198–199)

It may be surprising to find Descartes saying this. After all, if there is such a great difference between dreams and waking experiences, why was it not noticed in the First Meditation?

The answer, of course, is that we must distinguish between Descartes' position and that of the empiricist who wants to use connection with other experiences as a way of selecting some experiences as certainly veridical. Descartes, I think, recognizes that, on a purely empiricist approach, if dreams are never connected in the right way with waking experience, this is at best a fortunate accident. If some dreams are intrinsically as similar to waking experience as Descartes claims they are, then there is no reason why some dreams should not also cohere with the rest of our experience. The coherence of some of our experiences could not, by itself, be a sufficient reason for selecting them as certainly veridical. Coherence, on Descartes' view, can provide certainty about the external world only if it is supplemented by some form of a priori guarantee, like a proof that there is a God who is not a deceiver.

Now insofar as Descartes denies the adequacy of coherence empiricism, it seems to me that he is on solid ground. But quite apart from any difficulties which may be inherent in his project of proving that there is a nondeceiving God, his approach shares an embarrassing defect with coherence empiricism. Both Descartes and the coherence empiricist presume that dreams *are* never connected with the rest of the actions of our life. But in fact some people—narcoleptics, for example—do experience dreams which cannot be distinguished from waking experience in the way both Descartes and the coherence empiricist require. They often fall asleep quite unexpectedly and go immediately into vivid, but quite prosaic, dreams. The environment of the presleep period is maintained as a background, and extraordinary sequences of events do not occur.[12] So both Descartes and the coherence empiricist make false empirical assumptions.

12. Cf. Dement, "An Essay on Dreams," p. 221. These cases are also discussed briefly in my "Dreaming and Conceptual Revision."

Someone may, of course, object that the dreams of narcoleptics are not coherent with *all* the rest of their experience. After all, if there were not, at some stage—say after he wakes—some incoherence, how could we be justified in calling the narcoleptic's experience a dream? But Descartes makes it quite clear that the connections he is concerned with are ones which might be supplied by memory. If I want to decide *now* whether or not I am dreaming, the incoherence of my present experience with *future* experience is necessarily not available to me. So "coherence" here means "coherence with past experience."[13]

Both Descartes and the coherence empiricist reject (4) on the ground that something other than intrinsic features of our present experience can justify claims to certainty about the external world. The coherence empiricist recommends the extrinsic feature of relations with other experiences. Descartes relies on that criterion, supplemented by a divine guarantee of its validity. But neither succeeds in showing us an alternative route to certainty.

So I agree with the Stoic empiricist to this extent: if any of our beliefs about the external world were certain, it would have to be because some of our experiences possessed intrinsic features which enabled us to say that they were certainly veridical. So I accept (4). Unfortunately, however, the Stoic empiricist is wrong to think there are any "apprehensive presentations." The denial of such presentations is what we are committed to by (2). So I see no real escape from the conclusion of the dream argument.

I V

I CONCLUDE with a historical note on a possible connection between the dream argument and the argument from God's omnipotence. In antiquity dreams were frequently thought to be of divine origin. It is not surprising, then, that a discussion of the dream argument should sometimes involve questions about divine powers. An instance occurs in Cicero's *Academica*, when Lucullus presents the following skeptical argument:

13. Cf. Cicero: "The question is not what sort of recollection is usually experienced by those who have woken up or have ceased to be mad, but what was the nature of the visual perception of men mad or dreaming at the moment when their experience was taking place." *Academica* II, xxviii (Rackham trans.).

> If a presentation put by the deity before a man asleep is of such a character that it is probable, why not also of such a character that it is extremely like a true one? Then, why not such that it can with difficulty be distinguished from a true one? Then, that it cannot even be distinguished? Finally, that there is no difference between the one and the other? (*Academica*, II, xvi)

Lucullus is one of the characters in the dialogue who are charged with defending the dogmatism of Antiochus, so he puts this argument up only to knock it down. What is particularly interesting here is one of the objections he makes to this skeptical argument: "Who will have granted you either that the deity is omnipotent, or that even if he can do as described, he will?" Perhaps this is a bad objection to a bad argument. It is hard to see why God would have to be omnipotent to produce in men dreams indistinguishable from waking experiences. But then it is not easy to see why God would have to be omnipotent (much less the creator of eternal truths) in order to produce in men unshakeable beliefs in some mathematical falsehoods. The point of interest, however, is that assumptions which might have seemed extravagant to a contemporary of Cicero would not necessarily seem extravagant to a contemporary of Descartes. So the doubt based on God's omnipotence might well have been suggested to Descartes by a reading of the *Academica*.

However, this brief allusion to the powers of a deity in Cicero occurs only in the context of a discussion of sense perception and not, as in Montaigne, in a context in which eternal truths are being questioned. Moreover, when Cicero later takes up the defense of skepticism, he does not invoke God's omnipotence as a ground of doubt, either in discussing perceptual beliefs or in discussing beliefs in propositions of the kind Augustine and Descartes were to call eternal truths. So Montaigne is a more probable source for the Cartesian doubt based on God's omnipotence.

4

THE COGITO

THE DREAM argument is intended to provide a reasonable ground for doubting anything we may believe because of sense experience. If none of my experientially based beliefs about ordinary-sized objects in my immediate vicinity are certain, then no experientially based belief can be certain. And though the precise sense to be attached to the term "reasonable" has not yet been explained, readers not committed to some contemporary form of dogmatism should by now be inclined to grant that the dream argument does provide such a ground of doubt for that class of beliefs.

But though the Descartes of the First Meditation begins philosophizing as an empiricist, who bases all beliefs on experience, he does not keep up that literary fiction for very long. About halfway through the First Meditation he recognizes a class of beliefs which will, on the face of it, be true whether his experience is that of one who is awake or that of one who is asleep: the truths of arithmetic and geometry, and others of that kind, "which treat only of the simplest and most general things, and care little whether these things exist in nature" (AT VII, 20; HR I, 147). To doubt such propositions other grounds are required, and are found in the long-held belief that there is a God, who can do everything, who has made me as I am, subject to at least some errors, and who, even if he does not deceive me in everything, may still deceive me in any of the things I think I know most perfectly.

Now this second, more general ground of doubt, may be less persuasive than the first. The first, after all, starts from a proposition which can be represented either as a common sense belief, controversial only among philosophers (Sometimes in dreams we take things to be real which are not real) or as a highly plausible empirical proposition (Some of our dreams are so like our most vivid waking experiences that they cannot at the time certainly be distinguished from them). But that we have been created by an omnipotent being is neither a common sense proposition nor one which now commands so wide an assent as it did in the seventeenth century. (As Popkin has usefully reminded us, even belief in demons was much more prevalent in the seventeenth century than it is now.)

I have argued that the premises of Descartes' skeptical arguments need not be known to be true or believed without question. One of the themes of this chapter will be that they need not even be believed, in order to serve as the basis for a reasonable doubt. But I think it will be easiest to see why this is so if we begin by considering the first proposition to survive reasonable doubt.

Descartes tells us that the first and most certain principle which presents itself to someone philosophizing in an orderly way is that he exists.[1] Although some might question the priority thus attributed to our knowledge of the self's existence, I think a great many philosophers would agree with Descartes that it is quite certain knowledge—even though to admit this is, evidently, to

1. I cannot, in fact, find any one place where he says precisely this. I am conflating three passages.

"In the Second [Meditation], when the mind using its liberty, supposes that all those things do not exist whose existence can be doubted at all, it recognizes nevertheless that it cannot happen, that it itself does not, in the meantime, exist" Synopsis of the *Meditations*, AT VII, 12; HR I, 140. (The French version does not have "in the meantime," AT IX, 9.)

"And therefore this knowledge [LV; FV has *conclusion*] *I think, therefore, I exist* is the first and most certain which occurs to anyone who philosophizes in an orderly way" AT VIII-1, 7; HR I, 221.

"The term *principle* can be taken in different senses. It is one thing to search for a *common notion* which is so clear and general that it can serve as a principle for proving the existence of all the beings (*entia*) one will subsequently know, and another to search for *a being* whose existence is more known to us than that of any others, so that it can serve us as a principle for knowing them. . . . In this latter sense, the first principle is that *our soul exists*, because there is nothing whose existence is better known to us." Letter to Clerselier, June 1646; *Philosophical Letters*, 197. Cf. also AT VII, 480; HR II, 281.

admit that there can be certain knowledge of synthetic propositions.

When we try to say why Descartes can be certain of his existence, however, we immediately run into trouble. Descartes' "argument" for his existence, the famous *cogito, ergo sum*, is as obscure on examination as it is compelling at first glance. Descartes himself seems to give different accounts of the rationale for his certainty, and on no account that he offers is it clear that he is entitled to certainty.

Traditionally, the puzzle takes the following form: is Descartes' knowledge of his existence intuitive or inferential? Either answer bristles with difficulties, both textual and philosophical. In the *Regulae* Descartes says that everyone sees by an intuition that he exists, that he thinks, and many other things (AT X, 368; HR I, 7). This suggests that "I think" and "I am" are on a par with one another, that neither need be inferred from any other proposition, since each is, in its own right, as certain as we could wish it to be.

But the *Regulae*, as we have seen, is an early, immature work. And one respect in which it is immature is that it reposes a naive confidence in what we see by intuition. In his later, published works, Descartes seems to have lost that confidence and to think that there may be good grounds for doubting even the things that seem most evident to us (AT VII, 21, 36; HR I, 147–148, 158–159). In the later writings the proposition "I exist" is normally presented in a way which makes it look like the conclusion of an argument. "I think, therefore I exist."[2] The Second Meditation is notoriously an exception, but even there Descartes speaks of his existence as following from the fact that he judges that the wax exists (AT VII, 33; HR I, 156).

Still, if "I exist" is inferred from "I think," problems remain. It is natural to suppose that such an inference would be enthymematic, having a suppressed major premise, such as "whatever thinks exists," which should be made explicit. On this interpreta-

2. AT VI, 32; HR I, 101; AT VII, 140–141; HR II, 38; AT VIII–1, 7; HR, 221; Letter to Reneri for Pollot, April or May 1638, Alquié, *Oeuvres* II, 53–54; *Philosophical Letters*, 52; Letter to Colvius, 14 November 1640, Alquié, *Oeuvres* II, 282; *Philosophical Letters*, 83–84.

tion, as Spinoza pointed out,[3] it would seem that the premises would have to be better known than the conclusion. And that, on the face of it, is inconsistent with the status of "I exist" as a first principle. When Descartes is pressed on this point, sometimes he seems to deny that there is an inference, and sometimes he seems to concede it, as we shall see.

Such is the traditional problem. And each of the traditional answers to this problem has knowledgeable and interesting defenders in recent work on Descartes. Jaakko Hintikka's widely read article[4] on the *cogito*, for example, may be regarded as a sophisticated modern version of the view that "I exist" is certain on intuitive grounds. Hintikka, of course, does not deny that Descartes sometimes presents the *cogito* as an inference. There are too many contrary texts for such a denial to be plausible. But he thinks that viewed as an inference, the *cogito* is not a very good argument, and hence he prefers to emphasize what he calls its performatory aspect.

Considered as an inference, the *cogito* may be regarded as an instance of *modus ponens*, with a suppressed conditional premise of the form:

(1) $Ba \supset \exists x(x = a)$ [If I think, then I exist.]

Hintikka concedes that this conditional is provable in standard systems of predicate logic, but argues that in the systems in which it is true, it is of no use to Descartes in proving his conclusion. The systems of logic in which (1) is provable all tacitly assume that the singular terms employed refer to some actually existing individual. If we make this assumption, then before we can represent our categorical premise, "I think," as being of the form required for a sound argument:

(2) Ba

3. Spinoza, *Opera*, vol. I: *Descartes' Principles of Philosophy*, Prolegomenon, ed. C. Gebhardt (Heidelberg: C. Winters, Universitaets-buchhandlung), p. 144.

4. "*Cogito, Ergo Sum:* Inference or Performance?" *Philosophical Review*, 71 (1962), 3–32. Revised versions in A. Sesonske and N. Fleming, eds., *Metameditations* (Belmont, Cal.: Wadsworth, 1965), and Doney.

we must have already decided that the singular term a refers to something that exists. That is, we must have decided that our conclusion,

(3) $\exists x(x = a)$ [I exist],

is true.

Hintikka's point seems to be that on this interpretation the argument will be formally valid and will have true premises, but will be question-begging. 'Deciding on' the truth of the conclusion is supposed to be a necessary precondition for 'deciding on' the truth of the categorical premise. I take this to mean that the argument cannot be a *demonstration*, a valid argument with premises known to be true, unless the conclusion is known first. Hintikka's main criticism of the inferential interpretation of the *cogito*, then, turns out to be a relative of the familiar skeptical attack on all attempts at demonstration.

In any case, Hintikka proposes to regard the *cogito* as a performance, though he grants that this is only the better half of Descartes' insight. Descartes should be seen as recognizing the impossibility or absurdity of performing a certain kind of action, namely, denying his own existence. The sentence "I don't exist," though formally consistent, is "existentially inconsistent." Anyone who understands the language in which it is uttered, and the rules for the use of the first person pronoun in that language, must also understand that whoever utters such a sentence speaks falsely. So the sentence is impossible to believe. And its contradictory "I exist" is therefore self-verifying. Hintikka, then, does not simply appeal to intuition, and in this regard his interpretation is an improvement on more conventional versions of the intuitionist approach.

One problem, however, for any interpretation along these lines, if it is presented as being an account of what Descartes thought, as opposed to what he could or should have said, is to explain why Descartes so often gives the illusion that he is inferring his existence from his thought, when really he is recognizing the self-evidence of his existence. What are the words *cogito* and *ergo* doing in the *cogito ergo sum*?

Hintikka has an answer to this, and this is one further respect in which his interpretation improves on more conventional versions of the intuitionist approach. The "I think," according to him, expresses the performatory character of Descartes' insight. It is from an act of thought that Descartes comes to recognize the indubitability of his own existence, the act of trying to think the contrary. Descartes cannot think that he does not exist, not in the sense of making himself believe it. The attempt to make himself believe that he does not exist, to think it with assent, is necessarily self-defeating. So the relation of *cogito* to *sum* is more a causal one than a relation of inference. A certain (attempted) thought act necessarily produces a conviction of existence. *Ergo* is a trifle inappropriate. It would be more accurate for Descartes to say "By thinking I perceive my existence." But the thinking part is quite essential. Not just any action will do. It must be an act of thought, and specifically an act of trying to persuade myself that I do not exist.

It is, of course, misleading to speak of a performatory act here. Hintikka is not really concerned with speech acts, nor does he argue that asserting "I exist" has any important similarity to such standard examples of performatory utterance as saying "I now pronounce you man and wife." This has invited some criticism which is beside the point (for instance, in Caton, pp. 142–143n). The most relevant criticisms so far are those made by Frankfurt.[5]

Frankfurt's criticism centers on Hintikka's attempted explanation of the role of thinking in the *cogito*. Here he makes two useful points. First, Hintikka's interpretation requires that the thought act which results in my perception of my own existence have a very specific content: what I am trying to think and what I cannot persuade myself of is that I do not exist. In trying and failing to do this, I realize that I do exist. But in fact the thought acts Descartes regards as suitable are quite varied in their content—my existence follows from my being persuaded that there are no bodies, no heaven, no earth, etcetera (AT VII, 25; HR I, 150); it follows from my judging that the wax exists (AT VII, 33; HR I, 156); or from my thinking that I am something (AT VII, 25; HR I, 150).

Second, Hintikka's interpretation requires that the thought act be of a very special kind. It will not do for Hintikka if I simply

5. In "Descartes' Discussion of His Existence in the Second Meditation," *Philosophical Review*, 75 (1966), 329–356.

contemplate the possibility of my not existing, for that is something I certainly can do. The thought act must be an attempt to think my present nonexistence with assent. But for Descartes it is clear that a wide variety of thought acts will do. I can infer my existence from my doubting (AT X, 515; HR I, 316) or even from the fact that I merely entertain any proposition whatever (AT VII, 25; HR I, 150). And so Hintikka is driven to suggesting, in a footnote, that even in the *cogito* argument of the Second Meditation, the version he rightly regards as the most careful and authoritative, even there Descartes does not choose the most accurate way of expressing his insight. If Descartes was aware of the existential inconsistency of "I do not exist," he was only very dimly aware of it.

The difficulties faced even by the most sophisticated version of the intuitionist interpretation naturally make one wonder whether it would not be better, after all, to treat the *cogito* as an inference. One classical objection to the inferential approach is that in the Second Replies Descartes seems to deny that the *cogito* is an inference (AT VII, 140; HR II, 38). The short answer to that objection is that the most this passage shows is that Descartes does not regard the *cogito* as a syllogism with a suppressed major premise; it does not exclude the possibility of the *cogito* being a nonsyllogistic, immediate inference.[6] But though this is substantially correct, the situation is complicated in ways worth some discussion.

We may begin by pointing out that the whole issue of a suppressed major premise was first raised, not in the Second Objections, but in Descartes' own reply.[7] The difficulty raised about the *cogito* by Mersenne, who seems to have been the principal author of the Second Objections (cf. Alquié, *Oeuvres* II, 541n), was a very different one. He writes:

> Since you are not yet certain of God's existence and since you say nevertheless that you cannot be certain of anything, or that you

6. Cf. Bernard Williams, "The Certainty of the *Cogito*," pp. 88–107, in Doney, or Konrad Marc-Wogau, "Der Zweifel Descartes und das *Cogito ergo sum*," *Theoria*, 20 (1954), 128–152.

7. I owe this observation to Hiram Caton, but though we agree about the phenomenon, we differ greatly about the interpretation. Cf. Caton, 138–140.

cannot know anything clearly and distinctly unless you first know clearly and distinctly that God exists, it follows that you do not yet know clearly and distinctly that you are a thinking thing, since, according to you, this knowledge depends on the clear knowledge of an existent God, which you have not yet proved in those places where you conclude that you know clearly that you exist.[8]

Now there is no suggestion here of a suppressed major premise. Mersenne represents the *cogito* as having the form

I think (= I am a thinking thing)
Therefore, I am.

And his question concerns, not Descartes' knowledge of some suppressed major premise, but his knowledge of the premise "I think," that is, the premise which would be a minor premise if the *cogito* were a syllogism. In this he is like Hintikka and unlike most other critics of inferential versions of the *cogito*.

His objection is not quite the same as Hintikka's, however. It is not that the inference is question-begging, because we must know that "I exist" is true before we can know that "I think" is true. It is rather that Descartes cannot claim at this stage of his argument to know that anything is true, since he has not yet proved God's existence. That is, Mersenne raises the classic problem of the Cartesian circle as an objection, not to Descartes' proof of the existence of God but to his 'proof' of the existence of the self. Descartes does seem to lay himself open to such an objection. For he writes, at the beginning of the Third Meditation, *after* the supposed 'proof' of the existence of the self, that he does not seem to be able to be completely certain of anything so long as he does not know whether God exists and can be a deceiver (AT VII, 36; HR I, 159).

Descartes' reply to Mersenne's objection is very curious. He first claims that

When I said *that we can know nothing certainly unless we first know that God exists*, I said expressly that I was speaking only of

8. AT VII, 124–125; HR II, 26; Ross mistranslates the final clause, *quod sis*, as "what you are." In this he can claim to be following Clerselier (cf. AT IX, 98–99); but the translation makes Descartes' reply unintelligible, since there is then nothing in the passage to indicate that it is even the *cogito* which is being questioned.

> the knowledge of those conclusions *whose memory can recur when we are no longer attending to the reasons from which we have deduced them.* For the apprehension of principles is not usually called knowledge by the dialecticians. (AT VII, 140; HR II, 38)

There is a distinction, then, between knowledge of principles and knowledge of demonstrated conclusions. Apparently it is only the knowledge of demonstrated conclusions which requires a divine guarantee in order to count as knowledge.

Now this is not fair to Mersenne. It is true that Descartes does introduce such a distinction at the end of the Fifth Meditation (AT VII, 69–70; HR I, 183–185); and what he says there is quite consistent with his making an exception concerning our knowledge of principles, though he does not explicitly make such an exception there. But Mersenne seems to have had in mind the passage in the Third Meditation, which is much more sweeping and allows no exceptions (AT VII, 36; HR I, 159).

In any case, the implication of Descartes' reply so far is that "I think" can be known without first knowing "God exists," because "I think" is a first principle. Indeed Descartes does go on to say just that:

> When we perceive that we are thinking things, that is a first notion which is not inferred from any syllogism.

This is what we would expect. But then Descartes muddies the waters considerably:

> And when someone says, *I think, therefore I am or exist,* he does not infer his existence from his thought by a syllogism, but by a simple intuition of the mind recognizes it as a thing known by itself. This is evident from the fact that if he deduced it by a syllogism, he would first have had to know this major: *Whatever thinks is or exists.* But on the contrary, he learns that from what he experiences in himself, that it cannot be that he should think unless he exists. For it is the nature of the mind to form general propositions from the knowledge of particular ones.[9]

9. AT VII, 140–141; HR II, 38. Alquié's notes on this passage are instructive. Cf. *Oeuvres* II, 563–565. I follow the Latin version. The French is different, but not, I think, in any critical way.

One thing that is made clear by this portion of the passage is that Descartes is not here[10] willing to treat the *cogito* as a syllogism of the form:

Whatever thinks exists.
I think.
Therefore, I exist.

It is also clear that he thinks something is not inferred, but intuitively evident. Still, there is no telling from this passage just what that something is. It may be that what is seen by a simple intuition of the mind is the proposition "I exist," or it may be the inference, "I think, therefore I exist."

And although an inference might seem an unlikely thing to even consider inferring from anything else, on the ground that only propositions can be inferred,[11] the evidence seems to be that Descartes would not have thought so. He consistently blurs the distinction between inferences and propositions by referring to the whole formula "I think, therefore I am" as a truth, a first principle, a proposition, and a conclusion.[12] In one place he explicitly speaks of the whole formula as being known intuitively (Letter to the Marquess of Newcastle, March or April 1648; Bridoux, 1300–1301). And he does say, in the *Regulae*, that it is necessary to have some intuitions of logical connections before one can make any inferences at all (AT X, 369–370; HR I, 7–8).

All we can safely say about this passage is that in it Descartes displays a certain hostility toward regarding the *cogito* as a syllogism. But that issue looks like a red herring, since Mersenne had never suggested that the *cogito* was a syllogism. And if we focus on the first half of Descartes' answer, neglecting the ambiguous second half, we may want to say that the *cogito* is an asyllogistic

10. Elsewhere, however, it seems that he is willing so to treat it. Cf. *The Principles of Philosophy* I, 10, HR I, 222; AT VIII–1, 8, and the conversation with Burman, AT V, 147; Bridoux, 1356–1357.

11. Cf. G. Ryle, " 'If,' 'So,' and 'Because,' " in *Philosophical Analysis*, ed. Max Black (Ithaca: Cornell University Press, 1950): "An argument by itself cannot be the premiss or conclusion of an argument" (p. 326).

12. Cf. AT VI, 33; HR I, 101–102; AT VIII–1, 8; HR I, 221–222; AT V, 147; Bridoux, 1356–1357. Kenny's discussion of this issue is very helpful (Kenny, 51–55), as are Alquié's notes, *Oeuvres* I, 603–604.

inference, whose premise, "I think," is a first principle, and whose conclusion, "I exist," is known by demonstration.

That, of course, would be a complete reversal of the usual reading, and I have no wish to go so far. All I wish to insist on is that the passage from the Second Replies does not exclude the possibility of regarding the *cogito* as a nonsyllogistic inference from one premise, an inference whose conditionalization—"If I think, then I exist"—may best be construed as a rule of inference rather than a premise. And this much would be common ground with a number of other interpreters like Williams and Marc-Wogau.[13]

If the most prominent textual obstacle to an inferential interpretation is indecisive, how are we to deal with the fundamental philosophical obstacle, the accusation of begging the question? One solution, suggestive but not satisfactory, is offered by Williams. He states the objection in the following form:

> It might be said that a principle of inference is a principle authorizing us to infer one thing from another—say "*q*" from "*p*." But to infer "*q*" from "*p*" is to *come to know* "*q*" on the basis of "*p*"; and in the case that interests us, this is inconceivable . . . it is impossible for me to *come to know* that something is designated by "a" on the basis of the fact that "f(a)" is true. It follows from this that I cannot infer the first proposition from the second. (Doney, 96)

To this Williams replies that the objection confounds epistemological and logical considerations:

> It is extremely useful in logic to be able to say, for example, that there is a principle allowing us to infer "*p*" from "*p* and *q*" even on the assumption that it is in fact impossible to know the truth of "*p* and *q*", without first knowing the truth of "*p*." (Doney, 97)

Williams thinks that what is substantially Hintikka's objection does not really give us any reason for rejecting the inferential interpretation of the *cogito*.

What are we to say to this? It seems to me that Williams' reply to the charge of question-begging is not adequate. Epistemological considerations must be highly relevant to the *cogito*, since its

13. See the articles cited in n. 6 above.

purpose is to establish a firm foundation for knowledge. It will not do to say simply that it is useful in logic to call certain things rules of inference, even though they could not lead us from the known to the unknown.

Perhaps his point is that Hintikka's sort of objection proves too much if it proves anything. Hintikka seems to be saying that, since "I exist" is a necessary condition of "I think," knowing that I exist must be a necessary condition of knowing that I think. One might argue that, if this were the case, any valid deductive argument would have to be question-begging. For if it is valid, the truth of the premises will be sufficient for the truth of the conclusion and the truth of the conclusion will be a necessary condition of the truth of the premises. And the way will then be open for someone to argue that knowing the truth of the conclusion is a necessary condition for knowing the truth of the premises. So the accusation of question-begging, if applicable to the *cogito*, will be applicable to all deductive reasoning. And one might suppose, not being John Stuart Mill, that it is patently false that all deductive reasoning begs the question.

Still, I am not sure that Descartes would feel that he could take it for granted that some deductive reasoning is probative. As we have seen above, criticisms of the syllogism like Mill's had been raised by the skeptics as early as Sextus Empiricus, repeated by the Renaissance skeptics, and apparently accepted by Descartes himself in the *Regulae*. If Descartes would have taken Hintikka's objection seriously, that is reason enough for us to do so.

The results of our reflections so far have not been encouraging, but I would suggest that we can at least see some of the difficulties any interpretation must contend with. I want now to take up an interpretation which comes very close to being right, that offered by Frankfurt, in his recent book *Demons, Dreamers and Madmen*. Frankfurt focuses primarily on the discussion of the existence of the self presented in the Second Meditation, a discussion which does not contain the familiar formula. What he says about that version is quite helpful.

Frankfurt construes the argument as having four steps. Beginning with the question "I myself, am I not something?" Descartes then presents three objections to the proposition that he exists:

(a) But I have already denied that I have any senses or a body. Yet I am perplexed, for what follows from that? Am I so tied to a body and to senses that without them I cannot be?
(b) But I have persuaded myself that there is nothing at all in the world—no heaven, no earth, no minds, no bodies. Have I not, therefore, also persuaded myself that I am not? By no means. Surely if I persuaded myself of anything, I was.
(c) But there is a consummately powerful and crafty deceiver of some sort who assiduously deceives me at all times. Then, beyond doubt, I also exist if he deceives me. And let him deceive me as much as he can, still he will never bring it about that I am nothing, as long as I think that I am something.[14]

The consideration of the first objection leads to no definite conclusion, only questions. In considering the second and third objections, conditional statements[15] closely analogous to the *cogito* are made:

(i) If I persuaded myself of anything, I was.
(ii) If he deceives me, I exist.

Both (b) and (c) also contain categorical statements which could be used to detach the consequents of these conditionals. But Descartes' argument does not terminate in a categorical assertion of his existence. Instead, his fourth step is:

(d) Hence, now that more thorough consideration has been given to the matter, it must finally be concluded that this proposition: I am, I exist, is necessarily true as often as it is uttered by me or conceived by my mind.

This does not attribute necessary truth to "I exist," but to the proposition "When I utter or conceive 'I exist,' it is true" (Frankfurt, 101). Frankfurt concludes that Descartes' purpose is not to prove that "I exist" is true, but to prove that "I exist" is indubitable, in a very special sense of that term.

14. With one minor modification, I follow the translation given by Frankfurt, 91–92. Cf. AT VII, 24, 24–25, l. 13.
15. I do not follow here the strict letter of Frankfurt's interpretation. E.g., he seems to see only one analogue of the *cogito* in this passage: "Descartes does make a statement in the course of his discussion of *sum* that clearly resembles the *cogito*. This statement occurs in the second step of his argument" (p. 92). But his analysis of (c) shows clearly that he sees a *cogito*-like conditional there also (p. 100).

The concept of indubitability here is a normative one. It is not that "I exist" cannot be doubted, but that it cannot reasonably be doubted, that is, that there are not (or cannot be)[16] reasonable grounds for doubting that "I exist." For whenever "I exist" is considered, there is always available a ground for asserting it:

> Instead of showing that *sum* can be deduced from a premiss that is certain in its own right, Descartes in effect points out that a premiss from which *sum* can be elicited is an essential and inescapable element of every context in which the need for assurance concerning *sum* arises. (Frankfurt, 111)

Whenever we doubt "I exist," we consider it; and whenever we consider it, we have available to us a premise from which "I exist" can be inferred.

Now this last point, I suggest, is where the crucial difficulty lies. The notion of the availability of a premise from which "I exist" can be inferred needs explication and it does not get it. "A premise which entails *sum* is available" had better not mean "A premise which entails *sum* is known to be true," for Frankfurt does not (normally) present the *cogito* as a demonstration of its conclusion.[17] If it were a demonstration, "Descartes ought to establish . . . that *cogito* is in fact a statement of which he can be certain. He does not do so."[18] All Frankfurt seems entitled to mean by "a

16. Frankfurt is equivocal on this point. Cf. "What is indubitable is what there is no reason to doubt or what there can be no reason to doubt" (p. 103); "Descartes requires a foundation that *can never* be subject to doubt. He must have statements for which reasonable grounds for doubt are logically impossible" (p. 107); "Clear and distinct perception is a matter of recognizing that there are no reasonable grounds on which a proposition can be doubted" (p. 135). I should prefer to say that the indubitable is what one finds no reasonable ground to doubt, after a systematic search for reasons for doubt. The first rule of the method in the *Discourse* was to include nothing more in my judgments than what "would present itself so clearly and so distinctly to my mind that I *had* no occasion to put it in doubt" AT VI, 18, my emphasis. (HR I, 92 says "could have," but that is not, I think, warranted by the French.) I think the weaker criterion of indubitability is required to account for the passage at the beginning of the Third Meditation (AT VII, 36; HR I, 159).

17. Though Frankfurt does speak of having "conclusive grounds" for *sum* (p. 109).

18. Frankfurt, 110. Actually Frankfurt says "ought to establish or at least to claim that. . . ." But I take it that this is a slip, since the certainty of "I think" is at least claimed in the reply to Gassendi. What is crucial is that it is not established, nor even, so far as I can see, argued for.

premise entailing *sum* is available" is "A premise entailing *sum* is true," and he does not show how that is sufficient to establish that "I exist" cannot reasonably be doubted.

Nevertheless, Frankfurt seems to me to be on the right track, both in the emphasis which he places on the need to have reasonable grounds for doubt and also in his suggestion that the *cogito*, while it is an inference, is not intended to be a demonstration or proof of *sum*. It is not essential to a valid inference that the premises of the argument be known with certainty to be true, though this is essential to a proof, or demonstration, of the classical Aristotelian sort. It is because we think the *cogito* must be a proof if it is an inference at all, that we think the premise must be known to be true. And in that mood we listen willingly to talk about question-begging.

This is because we misunderstand Descartes' project. I take it that Descartes is concerned to avoid the difficulties in the notion of proof pointed out by the ancient skeptics and reiterated regularly by their Renaissance followers. Proof cannot go on to infinity. The process of establishing one proposition by citing others that entail it and are known to be true must come to an end somewhere in propositions which are not themselves proved. The problem is to find a premise, or set of premises, which can serve as first principles, without reasonably incurring the accusation that since the premises are themselves not proved, they are merely arbitrary.[19]

Aristotle himself was aware of this skeptical gambit and seems to have had two ways of dealing with it, neither very satisfactory. Sometimes (to put his point crudely, but not, I think, unfairly) he says that we do, after all, have demonstrations, so there must be indemonstrable propositions which can justifiably serve as their ultimate premises (72b18–24). And I can understand why a skeptic might regard that as question-begging. Sometimes he holds that the first principles of his demonstrations are indubitable in the sense that they cannot be disbelieved, even though they may be disavowed in words (72b20–34). But so far as I can see, this is not argued for, except in the case of the principle of contradiction (1005b20–1009a5).

19. Cf. Sextus Empiricus, *Outlines of Pyrrhonism* I, 14, 5th argum.; I, 15, 16; *Against the Logicians*, II, 1, 6.

Descartes, I suggest, does not want to rely, in his published works (that is, making an exception for the *Regulae*), on the contention that his first principles are self-evident. He knows that self-evidence will be dismissed by the skeptic as a matter of merely subjective conviction, liable to great variation from one person to another. And he wants a reply to that objection. So he adopts a negative procedure for getting his first principles, the method of systematic doubt:

> I know of no other way of properly judging which notions may be taken as principles except to prepare your mind for it by ridding yourself of all the opinions which you are predisposed to, and rejecting as doubtful whatever may be doubtful. (Letter to Mersenne, 15 November 1638; Alquié, *Oeuvres* II, 111)

He will doubt whatever he can find the least reason for doubting, giving his assent, initially, to all and only those propositions which he is able to find no reasonable ground for doubting (AT VII, 18; HR I, 145; AT VI, 31; HR I, 101). And he will systematically apply to each of his former beliefs the most powerful grounds of doubt he can imagine.

Now the notion of a reasonable ground of doubt is very important here. The first thing to notice is that it is not necessary that a proposition which is offered as a reason for doubting be itself very probable or even supported by any substantial body of evidence. It is sufficient that there not be any intellectually compelling evidence against it:

> A reason may be valid enough to force us to doubt, and nevertheless be doubtful itself, and so not to be retained . . . [such reasons] are indeed valid so long as we have no others which induce certainty by removing doubt.[20]

So Descartes will sometimes say that the reasons he offers for doubting are very slight and metaphysical, and that the beliefs they cast doubt on are nonetheless very probable (AT VII, 22, 36; HR I, 148, 159). And the point of setting the evidential requirements of reasonable doubt very low is to avoid skeptical com-

20. AT VII, 473–474; HR II, 277. This passage was emphasized by Alan Gewirth, in his classic article, "The Cartesian Circle," *Philosophical Review*, 50 (1941), 368–395. I am much indebted to Gewirth's article, as the following chapter will also illustrate.

plaints about relying on undemonstrated propositions. For if you accept as a first principle only what you have no reasonable grounds for doubting, and if you make the requirements for reasonable doubt very easy to satisfy, then what you accept cannot be said to be accepted arbitrarily. You are adopting very high standards of rationality.

You are not, however, adopting standards so high they cannot be met. For though the evidential requirements for a reasonable doubt may be very low, there are other requirements. The one most relevant to the *cogito* is that a reasonable ground for doubting a proposition must offer some explanation of how it is that we might erroneously believe the proposition even if the explanation is only conjectural.

That is why "I exist" survives the systematic doubt. Set up any skeptical hypothesis you like—that I am deceived by my senses, that I am dreaming, that I am deceived by an omnipotent demon, or any other you can imagine. Each of these hypotheses involves, in one way or another, the supposition that I am thinking. And it must involve that supposition if it is to explain how my thinking might be erroneous, and so satisfy the conditions for being a reasonable ground of doubt. But that supposition entails my existence. So "I exist" is inferred from "I think." But "I think" is not a premise of a proof. It is, rather, an essential element in any hypothesis which might cast reasonable doubt on my existence. The *cogito* is not question-begging, because "I exist" is not the conclusion of a proof. It is not inferred from premises Descartes need take any responsibility for defending as premises he knows to be true. It is a first principle which Descartes accepts, as he says in the *Discourse*, "without scruple," because he sees "that all the most extravagant suppositions of the skeptics are not capable of shaking it" (AT VI, 32; HR I, 101).

This analysis, I would argue, captures the elements of truth in the inferential and intuitionist interpretations and makes it intelligible that each of them should have had the appeal they have had. But its explanatory power may best be seen by considering a possible objection.

We saw earlier that in the Second Replies Descartes showed signs of treating "I think" as a first principle. And in some of

Descartes' discussions of the *cogito*—notably in the reply to Gassendi—Descartes pretty definitely suggests that the superiority of "I think, therefore I am" to other analogous inferences, like "I walk, therefore I am," or "I breathe, therefore I am," is that we can be certain of "I think," but that we cannot be certain that we breathe or that we walk.[21]

Frankfurt dismisses such passages as a mistake on Descartes' part, principally because he does not see any argument in Descartes for the certainty of "I think" (p. 110). Now it might be suggested that Descartes does have an argument for the certainty of "I think." In the Geometrical Exposition in the Second Replies, Descartes defines thought as "whatever takes place within ourselves insofar as it is an object of our consciousness."[22] From this definition it follows, arguably, that

(1) If I think, then I know that I think.

And since Descartes holds (AT VII, 473; HR II, 276) that

(2) If I know p, I cannot doubt p,

it follows that

(3) If I think, I cannot doubt that I think.

However, if this argument is meant to issue in a categorical assertion of the certainty of "I think," it manifestly does not succeed. All we have so far is a conditional assertion to the effect that "I think" is certain whenever it is true. That is not sufficient to make the *cogito* a demonstration from a certain first principle, "I think." If we try to detach the consequent of (3), we invite an infinite regress. (A further difficulty with this line of argument is that Descartes does not always seem prepared to accept (1), as we shall see in Chapter 7.)

Nevertheless, Descartes does often suggest that "I think" is peculiarly certain. That is a prima facie embarrassment for me,

21. AT VII, 352; HR II, 207; Letter to Reneri for Pollot, April or May 1638, Alquié, *Oeuvres* II, 53–54; *Philosophical Letters*, 52.
22. There is a passage in Kenny (pp. 47–51) which seems to offer Descartes this line of defense. In correspondence Kenny has said he did not mean it to be so construed. But the train of thought is seductive enough to be worth discussing even if it has no actual proponent.

because it suggests that "I exist" is not a first principle at all, but the conclusion of a demonstration. But I am prepared to allow that "I exist" might be the conclusion of a demonstration. For it seems to me that the claim of "I think" to be a first principle can be defended in the same way that the claim of "I exist" can, that is, a proposition entailing "I think" is a common element in any reasonable skeptical hypothesis which might be invoked as a ground for doubting that I think. Any supposition that explains how my thinking might be erroneous must entail not only that I exist, but also that I think. So "I think" would also survive systematic doubt, and the two propositions are on a par. And if that is so, then we have the making of a demonstration of "I exist."

This is why Descartes sometimes is tempted to treat "I think" as certain and "I exist" as the conclusion of a demonstration. But to Descartes there would be no advantage in using such an argument for the certainty of "I think" to establish the certainty of "I exist." For if the fact that a proposition is immune to reasonable doubt is sufficient to make its acceptance as a first principle rational, then we might as well take "I exist" as a first principle to begin with.

Suppose we grant that Descartes' argument does proceed in the way I have suggested, that the notion of a reasonable ground of doubt is central to it, and that Descartes does require that a reasonable ground of doubt offer some explanation, even if only a conjectural one, of my error. Still, it may be argued, to make this requirement is to stack the cards in Descartes' favor. A skeptic who is sufficiently on his guard to see what Descartes is up to will reject the requirement. Why should he offer any explanation of my error? And if he does offer an explanation, why should it be one which implies that I think and that I exist?

One answer to this is that if he does not offer some conjectural explanation of my error, then his attempt to cast doubt on my belief is not likely to be very persuasive. As a matter of fact, the classical skeptics did accept the responsibility for providing an explanation, by offering as grounds of doubt arguments of the sort Descartes considers in the First Meditation.[23] And surely they had

23. Cf. V. Brochard, Les sceptiques grecs (Paris: Vrin, 1923): "It is important to note that the skeptical doubt does not bear on the appearances or phenomena . . . which are evident, but only on the things which are obscure or

to offer some explanation of error, if their position was to have any plausibility at all.

Does the skeptic have to offer an explanation of error which presupposes that I think? Might he not say, more cautiously: "I don't know whether or not it seems to you that you are seated by the fire, attired in a dressing gown, and so on. But *if* it does so seem to you, that may be because your senses are deceiving you, or because you are asleep, or because a demon is deceiving you. Or it may have some other explanation, I know not what"? And the point here is that the explanations are not only conjectural (in the sense that we are not concerned about having evidence for them) but also wholly couched in hypothetical form. "*If* it seems to you, that may be because . . ." An explanation need not presume that what it purports to explain is the case.

And now the question is: "Would a ground of doubt which offered an explanation of error in this very tentative way be a reasonable ground of doubt?" I think not. For as soon as the skeptic attempts to put forward any set of propositions as grounds for my doubting *p*, he is presuming some tendency on my part to believe *p*, he is presuming that in some measure it seems to me that *p*.

The skeptic tells me that I must be sober and doubt all things, that I must suspend judgment even about such things as that I am seated by the fire, attired in a dressing gown. These injunctions certainly presuppose that if I am not sober, I will believe those things, that I have at least some tendency to believe them. And his grounds of doubt are *grounds for doubting* precisely because there is that tendency which must be overcome. So the skeptic must offer as an explanation of the possibility of my believing erroneously, a ground of doubt which assumes that I do think.

A number of problems about the *cogito* remain, problems concerning the principle that whatever thinks exists and its role in the argument. We have already seen one passage in which Descartes denies that the *cogito* is an enthymeme with "Whatever thinks exists" as a suppressed major premise. But to say that the *cogito* is not a syllogism is not to say that the principle relating thought to

---

hidden. . . . . No skeptic doubts his own thought. . . . He does not contest that such an object appears white to him, or that the honey sweet. But is the object white? Is the honey sweet? That is what he does not know" (p. 56).

existence plays no role in the argument. Our earlier discussion of Descartes' views about deduction in general would lead us to expect him to treat the *cogito* as an asyllogistic inference, with the principle functioning as a rule of inference.

This expectation receives support in the texts dealing with the *cogito*. For example, Descartes writes in the *Principles* that:

> When I said that this proposition, *I think, therefore I am*, is the first and most certain of all, which presents itself to someone who philosophizes in the proper order, I did not on that account deny that one must first know what thought is, and existence, and certainty, and that it cannot be the case that what thinks does not exist. (AT VIII–1, 8; HR I, 222)

Here it is granted that knowledge of a principle very similar to "Whatever thinks exists" is a necessary condition for certainty regarding our existence. But in the light of our discussion in Chapter 2 it is interesting that the principle is here given a modalized form: "It is not possible that what thinks does not exist," that is, "Necessarily, what thinks exists." For if the premise which would have to be supplied to make the argument formally valid is a necessary truth, then the original premise must itself have been sufficient for the conclusion.

This, perhaps, is what those scholars[24] sensed who have argued that Descartes distinguishes between two maxims: "Whatever thinks exists," the principle of the Second Replies, which has existential import and is not presupposed by the *cogito*, and "To think it is necessary to be," the maxim cited in the *Principles* (FV), which lacks existential import and is presupposed by the *cogito*. Certainly awkward consequences follow if necessary truths are accorded existential import.

The question of the consistency of the *Principles* with the Second Replies was raised by Burman in his interview with Descartes. And if Burman's report of Descartes' reply is accurate, the apparent distinction of the two maxims is blurred (cf. Caton, 138n):

> Before this conclusion, *I think, therefore, I am*, one can know the major, *whatever thinks, is*, [*sic*], because it is really prior to my

24. Cf. Alquié, *Découverte*, 152, and Gueroult, *Ordre* II, 310.

conclusion, and my conclusion rests on it. And so in the *Principles* the author says that it is prior, because it is always implicitly presupposed and prior. But I do not on that account always know expressly and explicitly that it is prior, and I do know my conclusion first, because I attend only to what I experience in myself. (AT V, 147; Bridoux, 1356–1357)

Here Descartes does not seem to distinguish between "Whatever thinks exists" (the maxim apparently disavowed in the Second Replies) and "To think it is necessary to be" (the maxim apparently acknowledged in the *Principles*), though as Kenny has pointed out (in correspondence), if Burman thought there was no difference between the two formulations, he may have unintentionally distorted Descartes' response. And we cannot, in any case, have the confidence in Burman's report of his conversation with Descartes that we would have in a work Descartes himself wrote and published (cf. Alquié, *Oeuvres* III, 765–766).

The reading of Descartes which seems to me to do the least violence to the texts would run as follows: Yes, there is a general maxim whose correctness is a necessary condition of the validity of the inference from thought to existence; this maxim is a necessary truth, not merely a contingent one; so it is best regarded, not as a suppressed premise, but as a rule of inference; the argument, therefore, need not take the form of a syllogism, and it is artificial to put it in that form, since what comes first in the order of discovery is the realization that the inference is valid in the particular case; but later, reflecting on the inference, we recognize that justifying it requires us to justify the maxim.

At this point, two sorts of question arise: first, what precisely is involved in this principle? In particular, is it simply a special case of some still more general principle of logic or language? Second, if the correctness of this principle is a necessary condition of the validity of the *cogito* argument, how might Descartes defend his reliance on the principle?

Recent Anglo-Saxon work on Descartes has tended to treat the principle relating thought to existence as being very much a special case of more general principles. So, for example, Hintikka presents it as a theorem of the predicate calculus, and Williams identifies the maxim "To think it is necessary to be" with a rule of language which says that propositions of the form a is F presuppose that a designates something.

As Williams' view applies to the case of the *cogito*, it implies the following reconstruction of the argument:

(1) If it is either true or false that I think, then I exist.
(2) *A fortiori*, if it is true that I think, then I exist.
(3) But it is true that I think.
(4) So, I exist.

But Descartes would not have accepted the first step of this argument. It follows from the principle of presupposition that if it is true that I think, then I exist. But it follows equally from the principle of presupposition that if it is false that I think, then I exist. (For if p presupposes q, q is a necessary condition of p's being either true or false.) And it is clear that Descartes would have rejected this consequence of (1). He would not have agreed that his existence could be inferred from his not thinking. For he goes on to say, after the *cogito* argument of the Second Meditation, that the proposition "I am" is certain only so long as I think, and that it could be that I would cease to exist if I ceased to think (AT VII, 27; HR I, 151–152).

This is not to say that the principle "Whatever thinks exists" is not a special case of some more general principle. But the more general principle is not anything quite so general as "Whenever a predicate can be truly or falsely applied to a subject, that subject exists." The more general principle is rather something like "Whenever there is an activity, we may infer an agent" (AT VII, 173–174; HR II, 62–63), or "Whenever we perceive any positive or real attribute, we may infer the existence of a subject of that attribute" (AT VIII–1, 25; HR I, 240; AT VII, 161; HR II, 53). So no purely formal principle will do. This applies as much to Hintikka as to Williams. Descartes would think Hintikka's leading principle,

(1) $Ba \supset \exists x(x = a)$,

to be simply false unless the possible interpretations of Bx were restricted to positive or real attributes, ones not involving a negation. The principle on which the *cogito* rests is a consequence of the general metaphysical doctrine that nothing has no real attributes.

But if the *cogito* argument does depend on a metaphysical doctrine of this sort, the question of Descartes' entitlement to rely on it becomes quite pressing. In the Second Replies Descartes speaks of his metaphysical doctrine as being known by the natural light (AT VII, 161; HR II, 53). But at the beginning of the Second Meditation, where the *cogito* argument occurs, Descartes is apparently barred from relying on the natural light by his confession, at the end of the First Meditation, that there is nothing he formerly believed to be true which he cannot at that stage doubt, "not merely through want of thought or levity, but for reasons which are valid and well considered" (AT VII, 21; HR I, 147–148).

Moreover, the metaphysical maxim cannot be defended in the same way that the proposition "I think" can. The premise of the *cogito* argument can be represented as being supplied by the opposition, as being a necessary ingredient in any skeptical hypothesis which would provide a reasonable ground of doubt. But no such claim can be made for the inferential principle that whatever thinks exists, or for the more general rule that from the existence of a real attribute we may infer a subject. The premise does not raise a problem of circularity, but the inferential principle does.

I want now to argue that this difficulty about the *cogito* argument is not only recognized but insisted on by Descartes. My text is a passage at the beginning of the Third Meditation. In rehearsing his grounds for doubting the simplest and easiest matters in mathematics, Descartes maintains that his only reason for doubting them is the thought that "some God" might have endowed him with a nature liable to be deceived even concerning the things most manifest to him:

> As often as this preconceived opinion concerning the supreme power of a God occurs to me, I cannot but confess that, if he wishes, it is very easy for him to bring it about that I should err, even in those things which I think that I intuit most evidently. (AT VII, 36; AT IX, 28; HR I, 158)

Those things do, nevertheless, retain a hold on his belief:

> As often as I turn my attention to the things themselves which I think I perceive quite clearly, I am so fully persuaded by them that

9 3

> I break out spontaneously in these words: Let whoever can deceive me, he will never bring it about that I am nothing so long as I think that I am something, or that it should, at some time, be true that I have never been, since it is true that I am; or perhaps that two and three are more or less than five, and such things, in which I recognize a manifest contradiction.

But though these propositions do arouse a spontaneous and invincible belief when they are considered, Descartes recognizes that they are not yet fully certain:

> And certainly since I have no reason for thinking that there is some God who is a deceiver, and indeed since I do not yet sufficiently know [FV: have not yet considered] whether there is a God, the reason for doubting which depends on this opinion is quite slight, and, as it were, metaphysical. Nevertheless, to remove it I must, as soon as possible, examine whether there is a God, and if there is, whether he can be a deceiver; for so long as I am ignorant of this, I do not seem to be able ever to be fully certain of anything else.

There are two things which particularly require note here.

First of all, Descartes explicitly mentions, among the propositions which he thinks he intuits most evidently, a principle which has a direct bearing on the *cogito* argument:

> So long as I think that I am something, I am not nothing.

This is only stylistically different from the inferential principle of the *cogito*, the principle whose correctness is admitted by Descartes to be a necessary condition of the validity of his argument. And he says quite plainly that, at this stage of the argument, this principle is still doubtful—doubtful in the normative sense that it merits doubt, even though it may compel belief whenever it is itself attended to.[25] But if a principle on which the *cogito* argument

25. Marc-Wogau, "Der Zweifel Descartes und das *Cogito ergo sum*," p. 145, cites a subsequent passage in the Third Meditation as showing that Descartes holds the inferential principle to be indubitable (and Marc-Wogau appears to mean indubitable in a normative sense), viz., AT VII, 38–39; AT IX, 30; HR I, 160–161; both the Latin and the French seem to be ambiguous, suggesting either the normative or the descriptive indubitability of the deliverances of the natural light. But since, in the two pages separating this passage from the one quoted in the text, nothing has been said which would justify, or even motivate, such a striking reversal of view, I infer that Descartes means descriptive indubitability. The passage would thus be saying that because

depends is doubtful, then the conclusion of the *cogito* argument must itself still, at this stage of the argument, be doubtful.

And Descartes says, at the end of this passage, that so long as he does not know whether or not God exists and can be a deceiver, he cannot be fully certain of *anything*. He makes no exception in favor of his own existence, as he might easily have done. If he thought that the Second Meditation did put his own existence beyond all reasonable doubt, this would be an incredible omission.

If we accept the view that Descartes regards his own existence as still doubtful at the beginning of the Third Meditation—a conclusion also reached by Gueroult, *Ordre* I, 155—two important consequences follow. First, we can now understand why Descartes responded as he did to Mersenne's objection to the *cogito*. Mersenne represented the *cogito* as an asyllogistic inference from the premise "I think" to the conclusion "I exist" and questioned Descartes' right to rely on this premise prior to his proof that God exists. And Descartes confused matters considerably by denying that the *cogito* is an enthymeme with the suppressed major premise "Whatever thinks exists."

The reason for this, I suggest, is that the accusation of committing a Cartesian circle is quite inappropriate with respect to the premise of the inference. Descartes need not claim to know that premise, which is supplied by the skeptical opposition. The accusation of committing a Cartesian circle—of engaging in a circularity stemming from specifically Cartesian doctrines—can arise only concerning the principle governing the inference. This is why Descartes thinks Mersenne must be raising a question about that principle.

Second, we must reverse a very common judgment about Descartes' system. It is often said that Descartes, in his quest for absolute certainty, is able to establish his own existence, but unable to establish the existence of anything else. If what has been argued here is correct, Descartes would hold that even the proposition "I exist" is fully certain only if the rest of the argument of the Meditations goes through. We must buy all or nothing.

I cannot, in fact, doubt the teachings of the natural light (when I attend to them), I must, at least provisionally, treat them as though they ought not to be doubted in examining whether there is a God.

5

THE CIRCLE

According to the title page of the first edition, the central contentions of Descartes' *Meditations* are that God exists and that the soul is immortal. In his dedication to the Sacred Faculty of Theology at the Sorbonne, Descartes writes that he has always thought that these two doctrines, concerning God and the soul, were the principal ones which should be demonstrated by philosophy rather than by theology. It may be sufficient for the faithful to believe them by faith; but it will never be possible to persuade infidels of any religion or even of any moral virtue without a demonstration by natural reason that God exists and that the soul is immortal. "Although it is absolutely true," writes Descartes,

> that we ought to believe in the existence of God because it is taught in the Holy Scriptures, and, on the other hand, that we ought to believe the Holy Scriptures because they come from God . . . nevertheless this cannot be proposed to infidels because they would judge it to be circular. (AT VII, 2; HR I, 133)

Descartes does not actually say that the reasoning thus described *would be* circular, just that infidels would think it so. Still, if we keep in mind who the intended recipients of the dedication were, we will be apt to put this reserve down to Descartes' instinct for diplomacy. A group of theologians, whose discipline is virtually defined by its willingness to accept arguments from scriptural authority, might be expected not to take kindly any very direct challenge to the credentials of that authority. But surely Descartes, as a philosopher, would think the infidels right to reject the proposed argument as circular.

This makes it very curious that precisely the same objection should have been made against Descartes himself. One of the things Descartes is concerned to argue in the course of the *Meditations* is that whatever we conceive clearly and distinctly is true. He apparently maintains this on the grounds that our clear and distinct conceptions, being "real and positive," must have God as their author and that God, being supremely perfect, could not be the cause of any error (AT VII, 62; AT IX, 49–50; HR I, 178). But if we ask why we ought to believe that God exists, the short answer seems to be that we infer his existence from the fact that we possess a clear and distinct idea of him (AT VII, 53; HR I, 171–172). And it is natural to wonder whether this is any less circular than the argument Descartes rejects. If we substitute "our faculty of clear and distinct perception," or what Descartes sometimes (AT VIII, 1, 16; HR I, 231) calls "the natural light," for the supernatural light of revelation, "Holy Scripture," we have a parallel argument. We ought to believe what the natural light tells us, because it comes from God, and we ought to believe that God exists and is not a deceiver, because the natural light tells us so. And so Descartes has been accused, by critics from Arnauld on, of reasoning in a circle.

That, in essence, is the problem of the Cartesian circle. But it is a problem which has far-reaching implications for the interpretation of the whole Cartesian system. If we find that Descartes is guilty of reasoning in a circle, we will, of course, want to know how a philosopher of his ability could have fallen into such a trap, and how he could have failed to see his mistake when it was pointed out to him, as it was, by various people. On the face of it, Descartes was never convinced that he had reasoned in a circle. Was this the natural reluctance of an author to admit error? obtuseness? a failure on the part of the critics to see some subtlety in the argument? Or does it have a more sinister explanation?

A great deal of scholarly labor has been devoted to trying to show that Descartes' argument is not what it appears to be and that the claim of obvious circularity is too hasty. Some argue that Descartes never intended to provide a rational defense of reason

DESCARTES AGAINST THE SKEPTICS

itself; others, that he did, but that the argument was complex
enough that its circularity was not obvious, so that Descartes'
failure to see it is not a mark against his intelligence.

In the eyes of some knowledgeable interpreters of Descartes all
of this effort is rather comic.[1] They would hold that not only is the
argument of the *Meditations* circular, it is known by Descartes to
be circular and is part of an elaborate deception on his part. On
this view, the arguments for the existence of God and the apparent
attempt to justify reliance on reason on their basis are intended
only to give a patina of piety to a work whose true implications are
radically subversive of religion. They are "a lightning rod against
ecclesiastical thunderbolts." But the circularity of the argument is
only one of many indications to the book's true audience that they
must read between the lines. If they do, they will find that Descartes is not the theist and dualist he appears to be, but an atheist
and materialist.

An approach as radical as this, as contrary to the general tendency of modern scholarship, is apt to be dismissed without a
proper hearing. So it is worth saying that a good deal of evidence
can be adduced in its favor. That Descartes engaged—*to some
extent*—in dissimulation cannot be denied. He certainly suppressed
work which he feared would get him in trouble and was less than
candid about expressing his disagreement with orthodox views. His
advice to Regius in the controversy with Voetius surely should
give cause for concern to those who think Descartes' sincerity can
be taken for granted:

> I agree entirely [with M. Alphonse] that you should take care not
> to arouse people against you by words that are too hard. I would
> also wish, indeed, that you had not advanced any new opinions,
> but had nominally retained the old, contenting yourself with giving
> new reasons, which no one can find fault with. Those who grasped

1. The principal contemporary exponent of this approach is Hiram Caton,
in his book, *The Origin of Subjectivity*, and in numerous articles, of which
"The Problem of Descartes' Sincerity" (*Philosophical Forum*, 2 [1971], 355–
370) is the most relevant. But as Caton emphasizes, skepticism about Descartes' sincerity has a long history and many distinguished adherents (e.g.,
More, Leibniz, La Mettrie, d'Holbach, and Adam). And Caton is not its only
contemporary exponent. See also Kenneth Dorter's "Science and Religion in
Descartes' *Meditations*," *Thomist*, 37 (1973), 313–340.

your reasons properly would have drawn their own conclusions about what you wanted them to understand. For example, why was it necessary to reject, openly, substantial forms and real qualities? (January 1642 (?); Alquié, *Oeuvres* II, 913)

And he goes on the contrast Regius' practice with his own in the *Meteors*, where he said expressly that he did not deny substantial forms, that he merely did not find them necessary to explain the things he wanted to explain.

Once one takes the dissimulation hypothesis really seriously, one is apt to see evidence for it everywhere. The passage we cited at the beginning of this chapter, from the dedication to the Faculty of Theology at the Sorbonne, will take on an entirely different meaning. Descartes' rejection of the circular argument from Scripture will not be just an ironic anticipation of a widespread objection to his own work but a broad hint to the critical reader not to take the apparently central contentions of that work too seriously.

This interpretation will be further confirmed by other paradoxes. For example, the title page and the dedication to the Sorbonne announce a work whose two main themes are the existence of God and the immortality of the soul. But though the dedication claims that knowledge of God is so easy that atheists are inexcusable and claims that Descartes' own proofs of God are peculiarly clear and evident, it also concedes that few people will be able to follow them and begs the theology faculty to lend the weight of its authority to these arguments, so that the atheists may—on that ground—be persuaded to grant the adequacy of proofs they do not understand.

As for the other supposedly central theme of the *Meditations*, Mersenne had already objected, before the *Meditations* were published, that Descartes had not said a word in them about the immortality of the soul (Letter to Mersenne, 24 December 1640; Alquié, *Oeuvres* II, 300). And though the title page was altered for the second edition, so that it claimed only a proof that the soul is distinct from the body, one might well wonder why the apparently stronger claim was ever made.

This is the kind of argument which can be mounted in favor of the dissimulation thesis, and I think enough has been said to give some idea why some interpreters find it so persuasive. It is not part of my project to give a point for point rebuttal of such arguments.

That would be as unrewarding a task as trying to convince a paranoid that people are not plotting against him. What I do hope to do is to remove some of the philosophical motivation for such an interpretation.

Dissimulation theorists typically do not see much force in the skeptical arguments Descartes professes to reply to and typically find the Cartesian defense of reason most unconvincing. In preceding chapters I have tried to present the skeptical arguments at their best, and I contend that at their best they have considerable force. I shall now argue that Descartes' defense of reason is much stronger than it is generally given credit for being. In particular, I shall argue in this chapter that Descartes *is* attempting a rational defense of reason (not something else), and that this defense is neither obviously nor subtly circular, that on a proper understanding of the skeptical opposition, there is no reason in principle why Descartes' defense should not succeed. I shall then argue that, though the defense of reason does fail in the end, it fails because Descartes' arguments for God's existence are not good enough, not because the project itself is inescapably circular. I would add, however, that the arguments are better than they are usually thought to be.

First we must deal with the accusation of circularity. One way to approach this puzzle is to start with a solution which now has less support than it once did, but which does bring out important features of the problem.[2] We can then move on to a solution which, if not quite right, is much closer to being right.

A. K. Stout, in an article entitled "The Basis of Knowledge in Descartes,"[3] calls our attention to the fact that, according to Descartes, we *cannot* doubt our clear and distinct perceptions *at the*

2. Willis Doney, who once argued for a solution along these lines ("The Cartesian Circle," *Journal of the History of Ideas*, 16 (1955), 324–338), has now apparently rejected it in favor of a solution more like that of Frankfurt (see "Descartes's Conception of Perfect Knowledge," *Journal of the History of Philosophy*, 8 (1970), 387–403). But a version of this interpretation still has an active defender in George Nakhnikian. See his *Introduction to Philosophy* (New York: Knopf, 1967), pp. 234–240, and "The Cartesian Circle Revisited," *American Philosophical Quarterly*, 4 (1967), 251–255.

3. Originally published in *Mind* (1929) and now reprinted in Doney's collection of critical essays. References will be made to this latter source.

time that we are having them. Whenever we are actually perceiving something clearly and distinctly we have an irresistible inclination to assent to the proposition; it is only propositions which are not clearly and distinctly perceived that our will is indifferent to. This is plainly the doctrine of the Fourth Meditation, and one way it is relevant to the problem of the circle is this: suppose we did establish that all clear and distinct ideas are true—of what use would this principle be to us? It would seem that in the only circumstances in which the rule would be applicable, namely, when we perceive something clearly and distinctly, we would have no need of reassurance, since we would already have an invincible conviction of the truth of the idea so clearly perceived.

If we think the rule useless on these grounds, however, we are too hasty. It can occur that we recall having perceived something clearly and distinctly in the past without our perceiving it clearly and distinctly now. In this sort of situation we might use the criterion of past clarity and distinctness to resolve present doubts. For instance, I might remember having proved a certain theorem in geometry, having seen that it followed from premises which themselves needed no proof. But if I am not now attending to the reasons which convinced me of the truth of the theorem, I may not now perceive it clearly and distinctly, and so I can have a doubt about it which could be resolved by using the rule that all our clear and distinct ideas are true. This would not apply to propositions so simple as not to need proof—in their case the rule would not be useful.

Descartes draws this distinction between our present clear and distinct perception and our recollection of past clear and distinct perception toward the end of the Fifth Meditation, and he indicates there that it is in connection with recollected perceptions that our knowledge of the existence of a veracious God will be useful. He evidently believes also that it has some relevance to the charge of circular reasoning. For he invokes the distinction when that charge is made by the authors of the Second and Fourth Objections; for example, he writes to Arnauld that

> We are assured that God exists because we fix our attention on the reasons which prove his existence to us; but after that it suffices that we remember having conceived a thing clearly in order to be

assured that it is true, which would not suffice if we did not know that God exists and that he is not a deceiver. (AT VII, 246; HR II, 115)

And to Mersenne he writes that

When I said that we can know nothing certainly if we do not first know that God exists, I said, expressly, that I was speaking only of the knowledge of those conclusions which we can recollect when we no longer think of the reasons from which we have drawn them. (AT VII, 140; HR II, 38)

(The immediate issue in this latter passage, it will be recalled, is not an accusation of circularity in proving that all clear and distinct ideas are true, but the question whether Descartes is entitled to claim certainty about his own existence before proving that God exists.)

Now the question is: What is the precise relevance of this distinction? Stout thinks there are two possible ways of reading Descartes here (Doney, 174). According to the first, what I perceive clearly and distinctly may be false unless a veracious God exists— even though I cannot help believing what I perceive clearly while I am perceiving it. It is only on reflection, in retrospect, that a doubt about my clear and distinct perceptions can occur. When I prove the existence of God, I can dispel this doubt. On the second reading, what I perceive clearly and distinctly cannot be false, whether God exists or not. The appeal to the veracity of the creator is made, not to justify the principle that clear and distinct ideas are true, but to guarantee the accuracy of our memory when we recall having perceived something clearly. The first reading represents Descartes' original position and involves a circle. The second reading represents the position he tended to shift into under criticism and involves a weakening of God's role as the guarantor of our knowledge, but no circle.

This is, in some ways, an attractive solution and some interpreters of Descartes have thought that the second reading must be correct. Some of the things Descartes says about inference in the *Regulae* strongly suggest the second reading. Descartes there distinguishes between intuition and deduction. Our knowledge of first principles depends on the faculty of intuition; our knowledge of the remote consequences of these first principles depends on deduction; and our knowledge of the immediate consequences of first principles may be regarded as either intuitive or deductive, depending, apparently, on whether or not, in attending to one of these consequences, we attend at the same time to the principles from which it follows and to the connection between them. If we do, our knowledge is intuitive—if not, it is deductive (AT X, 379; HR I, 8).

Descartes speaks, in the *Regulae*, of both intuition and deduction as being "acts of the understanding through which we can arrive at a knowledge of things without any fear of deception" (AT X, 368; HR I, 7), but he evidently regards arguments which are so complex and involved that the mind cannot grasp the whole of the argument at once as less than fully satisfactory. The certainty of the conclusion in such arguments depends in some measure on the memory, and Descartes thinks it desirable to try to avoid this dependence by repeatedly running over the steps of such an argument, reflecting on the individual propositions and their relations to one another, until we can pass so quickly from first step to last that the whole argument is seen at the same time. Unless we can do this without interruption and without leaving out any essential steps, the certainty of the conclusion will disappear (AT X, 387–388; HR I, 19).

Nevertheless, the interpretation which makes Descartes' defense a defense of memory will not do. It has seemed attractive because it has seemed to rescue Descartes from an impossible situation and because it has seemed to fit in well with the doctrine of the *Regulae*. But the latter 'advantage' is not a very substantial one. The *Regulae* is an early work and is inconsistent with the teaching of Descartes' mature works on precisely the sorts of issue here in question. The *Regulae* treats the things we perceive intuitively as providing a paradigm of certainty and finds no problem in accepting a proposition just because it is seen clearly and distinctly to be true. But in his published works, as we have seen, Descartes holds that he cannot be fully certain of anything so long as he does not know whether God exists and can be a deceiver. So in the later works, our dependence on intuition needs theoretical justification. Perhaps the universality of Descartes' initial, antecedent skepticism does then put him into an impossible situation, but that in itself is insufficient evidence that he did not adopt the more skeptical view in the *Meditations*.

There are other difficulties with the interpretation which makes Descartes' defense one of memory rather than of reason. Frankfurt has argued that the passages in the *Meditations* and the *Objections and Replies* which seem to support the memory interpretation show, on close inspection, that while the "metaphysical" doubt arises only in situations "involving memory," it is not a doubt about the reliability of memory.[4] I find Frankfurt's argument on this point convincing, but will not attempt to go into its details here. Instead let us turn to his own solution.[5]

Frankfurt points out that if being sure is equivalent to being unable to doubt, then Arnauld and Descartes' other critics are simply wrong to say that we can be sure of God's existence only if we already know that whatever is intuited is true. So long as we intuit that God's existence and veracity follow from premises also intuited, we will be unable to doubt God's existence and veracity, just as we are unable to doubt any present clear and distinct idea. So in that sense we can be sure that God exists and is not a deceiver. All we need do is rehearse the proof to the point where we can keep all the necessary intuitions in mind at once. So long as we keep them in mind, we will be unable to doubt and will, in that sense, be sure.[6]

Of course, being sure, in this sense, is not equivalent to knowing in any sense in which knowing *p* entails that *p* is true. It is a purely psychological state of complete conviction. And it would seem that we might fall out of this state of conviction and come to doubt God's existence and veracity when we are no longer attending to the reasons which have produced our conviction. Descartes, however, denies this:

> After I have recognized that there is a God, because at the same time I have also recognized that all other things depend on him

4. "Memory and the Cartesian Circle," *Philosophical Review*, 71 (1962), 504–511.

5. First stated in "Descartes' Validation of Reason," *American Philosophical Quarterly*, 2 (1965), 149–156, but subsequently reprinted in Doney and presented in an expanded form in *Demons, Dreamers and Madmen*.

6. Interesting in this connection is Descartes' reply to the objections of Burman, AT V, 148–149; Bridoux, 1358–1359.

and that he is not a deceiver, and consequently have judged that whatever I conceive clearly and distinctly cannot fail to be true— even if I no longer think of the reasons for which I have judged [some proposition which I have conceived clearly and distinctly] to be true, provided that I remember having clearly and distinctly understood it, no contrary reason can be brought forward which would make me call it in doubt, and so I have a true and certain knowledge of it.[7]

Once I have gone through the proofs of God's existence and veracity, not only am I at that moment convinced that what I conceive clearly and distinctly is true, but I am also convinced in such a way that nothing can ever persuade me later to the contrary, so long as I can recollect my clear and distinct idea. And Descartes identifies this state of immutable conviction with having certain knowledge.

Now this is strange. It is not in general true, according to Descartes, that my recollection of having seen something clearly and distinctly is sufficient to remove doubt about the truth of what I have seen thus. But it is true, according to Descartes, that my recollection of having seen clearly and distinctly that God guarantees the truth of our clear and distinct ideas is sufficient to remove doubt about the truth of our clear and distinct ideas. Why is this?

Frankfurt suggests that what Descartes is claiming is not that, after we have seen clearly and distinctly that God exists and is not a deceiver, we can never state or experience doubts about the truth of our clear and distinct ideas, but that, once we have seen our way through the Cartesian argument, those doubts will never be reasonable. Descartes' method of systematic doubt requires him to reject as false whatever he can find some ground for doubting, but the ground of doubt is required to be not entirely frivolous. It must, in some sense, be a valid ground for doubt. And Descartes' point, according to Frankfurt, is that after we have seen a demonstration of God's existence and veracity from clear and distinct premises, we can never again have a reasonable doubt of the truth of our clear and distinct ideas. The hypothesis which was invoked

7. AT VII, 70; HR I, 184. The bracketed phrase replaces a demonstrative pronoun [istud] which refers to a previous geometrical example.

in the First Meditation as a ground of doubt for our clear and distinct ideas—the hypothesis of a deceiving God—will be seen to be contrary to reason. Reason does not support the hypothesis of a deceiving God but supports, instead, belief in a perfect creator, for whom deception would be impossible.

Frankfurt's approach to the problem of the Cartesian circle is analogous to what I believe to be the correct solution to certain problems about the *cogito*. He stresses the methodological requirement in Descartes' program of doubt that the doubt be motivated intellectually by some reasonable ground of doubt. The proposition "I exist" cannot reasonably be doubted, because any reasonable ground of doubt we imagine will be self-defeating, entailing the truth of the proposition it is supposed to cast doubt on. Similarly, the proposition "Whatever we understand clearly and distinctly is true" cannot, in the end, reasonably be doubted because the only ground we can find for doubting the truth of our clear and distinct ideas is a hypothesis which turns out to be inconsistent with everything reason leads us to believe. Frankfurt construes Descartes as concerned to counter the skeptic's claim that the careful use of reason leads to the conclusion that reason is unreliable. Descartes' reply is that, on the contrary, the most scrupulous use of reason leads to the conclusion that reason *is* reliable.

Now it seems to me that all of this is very suggestive. Descartes does stress in the First Meditation that he requires a reasonable ground for doubting his former beliefs (AT VII, 18; HR I, 145). Toward the end of that meditation he says that

> of all the opinions which I had previously received as true, there is not one which I cannot now doubt—and that not from thoughtlessness or levity, but for reasons very strong and maturely considered. (AT VII, 21; HR I, 147–148; cf. AT VII, 171, 460; HR II, 60, 266)

So the hypothesis of a deceiving God is regarded *at that stage* as a valid ground for doubt.

As Descartes remarks in his reply to Bourdin, however, doubtfulness and certainty are "relations of our thought to objects," not "properties of the objects . . . inhering in them eternally":

> We may well enough be compelled to doubt by arguments that are in themselves doubtful and not afterwards to be retained . . . they

are indeed valid so long as we do not possess any others to remove our doubt and introduce certainty. It was because I found none such during the course of Meditation I, however much I looked around and reflected, that I therefore said that my reasons for doubting were valid and well considered. (AT VII, 473–474; HR II, 277)

After we have an argument from clear and distinct ideas to the existence of a perfect being in the Third Meditation and a similar argument that such a being cannot deceive in the Fourth Meditation, the hypothesis of a deceiving god is no longer a valid ground for doubting the truth of our clear and distinct ideas.

That this is Descartes' procedure is confirmed by his statement toward the beginning of the Third Meditation that

> Since I have no reason to believe that there is a God who is a deceiver and have not even considered those which prove that there is a God, the reason for doubting which depends only on this opinion is very light, and, as it were, metaphysical. But in order to remove it, I must examine whether there is a God . . . and if I find that there is one, I must also examine whether he is a deceiver. (AT VII, 36; HR I, 159)

Descartes' doubt is laid to rest, in the end, by the discovery that the reasons which lead him to conclude that there is a God also lead him to conclude that God, though omnipotent, could not deceive him. The result is that by that stage the truth of our clear and distinct ideas cannot rationally be doubted.

Frankfurt maintains that this procedure does not involve Descartes in any vicious circularity, or at least that it does not do so in the way in which it has generally been thought to. And it seems to me that he is right to claim this. But on his reconstruction of the argument, the certainty Descartes achieves is more modest than the certainty he has usually been thought to want. Frankfurt's Descartes establishes, not that all our clear and distinct ideas are true, but rather that it would never be reasonable to doubt the truth of our clear and distinct ideas. Descartes' conclusion, that it would never be reasonable to doubt what we perceive clearly and distinctly, may be true without its being true that all our clear and distinct ideas are true. It always remains possible that what we intuit is false, even though we have no reasonable grounds for suspecting this to be the case. And Frankfurt cites an important passage in which Descartes himself seems to allow this possibility. In the Second Replies Descartes writes that

> As soon as we think we conceive some truth clearly we spontaneously persuade ourselves that it is true. And if this persuasion is so strong that we could never have any reason for doubting what we believe in this way, then there is nothing further to seek; we have all the certainty that can reasonably be wished.
>
> For what does it matter to us if perhaps someone feigns that that same thing, of whose truth we are so strongly persuaded, appears false to the eyes of God or of the angels, and that therefore, absolutely speaking, it is false? Why should we care about this absolute falsity, since we do not believe it at all or even have the least suspicion of it? For we are supposing a persuasion so firm that it cannot be destroyed in any way, a persuasion, which, therefore, is just the same as the most perfect certainty. (AT VII, 144–145; AT IX, 113–114; HR II, 41)

Descartes recognizes that perfect certainty—understood as a conviction so strong that it cannot be overthrown—is compatible with absolute falsity. But he also regards the demand for anything more than his perfect certainty as quixotic.

So far my exposition of Frankfurt on Descartes has been based mainly on material coming from his article in the *American Philosophical Quarterly* (reprinted in Doney). And so far what Frankfurt says strikes me as most illuminating, though I shall want to come back and examine it more closely later. However, in the subsequent development of Frankfurt's position in his book *Demons, Dreamers and Madmen* there are things which must be wrong, if they are taken as an account of what Descartes thought.

The most important of these concern the interpretation of the maxim that whatever we perceive clearly and distinctly is true. Frankfurt writes that

> following the realistic bias of common sense, it is rather natural to assume that when he asks whether what is clear and distinct is true, Descartes is asking whether it corresponds with reality. (Frankfurt, 170)

But Frankfurt maintains that this is a mistake and shown to be a mistake by the passage cited above from the Second Replies, in which Descartes asks rhetorically why we should be concerned if someone suggests that a belief which we could never have any reason for doubting might, nevertheless, appear false to God and so might, absolutely speaking, be false. The concepts of absolute truth and absolute falsity, according to Frankfurt, are irrelevant to the purpose of inquiry. The concept of truth that is relevant to inquiry is the concept of coherence.

This leads Frankfurt to suggest that Descartes would take a Kantian approach to the question of the truth of scientific theories. He points out that the seventeenth-century controversy over the Copernican system had made the status of scientific theories a very important issue. Galileo had wanted to maintain that the use of natural reason gave a basis for deciding between the "two great systems" and that it showed the Copernican system to be correct. The Church, as represented by Cardinal Bellarmine, held that the empirical evidence was not decisive, that both systems "saved the appearances," and that the fact that the Copernican system was more economical in its assumptions did not show it to be correct. There is no way of knowing by the natural light of reason which theory is correct. So we can safely allow the supernatural light of revelation to decide the matter for us in favor of the Ptolemaic system.

Frankfurt argues that Descartes must have had a position on this controversy, that we are to look for his answer in the *Meditations*, and that they can be read as giving, implicitly, the following answer:

> Reason . . . can give us certainty. It can serve to establish beliefs in which there is no risk of betrayal. This certainty is all we need and all we should demand. Perhaps our certainties do not coincide with God's truth. . . . But this divine or absolute truth, since it is outside the range of our faculties and cannot undermine our certainties, need be of no concern to us. (Frankfurt, 184)

What we are looking for in the sciences are beliefs which are "solid and permanent," beliefs which we shall never have a reason to question, coherent beliefs, whether they correspond with reality or not. Science is sovereign in its own domain, but its domain is that of the phenomena, not things in themselves.

Now this, it seems to me, was pretty certainly not Descartes' position. On Frankfurt's interpretation, what God's veracity is supposed to guarantee—and this is *all* it is supposed to guarantee—is that certain of our beliefs "can confidently be expected to remain unshaken by any further inquiry" (Frankfurt, 180). But when Descartes sets out on his quest for a divine guarantee in the Third Meditation, his preliminary analysis of error certainly suggests a correspondence theory of truth. He writes that falsity can be found, not in ideas alone, nor in volitions alone, but only in judgments. And the principal error to be feared there consists in judging that "the ideas which are in me are like or conform to certain things which are outside me" (AT VII, 37; HR I, 160). And by the time he has reached the Sixth Meditation, he certainly writes as if he thought then that God was guaranteeing more than mere coherence:

> Since God is not deceptive, it is entirely manifest that he does not produce those ideas [of bodies] in me immediately, by himself, nor even mediately by some creature who contains their objective reality only eminently, and not formally. For since he has not given me any faculty for recognizing this, but, on the contrary, a strong inclination to believe that they are produced by corporeal things, I do not see how he could be understood not to be deceptive if these ideas were produced by anything other than corporeal things. (AT VII, 79–80; HR I, 191)

Our ideas, then, must be produced by things which are as our ideas represent them to be. As Alquié notes with respect to this passage, a God like Berkeley's, who produces coherent sets of ideas, would still be a deceiving God, since those ideas do not correspond to external reality. That we might be incapable of discovering the deception would not clear God of the charge of deception.

Again, the view of the Copernican controversy and of the status of scientific theories which Frankfurt's Descartes adopts is just not that which the real Descartes held. We need not speculate about what position is implicit in the *Meditations*. Descartes speaks directly to the question in the *Principles*. He does not there see the issue as one of a choice between two theories, each equally adequate from an empirical point of view. There are three competing theories, the Ptolemaic, the Copernican, and the theory of Tycho Brahe (*Principles* III, 15–41). The Ptolemaic theory Descartes dismisses in one sentence, as being contrary to the empirical evidence. Many observations disconfirm it, though the only one Descartes specifically mentions is the then very recent discovery of the phases of Venus (*Principles* III, 16).

But there is a rival to the Copernican theory which does account equally well for the phenomena, the Tychonic theory. As Descartes points out, if you consider the Tychonic and Copernican theories only as hypotheses, there is little difference between them (*Principles* III, 17). They are, as we would say today, mathematically equivalent. But Tycho was not trying merely to save the phenomena. He wanted to explain "how things are *in fact*." And Descartes devotes most of his energy to trying to show that Tycho is wrong by arguing that—if you define motion properly—the Earth moves on a Tychonic theory but not on a Copernican one. *This* is Descartes' device for dealing with the Church, so to define motion that he can adopt a heliocentric account of the solar system without, "strictly speaking," ascribing motion to the Earth.

Is it quixotic of Descartes to hope to know "how things are in fact"? He does not think so. At the end of the *Principles* (IV, 204–206) Descartes returns to the question of the status of his scientific theories and imagines someone objecting that he has done no more than explain how the phenomena *may* have been caused:

> Just as the same craftsman can make two clocks which, though they show the time equally well and are exactly alike externally, have an altogether different internal mechanism, so there is no doubt that the supreme maker of things could have brought about everything we see in an infinity of different ways, without its being possible for the human mind to know which of all these ways he has chosen. (AT IX-2, 322; HR I, 300)

At first Descartes appears to concede the soundness of this objection, arguing that it will be sufficient for all practical purposes to have a theory which accounts for all the phenomena.

But in sections 205–6 Descartes takes back what he has given away in section 204. In order not to "do wrong to the truth" it is necessary to draw a distinction between moral and metaphysical certainty. The scientist who is innocent of Cartesian metaphysics is nonetheless able, by using the hypothetico-deductive method, to attain a certainty sufficient for the purposes of life, or moral certainty. He is like a man trying to decipher a coded letter. If it is a long letter and he happens upon a simple key which makes an intelligent message of all of it, he will not doubt that he has found the right key, even though he recognizes the abstract possibility that the author may have been using a different key. This is moral certainty. And Descartes regards the scientific theories of the *Principles* as at least morally certain because, like the key to a cryptogram, they explain very simply *all* the phenomena.

Still, this moral certainty can be surpassed when science is supplemented by Cartesian metaphysics. When we know that God is supremely good, and not at all deceptive, we can be certain that the faculty he has given us for distinguishing truth from falsity "cannot err," so long as we use it rightly (AT VIII–1, 328; AT IX–2, 324; HR I, 302). On Frankfurt's interpretation this inability to err would have to be construed as an inability to detect error. For him, God's veracity guarantees only that we will never discover grounds for doubting our theory, either by encountering recalcitrant experiences or by developing an incompatible theory which accounts equally well for the phenomena. But, as we have seen, God's veracity guarantees more than invincible ignorance (AT VII, 79–80; HR I, 191).

Now the question which interests me is this: How is it that a generally correct account of Descartes' defense of reason leads to demonstrably mistaken conclusions about his theory of truth and his philosophy of science? Did Descartes simply fail to see the implications of his views about reason or has Frankfurt drawn the wrong conclusions from them? I think the latter is the case, and I suggest that the mistake comes about in the following way.

Frankfurt sees, clearly and correctly, that Descartes is very much concerned with achieving a certainty about his beliefs which cannot be shaken by skeptical questioning; he sees that Descartes is led by this concern with certainty to take indubitability as a criterion of truth, and that the indubitability which is offered as a criterion of truth must be understood normatively, in the sense that indubitability is a matter of not having reasonable grounds for doubt. He also sees, and offers good evidence that Descartes saw, that the indubitability which is offered as a criterion of truth is not a logically sufficient condition of truth, that is, that it is logically possible that we should find indubitable a proposition which is nonetheless false, if truth and falsity are given any absolute sense. All of this seems to me to be right.

The mistake comes, I think, when Frankfurt infers that Descartes must not be taking indubitability as a criterion of absolute truth, that he must be implicitly redefining truth in terms of indubitability and therefore adopting a conception of truth which identifies it with coherence. This is wrong, as a matter of fact; and if it were right, it would make the whole enterprise an empty one. On Frankfurt's reading, Descartes is not concerned to show that all his clear and distinct ideas are true in the sense that they correspond with reality, but only to show that they are indubitable (Frankfurt, 170, 173, 179–180). But clarity and distinctness are themselves to be understood in terms of indubitability (Frankfurt, 135). And so all of Descartes' laborious argument would only establish the unexciting conclusion that indubitable beliefs are indubitable. There must be more to it than that.

The problem, I think, is to see how we can justifiably treat indubitability as a criterion of truth without denying what cannot be denied, that truth is not the same thing as indubitability. The solution will involve going back and looking again at Frankfurt's answer to the charge of circularity.

At one level, his answer is this. Descartes does not reason in a circle when he argues that all our clear and distinct ideas are true because he does not in fact assume the truth of that principle at any stage of his argument. We do not argue: I perceive p clearly and distinctly, but whatever I perceive clearly and distinctly is true, so p is true. We do not argue that way because when in fact we do perceive something clearly and distinctly, we cannot but believe it and so are not in need of any further argument.

This helps to meet the charge of circularity but does not take us very far.[8] For then the question arises, "What happens when I do not at the moment perceive p clearly and distinctly, but only remember doing so? I do not need to go back over my grounds for

<hr/>

8. I take it that it is a valid criticism of Kenny's solution to the problem of the circle that it goes no further than this. Cf. the review of *Demons, Dreamers and Madmen* by Charles Parsons in the *Journal of Philosophy*, 69 (1972), 38–46, particularly pp. 39–41.

p to remove doubt about p, but why not?" Frankfurt's answer at this level is that once we have an argument from clear and distinct ideas which has the conclusion that all our clear and distinct ideas are true, retrospective doubt about our clear and distinct ideas can no longer be reasonable. Why not? Well, because once we have that argument, skepticism has been shown to be an untenable position. If skepticism is to be reasonable, it must argue, and argue in the following way: assume that reason is reliable; the best, most careful use of reason now leads you to the conclusion that reason is unreliable, that there are good reasons for doubting the reliability of reason; so the assumption that reason is reliable has been reduced to absurdity (Frankfurt, 174–175).

Frankfurt's Descartes counters this by showing that the most rigorous use of reason does not lead to the conclusion that reason is unreliable, but leads, rather, to the conclusion that reason is reliable. That is the point of producing an argument from clear and distinct ideas which has the conclusion that all our clear and distinct ideas are true. It shows that the skeptics' attempt at a reduction of reason to absurdity fails.

Or at least it nearly shows this. For Frankfurt does think Descartes' reasoning is defective, and perhaps circular, though "in a rather different way than has generally been thought" (Frankfurt, 177). Descartes has overlooked the following "embarrassing question":

> Given that reason leads to the conclusion that reason is reliable because a veracious God exists, may it not also lead to the conclusion that there is an omnipotent demon whose existence renders reason unreliable?

Frankfurt thinks that Descartes simply takes for granted that the proper use of reason will not also lead to such incompatible results and that in doing so, he begs the question. In the end, Descartes' defense of reason breaks down.

I am more hopeful than Frankfurt about the success of Descartes' project. I think Descartes does have a reply to the skeptics' objection. But to see that it is a cogent reply requires a somewhat different account of the skeptical challenge from the one Frankfurt offers. I have argued that Descartes is fundamentally concerned to avoid difficulties in the notion of proof which had been pointed out by successive generations of skeptics since the time of Sextus Empiricus. Proof cannot go on to infinity. A demonstration of the classical Aristotelian type, which establishes one proposition by citing others which are known to be true and seen to entail it, must come to an end somewhere in propositions which are not themselves proven. One problem is to find a premise or set of premises which can serve as first principles without plausibly incurring the accusation that since they are not themselves proven they are arbitrary.

Descartes does not want, in his published works, to rely simply on the contention that his first principles are self-evident. He knows that this will be dismissed by the skeptic as a matter of merely subjective conviction, liable to great variation from one person to another. He knows also that many of the principles he wants to take as fundamental in physics and metaphysics—principles about causality and motion—are going to run contrary to the Aristotelian intuitions of common sense and are even going to seem to be disconfirmed by empirical evidence.[9]

Part of Descartes' strategy is to try to counteract our natural tendency to accept the evidence of the senses uncritically, by scrutinizing, in the First Meditation, various possible rules for the acceptance of empirical evidence. But part of the strategy is to adopt a subjectivist conception of proof, tailored to meet the requirements of the skeptical dialectic. Descartes will accept an argument as a proof if, as he is going through it, it compels his assent, and if, at the end of the argument, he finds that he has no valid

9. See, e.g., the discussion of the law of inertial motion (*Principles* II, 37; AT IX-2, 84–85; HR I, 267). Again, the generation of certain forms of animal and plant life out of inanimate matter was accepted on empirical grounds by many of Descartes' contemporaries, and cited as a counterexample to the causal maxims of the Third Meditation in the Second Objections (cf. HR II, 25, and for Descartes' reply, HR II, 33–34). Cf. also the discussion of the need for using analysis in metaphysics, AT IX, 122–123. On the other hand, in the *Regulae*, Descartes had written that the certainty of the mathematical sciences stemmed from the fact that they dealt with objects so pure and simple that "they do not admit of anything which experience has rendered uncertain" (AT X, 365; HR I, 5).

ground for doubting the conclusion. It is this latter condition, intended to rule out objections of arbitrariness, that is crucial to understanding how Descartes avoids circularity.

Descartes maintains that doubt must always be reasonable doubt in the sense that some valid ground must always be offered for doubting whatever proposition is to be doubted. This is not an unreasonable requirement, but one the classical skeptics implicitly accepted, and one which, arguably, they had to accept if their position was to be at all plausible. The important question is: What are the criteria for a proposition's being a valid ground of doubt? I have argued in the preceding chapter that Descartes deliberately establishes criteria of validity which are very weak. A proposition which is offered as a ground for doubt need not have any evidence in its favor; all that is required is that there should not be compelling argument against it (AT VII, 473–474; HR II, 276–277). The reason for setting the evidential requirements of a valid ground of doubt very low is a strategic one. The weaker the criteria for a valid ground of doubt, the more dramatic and persuasive it is if a valid ground of doubt cannot be found. Weak criteria of validity are what the situation requires.

But it follows from these evidential requirements that a proposition which counts as a valid ground of doubt at one stage of the argument may not count as a valid ground of doubt at a later stage. In the First Meditation, when Descartes lacks any compelling argument in favor of the proposition that there is a veracious God, the unsupported hypothesis that there is a deceiving God is a valid ground for doubting any proposition whatever. But by the end of the Fourth Meditation, this hypothesis will not count as a valid ground of doubt. By that stage we have—or are supposed to have—a compelling argument that God exists and is *not* a deceiver. So we then have an argument which not only compels assent but also constitutes a "proof" in the sense Descartes is implicitly giving that term.

This gives us an answer to the problem that bothered Frankfurt. He was concerned that a skeptic might say, at the end of the argument, "Yes, but there may be an equally compelling argument to show that reason is not reliable, by showing, perhaps, that there is also an omnipotent demon who deceives us. This would be incompatible with the conclusion of your argument, but perhaps the most scrupulous use of reason does lead to incompatible conclusions." The reply to *that* is that at this stage of the argument the skeptic cannot raise a valid ground of doubt merely by saying: it is possible that there is an equally compelling argument leading to a contrary conclusion. The ball is in his court, and he must produce the argument, not just assert its possibility. If he does not, it is Descartes' point, and it is match point.

It is important to recognize that Descartes is playing this game according to the skeptics' own rules. And by their rules, he wins. I take it to be established by the work of scholars like Popkin that the form of skepticism which Descartes was primarily concerned to counter was the pyrrhonian variety of skepticism, whose classic statement occurs in the works of Sextus Empiricus. Pyrrhonian skepticism differs from the less interesting academic variety chiefly in denying that in the end there is any difference in the apparent probability of any two propositions dealing with external reality (*Outlines of Pyrrhonism* I, 190). It holds, rather, that for any argument which purports to establish a conclusion about the reality lying behind the appearances an equally plausible argument leading to an opposite conclusion is available:

> When I say "To every argument an equal argument is opposed," what I am saying is "To every argument investigated by me which establishes a point dogmatically [that is, which has a conclusion which makes a claim about external realities—I, 13–15] it seems to me that there is opposed another argument, establishing a point dogmatically, which is equal to the first in respect of credibility and incredibility." (*Outlines of Pyrrhonism* I, 203)

When someone who holds *that* is confronted with a compelling argument leading to the conclusion that all our clear and distinct ideas are true, he is bound, I think, to produce an equally compelling counterargument and not merely to claim that it may be possible to produce such an argument.

Note that the pyrrhonian skeptic is concerned only with suspending judgment about propositions dealing with external reality. He does not suspend judgment about the appearances.[10] But since

10. Sextus, *Outlines of Pyrrhonism* I, 19–20. Cf. Popkin on the mitigated skepticism of Mersenne and Gassendi.

Frankfurt's Descartes abandons all hope of making a judgment about things in themselves, contenting himself with the phenomena, he is not really at odds with the pyrrhonian. To attribute a coherence theory of truth to Descartes is to render his opposition to skepticism unintelligible.

We need not do this, however. We can say, instead, that what is implicitly revised in Descartes is not the concept of truth but the concept of proof. Descartes is working with a concept of proof for which it does not hold that if there is a proof of p, then p is true. He admits that indubitability is compatible with falsity. But he is unconcerned about this, not because he is not interested in absolute truth, but because he thinks that rejecting a proposition which is, in his sense, indubitable is a patently arbitrary act.[11] The skeptic does not want to be, and does not think he is, patently arbitrary. Descartes' argument is designed to show that by the skeptic's own standards, the skeptic would be acting arbitrarily if he rejected the argument.

I think Descartes is right. There is no difficulty in principle about Descartes' procedure in the *Meditations*. The really serious objection to his argument is the substantive one that his arguments for the existence of a nondeceiving God are just not compelling.

The argument of this chapter is now substantially complete. But I should like to try to set out more precisely the view I am arguing for and to show that it accounts for various textual phenomena and enables Descartes to meet the objections of his critics. I have said that Descartes is implicitly redefining the concept of *proof*. How would the new definition go if it were made explicit?

11. In his comments on an earlier draft of this chapter, read to the Boston Colloquium for the Philosophy of Science in 1972, Frankfurt wrote that, according to Descartes, "we need not worry" about the fact that propositions of which we are perfectly certain "may not be absolutely true, because perfect certainty is quite sufficient for human purposes and because it is (by definition of 'perfect certainty') impossible that we should ever discover that a belief for which reason provides perfect certainty is absolutely false." (Cf. Frankfurt, 179–180.) But in the Cartesian passage this remark was intended to gloss (Second Replies, AT VII, 144–146; HR II, 41–42), there is no reference to human purposes. And the reason Descartes gives for disregarding the suggestion that perfectly certain propositions may be absolutely false is not that we cannot discover their falsity but that we cannot believe it, or even suspect it (AT VII, 145, ll. 4–6; cf. AT VII, 146, ll. 11–13).

One key element in the definition would be the notion of an *assent-compelling proposition*. This notion is at least coextensive with that of clarity and distinctness: all and only clear and distinct ideas are supposed to compel our assent. Descartes apparently does not wish to define clarity and distinctness in terms of this property, but it is the most important property of clear and distinct ideas for our purposes.

Some propositions compel our assent whenever we consider them (for instance, simple mathematical truths); when we consider them, we cannot but assent to them; others (such as more complex mathematical truths) compel our assent because we see that they can be made the conclusion of an assent-compelling argument, that is, an argument whose premises compel our assent and whose conditionalization also compels our assent. (By the conditionalization of an argument I mean the conditional proposition which has the argument's conclusion as its consequent and the argument's premise, or the conjunction of its premises, as its antecedent.) To be proved, a proposition must be assent-compelling in one or the other of these two ways, either assent-compelling in itself or capable of being made the conclusion of an assent-compelling argument.

But though the capacity to compel our assent is necessary for proof, it is not sufficient. To regard it as sufficient would be to adopt too subjective a concept of proof. It is also necessary, for a proposition to be "proved," that we have *no valid or reasonable ground for doubting it*. And the problem is to give an adequate account of what a valid ground of doubt is.

As a first approximation, we might say that

(D) Someone has a valid ground for doubting a proposition (say p) if and only if he can think of (that is, is able to state when requested) some other proposition (say q) such that
  (i) q is incompatible with p;
  (ii) he can think of no assent-compelling proposition incompatible with q;
  (iii) q explains how he might have erroneously thought p.

The first requirement, *i*, seems essential if q is to be a ground for doubting p at all, valid or otherwise. For to suggest a ground of doubt, it seems, is to suggest a hypothesis whose truth would exclude the truth of the proposition to be doubted. The third requirement, (iii), states the explanatory condition defended in the preceding chapter. The second requirement, (ii), states a very minimal evidential requirement, suggested by the passage from the Seventh Replies cited in the preceding chapter:

> A reason may be valid enough to force us to doubt, and nevertheless be doubtful itself, and so not to be retained . . . [such reasons] are indeed valid so long as we have no others which induce certainty by removing doubt. (AT VII, 473–474; HR II, 277)

Given (ii), we seem able to understand why Descartes would regard the hypothesis of a deceiving God as a valid ground of doubt in the First Meditation, but not at the end of the Fourth. To say that a ground of doubt will be valid so long as we are not irresistibly impelled to deny it is to adopt a very weak criterion of validity. But as we have seen, the situation requires a weak criterion.

This, of course, is only a first approximation, and is not satisfactory as it stands. On the proposed account of a valid ground of doubt, any proposition which compels our assent would have to be regarded as 'proved.' For if it compels our assent, we *could not* have a valid ground for doubting it. If the assent-compelling proposition is p, any valid ground for doubting p would have to be both incompatible with p (by (i)) and such that we cannot think of any assent-compelling proposition incompatible with it (by (ii)). But this defect can be fairly easily remedied by amending the account of a valid ground of doubt as follows:

(D') Someone has a valid ground for doubting a proposition, p, if and only if he can think of some other proposition, q, such that
  (i) q is incompatible with p;
  (ii) (a) if p is not assent-compelling, then he can think of no assent-compelling proposition incompatible with q;
    (b) if p is assent-compelling, then q is also assent-compelling;
  (iii) q explains how he might have erroneously thought p.

The effect of this change is to make the evidential requirement imposed on a valid ground of doubt vary with the 'evidence' of the proposition to be doubted. Where that proposition is not assent-compelling, then, as far as the evidential requirement is concerned, any hypothesis not excluded by an assent-compelling contrary proposition will do as a valid ground of doubt, however improbable it may seem. The strategic reason for setting this requirement so low should be clear by now. But where the proposition to be doubted *is* assent-compelling, then any hypothesis put up as a ground for doubting it should have an equally strong claim on our assent. That this condition is sufficient seems clear. If we were confronted with two incompatible propositions, each of which compelled our assent, we would have as much reason to accept the one as the other. That this condition is necessary may be less clear. But as I have argued above, the skeptical opposition could hardly object to it, given their doctrine that "To every argument an equal argument is opposed."

This account of reasonable doubt is still not satisfactory. For it is open to the following objection: Descartes wants to make a distinction (cf. AT VII, 141; HR II, 39) between the atheist, who may well see some proposition of mathematics clearly and distinctly, but lacks perfect knowledge of it, and the Cartesian theist, who not only sees the mathematical proposition clearly and distinctly (that is, is compelled to assent to it), but has perfect knowledge of it (that is, a 'proof' in the sense being defined here in terms of assent-compelling propositions and the absence of valid grounds of doubt). For as things stand, both the atheist and the Cartesian theist could reject the hypothesis of a deceiving God as unreasonable, since the truth of mathematics compels their assent, and the hypothesis of a deceiving God which is supposed to cast doubt on it does not. This difficulty springs directly from the amendment just made.

The solution, I suggest, lies not in reconsidering the evidential requirement, (ii), but in reconsidering the incompatibility requirement, (i). A valid ground of doubt *might* logically exclude the truth of *any* proposition I am compelled to assent to—for example, "An omnipotent being (God or demon) so arranges things that whenever I am compelled to assent to a proposition, it is false" (cf. AT VII, 21, 25; HR I, 147, 150). But it need not. It might take the form: "I have been so made by nature that I am *sometimes* deceived, even in the things I think I perceive with the maximum possible evidence." (Cf. AT VII, 70; HR I, 184; but Haldane follows the French version, which blurs this point slightly; cf. AT IX, 55.) Suppose that we try to accommodate this by the following amendment:

> (D″) Someone has a valid ground for doubting a proposition, p, if and only if he can think of some other proposition, q, such that
> > (i) q is incompatible with p or with some principle, r, which provides the basis for his assent to p;
> > (ii) (a) if either p or r is not assent-compelling, then he can think of no assent-compelling proposition incompatible with q
> > (b) if both p and r are assent-compelling, then so is q.
> > (iii) q explains how he might have erroneously thought p.

The new notion here is that of a principle which provides the basis for the person's assent to p. This might include the premises of his argument for p (if he has one), but more importantly, it would include any second-order principles used in the subsequent, reflective assessment of arguments. If p is a 'first principle,' then r would be any principle used to derive p from skeptical hypotheses (as, "Where we find an activity, we must infer an agent"). Or if p is the conclusion of an argument, r would include the principle governing the reliability of that kind of argument (as, "If a belief is based on vivid experiences which I take to be of ordinary-sized objects in my immediate vicinity, it is true" or "If a proposition compels assent whenever considered, or follows by compelling steps from compelling propositions, it is true").

This definition allows Descartes to make the distinction he wants to make. The atheistic mathematician is compelled to assent to some mathematical proposition, but not to the principle that assent-compelling propositions are true. So the evidential clause relevant to him is (ii) (a), and he can easily have a valid ground for doubting the mathematical proposition when he subsequently reflects on it. But the Cartesian theist is compelled to assent both to the mathematical proposition and to the principle that assent-compelling propositions are true. So the evidential clause relevant to him is (ii) (b), and he could only have a valid ground for doubting the mathematical proposition if that ground of doubt were assent-compelling.

It should be noted, incidentally, that though I have spoken of a revised concept of *proof*, this is somewhat misleading. For a proposition might be 'proved' in this sense and yet be a first principle, for example, if it were assent-compelling because it compelled assent whenever considered and were such that we had no valid ground for doubting it. So to be 'proved' does not imply that a proposition is the conclusion of an argument. If you find this use of "proof" too strange, you may treat this as an account of the normative sense of indubitability.

I want to conclude by applying the theory here constructed to the passage from the beginning of the Third Meditation with which we concluded the last chapter. The passage is a difficult one, and interpreters as diverse as George Nakhnikian and Frankfurt (p. 108) have wanted to disavow it as expressing an 'aberrant doctrine.' In that passage Descartes enumerates a number of propositions which he says compel his assent whenever he considers them:

So long as I think I am something, I am not nothing.
Since it is now true that I exist, it will never be
true that I never existed.
Two plus three equals five.

But after having said this, he goes on to say that so long as he does not know whether God exists and can be a deceiver, he cannot be fully certain of anything else (AT VII, 36; HR 158–159), including, it seems, these propositions which compel assent whenever considered. How do these propositions fare on this interpretation?

The first point is that even though they do compel assent whenever considered individually, they can be doubted when they are considered as a class, under the general description "propositions which compel my assent whenever considered." So a kind of doubt is possible, and the question is whether that doubt could be reasonable.

Well, what ground of doubt is proposed? That an omnipotent being sometimes deceives me, even concerning things I cannot help

DESCARTES AGAINST THE SKEPTICS

but assent to. How does this satisfy the criteria for being a valid ground of doubt? There is no difficulty about (iii)—it hardly seems that omnipotence would be required to lead me into an error I could not overcome. Nor is there any difficulty now about (i), since the hypothesis will be incompatible, not with any particular proposition compelling assent whenever considered, but with the general principle that assent-compelling propositions are true. But does this hypothesis satisfy (ii)? That depends on the status of the general principle just mentioned. If it does not compel assent, then the hypothesis of an omnipotent deceiver must satisfy (ii) (a), and at the beginning of the Third Meditation it does. So at that stage of the *Meditations*, the hypothesis of an omnipotent deceiver constitutes a valid ground of doubt, even concerning propositions which compel assent immediately. But by the end of the Fourth Meditation the principle that assent-compelling propositions are true is supposed itself to compel assent. So the hypothesis of an omnipotent deceiver, to be a valid ground of doubt, would by that stage have to satisfy (ii) (b), that is, it too would have to compel assent. But by then it has been carefully considered, and though part of it ("There is an omnipotent being") compels assent, part of it ("He deceives me") compels dissent.

There is no difficulty in principle about Descartes' procedure. The real question is the substantive one: Are his arguments for an omnipotent being compelling?

6

GOD

IF THERE IS, in principle, no difficulty about Descartes' procedure in the *Meditations*, it becomes all the more important to determine whether or not any of Descartes' various arguments for the existence of God are, by the criteria we have discussed, good ones. The *Meditations* contain three distinct arguments for the existence of God—two causal arguments in the Third Meditation and a version of the ontological argument in the Fifth. All three arguments are, I think, better than their reputations. But the first two are not *much* better than their reputations; with them the principal task will be to see why they seemed plausible to Descartes. The ontological argument is another matter. I find it very plausible indeed, and if wrong at all, then wrong for reasons quite different from those usually suggested.

I

FIRST, however, the causal arguments. Like some of the traditional Thomistic arguments for God's existence, these invoke God's existence in order to explain certain contingent facts. But the contingent facts appealed to here are of a different order than those appealed to by St. Thomas, and as a consequence the causal principles are uncomfortably unfamiliar. I begin with the first of the Third Meditation arguments, which may be presented in the following form:

(1) Some of my thoughts, namely, my ideas, are like images or likenesses of things in that they represent things external to me as having certain characteristics. (AT VII, 37; HR I, 159)

(2) Some of the objects of my ideas are represented as having more formal reality, that is, more being or perfection, than others are represented as having. (AT VII, 40; HR I, 162)

(3) Whatever exists must have an efficient and total cause which possesses at least as much formal reality as the effect does. (AT VII, 40; HR I, 162)

(4) Every idea must have a first and principal cause which possesses at least as much formal reality as the idea represents its object as having. (AT VII, 41–42; HR I, 162–163)

(5) I have an idea of God as an actually infinite, eternal, immutable, independent, all-knowing, all-powerful substance by whom I (and anything else which may exist) have been created. (AT VII, 40, 45; AT IX, 32, 35–36; HR I, 162, 165)

(6) I myself do not actually have all the perfections which my idea of God represents God as actually having (AT VII, 45; HR I, 166)

(7) I am not the first and principal cause of my idea of God.

(8) The first and principal cause of my idea of God is some being other than myself who possesses at least as much formal reality as my idea of God represents God as having.

(9) God exists.

Note that in stating Descartes' argument I have not used the term "objective reality." This seems to me legitimate. I take it that "objective reality" is definable in terms of "formal reality" and "representation," and that the argument is more perspicuous if the defined term is eliminated in favor of its defining ones, so that we talk about the formal reality an idea represents its object as having.

The structure of this argument is roughly as follows: (1) and (2), though they contain a definitional element, in that they introduce the terms "idea" and "formal reality," are basically contingent premises, whose justification must be that they are reports of what my consciousness contains. Descartes seems to have felt that beginning from this kind of contingent premise was an improvement on starting from the empirical premises of the five ways of St. Thomas. When Caterus invited him to compare his argument with the Thomistic ones, he wrote that

> I have not drawn my argument from the fact that I saw, in sensible things, an order or a certain succession of efficient causes . . . partly because I thought the existence of God was much more evident than that of any sensible thing . . . I preferred to use as the foundation of my argument my own existence . . . which is so

well-known to me that nothing can be better known. (AT VII, 106–107; HR II, 12–13)

This, perhaps, is unfair to St. Thomas. His arguments from change and contingency do not *have* to start from change and contingency in the objects of our senses. Change and contingency in minds would do as well. But we shall find that this difference between Descartes and St. Thomas is connected with other, more significant differences.

(3) is also a premise, though one which must be construed as an eternal truth, not a report on the contents of consciousness. When he introduces (3) Descartes says that it is manifest by the natural light. I take him to mean by that that (3) is a proposition which he *cannot* doubt when he considers it, and which he must therefore treat provisionally as beyond doubt while he is considering whether God exists and can be a deceiver. (Cf. AT VII, 38–39; HR I, 160–161; and the comment in Chapter 4 n25.) Modern readers are apt to feel that Descartes' strong conviction of the truth of propositions like (3) is no more than the result of his Jesuit education, and a good deal of Cartesian scholarship in this century has been devoted to arguing that Descartes did not make so clean a break with the past as he professed to. So it is worth pointing out that (3) is not a mere residue of childhood training, nor even a proposition which a good scholastic would wish to accept. From a scholastic point of view Gassendi's objection—that effects often owe their formal reality to their material cause (Alquié, *Oeuvres* II, 736)—is well taken. Descartes' version of the causal principle involves a rejection of the Aristotelian analysis of causation.

The status of (4) is debatable. When Descartes expounds this argument in geometric style at the end of the Second Replies (AT VII, 165; HR II, 56), he gives its analogue as an axiom, or "common notion." But he prefaces the list of axioms with the remark that some of his axioms might have been treated as theorems if he had wished to be more exact, and this proposition seems to be an example. The Third Meditation gives the impression that it is meant to follow from (3), in conjunction, perhaps, with (1) and (2).

The status of (5) is also obscure. Both in the Third Meditation and in the Geometrical Exposition Descartes tends to present it as a definition: "By the term 'God' I understand . . ." (cf. AT VII, 45; HR I, 165). But this is liable to encourage unnecessary objections: Can we define singular terms? and if so, Is this definition stipulative or reportive? and so on. I take it that all Descartes really wants or needs to say is that he can conceive of a being with a certain combination of attributes and this, again, seems to be a report of what his consciousness contains.

We need not trouble greatly over the rest of the argument, since it is clear, on reflection, that Descartes' conclusion follows directly from (4) and (5) alone. (6) and (7) are necessary only to establish that the being who is the cause of my idea of God, and who therefore possesses at least as much perfection as I conceive of God as having, is not myself. And I doubt that many readers will object to that.

I pass now to assessment of the argument. (1) raises no really serious difficulty. Fundamentally, it claims that some of my thoughts represent external objects as having certain characteristics. Just as a picture may, by showing someone engaged in some action, say something about that person, so an idea may, in virtue of its propositional structure, say something about its object.[1] But representation is an intentional relation, as one of Descartes' examples indicates. There may be no external object having the characteristics my idea of a chimera represents a chimera as having. So understood, the central claim of (1) should be uncontroversial.

(1) also proposes to call these representative thoughts "ideas," and certainly Descartes is free to stipulate a meaning for this technical term. It may be that he does not use that term with the same meaning everywhere in his writings; but that will be no criticism of this argument, unless it can be shown that there is equivocation on the term in this context.

What has caused the most difficulty has been the tendency of critics like Hobbes to assume that when Descartes says that ideas

---

1. I have discussed Descartes' doctrine of ideas in "Descartes, Spinoza, and the Ethics of Belief," in *Spinoza, Essays in Interpretation*, ed. M. Mandelbaum and E. Freeman (La Salle, Ill.: Open Court, 1975), pp. 159–189. Cf. also Kenny, *The Anatomy of the Soul* (Oxford: Basil Blackwell, 1973), pp. 90–95.

are like images he means that they *are* images.[2] Since it is agreed on all sides that there can be no image of God, this equation would permit an easy rejection of the claim that I have an idea of God. But Descartes does not equate ideas with images; he merely compares them with images. Images and ideas are alike in that both represent some object other than themselves as having some characteristic.

(2) is more problematic, since it involves ascribing to the objects of our ideas something called "formal reality," which is a very difficult notion. Clearly it cannot be equated with existence, since we can ascribe formal reality to the object of an idea without committing ourselves to the claim that that object exists. Descartes glosses "formal reality" as "being" or "perfection," which seems unhelpful, since formal reality is supposed to be something which admits of degrees and we do not naturally think of either being or perfection as admitting of degrees.

Nevertheless, it is possible to make some sense of the notion by considering Descartes' examples. "Perfection" may be more helpful than "being." Descartes would characterize such attributes of God as knowledge and power as perfections of God. By this I take it that he would mean that a being which has them is, in some sense, and other things equal, better than one which lacks them. Certainly he thinks that a being capable of choosing a perfection and clearly seeing it to be a perfection would choose it (AT VII, 166; HR II, 56). Since knowledge and power admit of degrees, we should, presumably, say that a being with a greater degree of knowledge has, other things equal, more formal reality than one with less knowledge.

Eternity and immutability are also supposed to be perfections, and, if eternity is identified with limitless duration, then things might be said to have lesser degrees of this perfection in proportion as their duration was more limited. So they would have less formal reality. Similarly, if immutability is identified with a capac-

---

2. Cf. AT VII, 80; HR II, 67. There still seems to be confusion on this point, even in Alquié who, in his comment on Hobbes' objection (*Oeuvres* II, 610n), concedes that, in the passage Hobbes cites, Descartes really does say that (some) ideas *are* images. Cf. also his notes to Descartes' reply (*Oeuvres* II, 612, nn1, 2), and Beck, *Metaphysics*, 153.

ity to resist change, we might conceive varying degrees of this capacity just as we conceive varying degrees of any power. God would have the perfection in the highest possible degree. But other things could have it in lesser degrees.

However, this line of thought cannot naturally account for all of the ways in which Descartes wants to use the notion of formal reality. For instance, Descartes apparently thinks that an object which is hot has, by virtue of that fact, a certain measure of formal reality. But heat does not seem to be a perfection in the sense in which we have been using that term.

In any case, this way of explaining "formal reality" suffers a more serious difficulty. If there are a plurality of attributes whose possession might contribute to the formal reality of a thing, then we would need some principle for comparing the contributions the varying degrees of the various attributes would make. Clearly, a being possessing both knowledge and power in a high degree will have, other things equal, more formal reality than a being possessing these attributes in a low degree. But how are we to compare a being possessing much knowledge and little power with one possessing much power and little knowledge? Which has the greater formal reality? I find nothing in Descartes which even suggests an answer to such a question. And until there is one, this way of understanding "formal reality" can give us only the most rudimentary grasp of the concept.

We may, however, take another tack. Arguably, Descartes has a different and much simpler account of what constitutes a difference in the degree of formal reality of something. In some passages it appears that differences in degree of formal reality are a function of differences in degree of *one* property, the capacity for independent existence (AT VII, 40, 44, 45, 165, 166; HR I, 162, 165, II, 56).

So substances are supposed to possess more formal reality than modes. And they do this because, as substances, they are things which of themselves are "apt" to exist or are capable of existing. Modes, on the other hand, are not of themselves capable of existing. They require a substance to inhere in. Similarly, an infinite substance has a greater capacity for independent existence than a finite one. For only the infinite substance, God, is literally such that he needs nothing else in order to exist (*Principles* I, 51). Finite substances are capable of independent existence only in the restricted sense that they require nothing other than the concurrence of God in order to exist.

On this reconstruction of the notion of formal reality the scale of being will have only three distinct points on it—modes, which depend on finite substances, finite substances which depend only on God, and God, who depends on nothing else, but on whom everything else depends, either directly, as is the case with finite substances, or indirectly, as is the case with modes.

Still, I want to say, there is great difficulty in the notion of formal reality. We need to understand the notion of formal reality in order to know whether we should assent to (3). (3) is plainly intended to state a form of what we might call "the principle of causality." Hume notwithstanding, I feel sure that there must be some way of stating the principle of causality which would command my assent. Admittedly I can *conceive* of something springing into existence ex nihilo. But I cannot *believe* that this ever happens. That is a fact about me and what I can believe, which may not be a fact about you and what you can believe. But if my interpretation of Descartes' defense of reason is correct, then facts about what I can, on reflection, believe, are important (not decisive, but important).

But though I agree that, stated in *some* way, the causal principle will compel my assent, I cannot agree that (3) commands my assent. I just do not understand the concept of formal reality well enough.

On one way of explaining "formal reality"—the way which emphasizes the notion of "being" or "perfection"—(3) is plainly a version of the principle of causality. But on that way, it is very difficult to know how, in general, to compare different things with respect to their formal reality. I do not understand the concept well enough to apply it outside of a special range of cases and so feel no compulsion to assent to any principle which essentially involves it.

On another way of explaining "formal reality"—the way which emphasizes the notion of a capacity for independent existence—(3) is not, so far as I can see, a version of what I understand by the principle of causality. It is not, so far as I can see, a principle which would, prima facie, be confirmed by instances of collision in which the quantity of motion is preserved, or instances of heat transfer, or would, prima facie, be disconfirmed by cases of spontaneous generation. Indeed it would seem to imply that although a substance could be caused only by another substance, a mode might be caused by anything at all.

So I do not find (3) assent-compelling. What about (4)? Since (4) is at least sometimes justified by appeal to (3), which we have already found to be dubious, it is tempting to dismiss (4) out of hand. But it does not follow that if (3) is dubious, (4) must also be dubious. Descartes might be offering us bad reasons for believing something we should believe on other grounds, or need no grounds for believing.

One interesting feature of (4)—and one which makes it very implausible to suppose that it could be derived simply from (3), or even from (3) in conjunction with (1) and (2)—is that it asserts the existence of a *first* cause for our ideas. How would Descartes justify this aspect of (4)?

It seems clear from the First Replies that he does *not* want to argue from the inconceivability of an infinite series of causes. Explaining why he did not argue, as St. Thomas had, from the succession of efficient causes in sensible things, he writes that this was partly

> because I did not seem to be able to reach anything by this succession of causes except a recognition of the imperfection of my intellect, in that I cannot grasp how an infinity of such causes have so succeeded one another from eternity that there has not been a first. For surely from the fact that I cannot grasp that, it does not follow that there must have been a first [cause]. (AT VII, 106; HR II, 12–13)

The implication is that St. Thomas was guilty of this non sequitur. And whether or not that is a fair criticism of St. Thomas (who is not easy to interpret on this point), it is clear that Descartes wants to avoid that move.

Descartes' grounds for asserting (4) probably come out best in the Second Replies. There it appears that he regards (4) as being presupposed by the claims we ordinarily make to knowledge of the external world. This principle must be regarded as a primary notion, he writes, because all our beliefs in the existence of things external to us depend on it alone:

> For how could we have come to think that they exist, except that the ideas of them reach our mind through the senses? (AT VII, 135; HR II, 35)

Similarly defending (4) in the Geometrical Exposition, Descartes writes that it

> must so necessarily be admitted that the knowledge of all things, both sensible and insensible, depends on it alone. For how do we know, for example, that the sky exists? Because we see it? But that seeing does not affect the mind except insofar as it is an idea—an idea, I say, inhering in the mind itself, and not an image depicted in the fantasy. Given this idea we can judge that the sky exists only if we suppose that the objective reality of every idea must have a cause which really exists, and which we judge to be the sky itself. (AT VII, 165; HR II, 56)

Descartes' language in these passages is ambiguous. He might be construed as maintaining either (a) that when someone has a perceptual belief, *he does, as matter of fact, hold that belief because* he assumes (perhaps tacitly) that his having an idea of an object of a certain sort must be explained by the existence of some cause which has at least as much reality as his idea represents its object as having, or (b) that when someone has a perceptual belief, *he can legitimately hold that belief only if* he assumes, and so forth. Quite possibly Descartes would maintain both (a) and (b). He evidently does think that most people in fact believe something rather like (4). For instance, at the beginning of *Le monde*, he remarks that

> Everyone is commonly persuaded that the ideas we have in our thought are entirely like the objects from which they proceed.[3]

Descartes cites this common opinion only to go on to cast doubt on it; he appeals, for example, to the fact that the idea of a sound which is formed in our thought bears no resemblance to the vibration of the air which is its cause. But he might well regard (4) as a defensible version of this common opinion. (4) would require only

---

3. AT XI, 3; Alquié, *Oeuvres* I, 315. Note, however, that in contrast to the *Meditations*, the ideas of *Le monde* are said to be formed in our imagination.

that there be something in the cause of our idea of sound which is at least as real as what our idea of sound suggests that there is. The vibration is a likely candidate.

If this interpretation is correct, then I think we can see somewhat more clearly the force of Descartes' asserting the existence of a 'first' cause of our ideas, and why he would feel entitled to make this claim. A 'first' cause, in the sense intended here, need not be an uncaused cause; Descartes is prepared to allow that the requirements of (4) would be satisfied in the case, say, of our idea of the sun, if that idea were caused by the sun. An inquiry into the causes of one of our ideas will come to a natural end if it traces the causal process back to something which is as our idea represents it as being, even if that thing in turn has a further cause.

If this is so, then it becomes easier to understand how Descartes could have thought he had improved on the Thomistic arguments. There is a tension in the Thomistic arguments between the universality of the causal principle and the affirmation of a first cause, a tension St. Thomas' interpreters sometimes resolve by saying that even if the series of causes extends back to infinity, the series itself requires explanation by a necessary being; the existence of a contingent being can never be really satisfactorily explained by positing either another contingent being or even an infinite series of contingent beings.[4] This line of defense leads inevitably to the Kantian criticism that the causal (or cosmological) arguments require the concept of a necessary being, which must in turn be justified by appealing to the ontological argument (which St. Thomas rejected). Descartes does not, in his first causal argument, seem to be required to take that unpromising route.

Nevertheless, his own alternative is not free of difficulties. First of all, though we can see (4) not as a consequence of general causal principles but as formulating a particular kind of causal theory of perception, that theory is hardly obvious, or even very intelligible, so long as we do not have a firmer grip on the notion of formal reality than we do. I suppose that any sensible theory of perception must regard perception as being the terminus of a complex causal process of some sort. But Descartes' version of a causal theory

4. See, e.g., Terence Penelhum, *Religion and Rationality* (New York: Random House, 1971), p. 22.

requires us to revise some of our beliefs about the nature of the things that cause our perceptions. Understanding and accepting it will require us to make comparisons of the degrees of formal reality of many different things. We would have to be able to say, for example, whether a vibration contains as much formal reality as our idea of a sound represents the sound as having. And I don't think we understand the notion of fomal reality well enough for that, certainly not well enough to be compelled to assent to (4).

Again, (4) gets whatever plausibility it has from common beliefs about perception. But it cannot be restricted to perceptual ideas. The idea to which we want subsequently to apply it is the idea of God, and this is not a perceptual idea but one we have because we can *conceive* a being with certain attributes. So the argument does seem to trade as well on a certain unclarity in the notion of an idea.

I conclude, then, that although (4) can be defended independently of (3), it is no better off than (3). And since (4) is essential to the argument in a way (3) is not, the argument must be regarded as unsuccessful if (4) is not acceptable. But as we shall see, there is some reason to think that Descartes does not want to rely too heavily on this first argument of the Third Meditation.

II

THE SECOND argument which Descartes produces in the Third Meditation may be summarized as follows:

(1) I exist as a thinking thing, or substance, and possess an idea of God as a supremely perfect being. (AT VII, 48; HR I, 167)

(2) Whatever exists has a cause possessing at least as much formal reality as the effect does. (AT VII, 49; HR I, 169)

(3) The cause of my existence is either myself, or God, or some other being or beings less perfect than God. (AT VII, 48; HR I, 167)

(4) Whatever causes its own existence can acquire any perfection it conceives. (AT VII, 48, 166; HR I, 168, II, 56–57)

(5) Whatever conceives a perfection it can acquire, does acquire that perfection. (AT VII, 48, 166; HR I, 168, II, 56)

(6) I conceive of perfections, such as knowledge, which, insofar as I doubt, I do not have. (AT VII, 48; HR I, 168)

(7) I am not the cause of my existence.[5]

5. AT VII, 48; HR I, 168. For the sake of simplicity, I am treating the two paragraphs beginning "Neque vim harum rationum effugio" ("Nor do I escape

(8) If the cause of my existence is some being (or beings) other than God, it (or they) must also be a thinking thing, possessing the idea of all the perfections I attribute to God. (AT VII, 49; HR I, 169)

(9) If a thinking thing possessing the idea of all the perfections I attribute to God is the cause of its own existence, it is God. (AT VII, 49–50; HR I, 169)

(10) If it is not the cause of its own existence, then it must be caused by some other thinking thing which also has an idea of all the perfections I attribute to God. (AT VII, 50; HR I, 169)

(11) The series of causes of thinking things having an idea of God cannot be infinite, that is, it must have a first member. (AT VII, 50; HR I, 169)

(12) The first member of the series of causes of thinking things having an idea of God must be the cause of itself. (AT VII, 50; HR I, 169)

(13) The first member of the series of causes is God.[6]

I take it that the structure of this argument is roughly this: (1) is a premise warranted by the arguments of the Second Meditation. Note that, whereas in the first argument the idea of God was specified by an enumeration of his attributes, here it is specified by a formula more characteristic of the ontological argument. The groundwork for this is laid in one of the transitional paragraphs between the first argument and the second (at AT VII, 46; HR I, 166), where the idea of God is said to be an idea "of a being supremely perfect and infinite." By the beginning of the second argument (at AT VII, 48; HR I, 167), God is designated, in a strikingly Anselmian way, as a being than whom "nothing more perfect, nor even as perfect, can be thought or supposed."

(2) is a deliverance of the natural light of reason. (3) is intended to follow from (1) and (2). I exist; my existence must have a cause; and given that God is conceived as a supremely perfect being, these three alternatives exhaust the possibilities.

(4) is justified by the subargument that it is more difficult to produce a substance than a mode, and that whatever can do the

---

the force of these arguments") as a digression in response to probable objections.

6. AT VII, 50; HR I, 169. Again I simplify by treating the two paragraphs beginning at AT VII, 50, "Nec fingi potest" ("Nor can it be supposed") as a digression in response to probable objections.

more difficult can do the less difficult. (5) is taken as axiomatic and is probably analytic; (6) is again warranted by the arguments of the Second Meditation. (7) follows from (4), (5), and (6). (8) is meant to follow from (2). (9) follows from (4) and (5), and (10) is supposed to follow from (2) and (8). (11) is held to be manifest once we reflect that what is in question is not the cause of a thing's coming into existence, but the cause of its continuing in existence. (12) follows from (11) and (2), and (13) follows from (12) and (9).

What exactly is the status of this argument? Certainly Descartes' presentation of the argument, both in the Third Meditation and in the Geometrical Exposition,[7] strongly suggests that he thought of the two arguments as distinct and independent of one another. And on the face of it, they *are* independent of one another, since the first argument involves no assumptions analogous to (4), (5), and (11) in the second argument, whereas the second argument does not require the dubious (4) of the first argument.

Descartes, however, does not consistently take that view of the relation between the arguments. For example, in the First Replies he writes that because the idea of God is the same in everyone's mind, and because

> we are never aware of its coming to us from anywhere but ourselves, we suppose that it pertains to the nature of our intellect. And indeed this is not wrong; but we neglect something else, which is the most important consideration, and the one on which the whole force and illumination of this argument depends: that this faculty of having in itself the idea of God could not exist in our intellect if this intellect were only a finite being, as it really is, and did not have God as its cause. That is why I asked further whether I could exist if God did not exist, *not so much to bring forward an argument different from the preceding one, as to explain it more completely.*[8]

Descartes' strategy in the Replies is to treat the second argument as a defensive position that he can fall back on when he is pressed about the distinctive doctrines of the first argument. When Mer-

7. Cf. Alquié, *Oeuvres* II, 448, n3, and 594–597.
8. AT VII, 105–106; HR II, 12, my emphasis. Cf. the similar passage in the letter to Mesland of 2 May 1644, Alquié, *Oeuvres* III, 69. Kenny, *Philosophical Letters*, 147.

senne argues in the Second Objections that we have a sufficient foundation in ourselves on which to construct the idea of God, Descartes, rather surprisingly, agrees:

> I said expressly at the end of the Third Meditation, that *this idea is innate in me*, that is, that it comes to me from myself . . . but . . . I warned that *the whole force of my argument consists in this, that it could not happen that the faculty of forming that idea should exist in me unless I was created by God.*[9]

Later, in response to the suggestion that he might have received the idea of God from reading or from the conversation of friends, he replies that it has no force, because

> the argument will proceed in the same way if I ask about those others, from whom I am said to have received it, whether they have it from themselves or from another, as if I were to ask this about myself, and I shall always conclude that he from whom it first proceeded is God. (AT VII, 136; HR II, 35)

Descartes plainly thinks that the proposed explanation would involve an untenable regress. And this is surely to rely on the dialectic of the second argument to defend the first.

If we view the second argument of the Third Meditation as the fundamental Cartesian causal argument, and not merely as a supplementary argument which Descartes hopes will be more acceptable to Thomists,[10] then the Kantian criticism becomes quite pressing. The principle of causality, (2), is not merely an idle wheel in this argument; it is required to do work at various stages of the argument. But on its face it is compatible with the equally necessary (11) only if something is its own cause. Descartes does not want to put a merely negative construction on the notion of a being causing itself (AT VII, 109–111; HR II, 14–16) by saying that to exist *a se* is to have no cause. He insists on applying the principle of causality to everything: "There is no existing thing of which one

9. AT VII, 133; HR II, 33. Here Descartes is evidently referring to (but not quoting very exactly) AT VII, 51–52; HR I, 170–171: "The whole force of my argument consists in this, that I recognize that it cannot happen that I should exist with a nature such as I have, that is, possessing the idea of God, unless God also really existed."

10. Cf. Alquié, *Oeuvres* II, 448, n3. A reasonable hope, as the reaction of Caterus illustrates. Cf. the First Objections and Alquié's notes thereto.

cannot ask what is the cause of its existence. That can be asked even of God" (Geometrical Exposition, Axiom 1). But it is difficult to see how the notion of something's causing itself could be given a positive construction without invoking the ontological argument. Indeed, in explaining the positive sense of existence *a se* Descartes does rely on "the immense and incomprehensible power contained in his idea" (AT VII, 110; HR II, 15).

Sometimes Descartes has a different way of resolving the tension between the universal principle of causality and the affirmation that there must be a first cause. Sometimes he argues that if our question is not "By what cause was the thing formerly produced?" but "By what cause is it conserved at the present time?" we must deny that this could have resulted from an infinite series of causes:

> since the whole period of my life can be divided into innumerable parts, each of which is in no way dependent on the rest, from the fact that I existed a little while ago, it does not follow that I must now exist, unless some cause, as it were, recreates me at this moment, that is, conserves me. (AT VII, 48–49; HR I, 168)

If I continue to exist from one moment to another, then some cause must be at work, continually re-creating me. And an infinite series of causes all operating at the same moment *is* impossible.

This is a puzzling doctrine, which may easily give rise to misunderstanding. Kenny, for example, has objected that even if we grant that the duration of an individual can be conceived as a logical construction out of a set of time slices—Descartes at t_0, Descartes at t_1, Descartes at t_2, and so on—we need not conclude that these time slices are causally independent of one another:

> Why may not each time slice be the cause of the existence of the next, dying phoenixlike in giving birth to its successor? There will be no violation of the principle that a cause must be as perfect as its effect; nothing can be imagined that more exactly equals in perfection a time slice of Descartes than an immediately preceding time slice of Descartes. (Kenny, 144)

This, I think, is to miss Descartes' point. It is not the degree of formal reality the preceding time slice has which disqualifies it as a cause. It is its temporal priority.

That a cause cannot be temporally prior to its effect does not come out very clearly in the Third Meditation, where Descartes admittedly offers a different ground for rejecting Kenny's objection. But in the First Replies, when Descartes is responding to the objection that nothing can be its own efficient cause because an efficient cause must be temporally prior to its effect, Descartes does reject that requirement:

> The light of nature does not tell us that the nature of an efficient cause requires it to be prior to its effect in time; on the contrary, it does not, strictly speaking, have the nature of a cause except when it produces its effect, and therefore is not prior to it. (AT VII, 108; HR II, 14)

I suppose the reasoning here is that a cause must be a sufficient condition of its effect; but if a cause were temporally prior to its effect, then it could not be sufficient for that effect, or else the effect would already exist and the cause would not be temporally prior to it. The conclusion is that anything which qualifies as a cause must be simultaneous with its effect.

No doubt this is a conclusion paradoxical enough to make us suspect sophistry in the reasoning that leads to it. But even if we grant it, it is not clear that it resolves Descartes' problem. What this doctrine leads to is a restriction on the kind of thing that could satisfy the universal principle of causality, on the kind of thing that would be counted as an answer to the request to specify a cause. It does not give us a reason for qualifying the principle, or for saying that there is some cause whose explanation we need not seek in some further cause. No doubt it is not so easy for us to imagine an infinite series of causes all acting at the same time as it is for us to imagine an infinite series of causes acting successively. But I suspect that this comes from our not taking simultaneity strictly, from our thinking instead that there must be *some*—perhaps infinitesimally small—temporal interval between cause and effect. So if the series of causes were very long, the temporal interval between an effect and its more distant causes would no longer be negligible. But if we are really serious about saying that a cause must be simultaneous with its effect, there seems to be no reason to set any particular limit to the causal series.

I conclude, then, that whatever other difficulties it may involve, Descartes' second causal argument does encounter the objection Kant raised against 'the' cosmological argument. It does depend on the ontological argument, in the sense that its premises can only be made consistent with one another if we accept the idea that a thing can be its own cause in the way the ontological argument is supposed to explain. The first causal argument does not, on the face of it, have *that* defect. But the fact that Descartes tends to fall back on the second argument when the first is questioned suggests that in the end the first argument too may depend on the ontological argument. To that extent Kant is vindicated, and the question of the ontological argument's soundness is very pressing.

III

THE ARGUMENT of the Fifth Meditation is Descartes' best known argument for the existence of God. But familiarity should not breed the illusion that understanding and assessment will be easy. The ontological argument raises much more difficult problems of interpretation and evaluation than the arguments of the Third Meditation do. No textually plausible interpretation of those arguments is likely to render them philosophically acceptable. But the acceptability of the ontological argument may well depend on contentious matters of interpretation.

I propose to begin by taking what seems to me to be the most natural reading of the argument as presented in the Fifth Meditation, to discuss classical objections to that argument, and then to consider whether any textually based reformulation of the argument can escape these objections. Tentatively, then, we summarize the argument thus:

(1) I have ideas of things which, whether or not they exist, and whether or not I think of them, have true and immutable natures or essences. (AT VII, 84; HR I, 179–180)

(2) Whatever property I perceive clearly and distinctly as belonging to the true and immutable nature of something I have an idea of really does belong to that thing. (AT VII, 84; HR I, 180)

(3) I have an idea of God as a supremely perfect being. (AT VII, 65; HR I, 180)

(4) I perceive clearly and distinctly that existence belongs to the

true and immutable nature of a supremely perfect being. (AT VII, 65; HR I, 180–181)

(5) A supremely perfect being really does exist.

(6) God exists.

The first step of this argument is meant to be a report on the contents of my consciousness. These ideas are something I discover in myself.

It may, of course, be objected that (1) is not *just* a report of what my consciousness contains. As Alquié rightly observes (*Oeuvres* II, 470, n2), the relative pronoun "which" must refer to "things," not to "ideas." So (1), it may be argued, makes a claim, not merely about my ideas, but about the things which are the objects of my ideas, namely, that whether or not they exist or are thought of, they have true and immutable natures. And the truth of this claim cannot be discovered by introspection.

This objection, however, is too hasty. Though it is the things that have the natures, what is central in (1) is that this is how my ideas represent the things, that is, as having such natures. This is not to say, however, that Descartes cannot offer further argument for (1). He can, and we shall return to that argument later.

The text of the *Meditations* suggests, somewhat implausibly, that (2) follows from (1):

> From this fact alone, that I can produce the idea of something from my thought, it follows that whatever I perceive clearly and distinctly to pertain to that thing really does pertain to it. (AT VII, 65; HR I, 180)

We shall see later that there is more merit than might at first appear in treating (2) as a consequence of (1). But the precise status of (2) raises some very complicated and far-reaching problems. So for now it is best left obscure.

(3), again, is a premise reporting on the contents of my consciousness. (4) is justified by the subargument (AT VII, 66; HR I, 181):

> (a) All perfections belong to the true and immutable nature of a supremely perfect being.
> (b) Existence is a perfection.
> (c) Existence belongs to the true and immutable nature of a supremely perfect being.

(a) is supposed to be analytic and, like (b), clearly and distinctly perceived. Hence, we perceive (c) clearly and distinctly.

(5) really does, I think, follow from (2), (3), and (4). And (6) is taken by Descartes to be equivalent to (5), though this, it seems to me, needs some argument.

Now the ontological argument, in one form or another, has a very long history,[11] and has been attacked on many grounds. But since Kant the most popular criticism has been that existence is not a property. If existence is not a property, then, a fortiori, it is not a perfection, that is, a property in virtue of which the things that have it are, other things equal, better than those that lack it. This would exclude Descartes' subargument for (4) by refuting premise (b) of that argument. And if only properties can be used in definitions (and so belong to the true and immutable natures of things), it would not merely exclude that subargument, but also entail that (4) is false.

The distinction of having first voiced this criticism belongs, perhaps, to Gassendi,[12] who wrote in the Fifth Objections that

Neither in God nor in any other thing is existence a perfection, but only that without which there are no perfections. In fact, what does not exist has neither perfection nor imperfection; but what exists and has various perfections, does not have its existence as one of those perfections, but only as that by which the thing itself and its perfections are existent. . . . So we do not say that existence is in a thing as a perfection, nor, if it lacks existence, that it is imperfect or deprived of some perfection; we say, rather, that it is nothing. (AT VII, 383; HR II, 228)

Descartes' immediate reaction to this objection was one of puzzlement:

I do not see what sort of thing you think existence is, nor why it cannot be called a property, just as omnipotence is, taking the term "property" for any sort of attribute, or for whatever can be pre-

11. Useful surveys are given in two recent anthologies: *The Ontological Argument, from St. Anselm to Contemporary Philosophers*, ed. A. Plantinga (Garden City, N.Y.: Doubleday, 1965); and *The Many-faced Argument, Recent Studies of the Ontological Argument for the Existence of God*, ed. J. Hick and A. C. McGill (London: Macmillan, 1968).

12. See, however, Schopenhauer on "the prophetic wisdom of Aristotle," in Plantinga, *The Ontological Argument*, p. 67.

dicated of a thing, as it surely must be taken here. (AT VII, 382–383; HR II, 228)

And it seems to me that puzzlement is, initially at least, the right reaction to have when someone says that existence is not a property.

The philosophical distinction between substances and their properties is a correlate of the grammatical distinction between subjects and predicates. Part of what we mean when we say that omnipotence is a property is that phrases like "is omnipotent" can occur sensibly as the grammatical predicate of a sentence. And by purely grammatical criteria, existence has as good a claim to be classed as a property as omnipotence does. The term "exists" can occur sensibly as the grammatical predicate of a sentence, as the debate over the truth of "God exists" illustrates.

Grammar, of course, is not everything. No one would want to claim that the term "it" in the sentence "It is raining" designates a substance. But the philosophical logician who thinks he can provide the grammatical predicate "exists" with a semantics analogous to those he provides for other paradigmatic predicate expressions will think there is a prima facie case for regarding existence as a property,[13] and that the contrary view needs to be argued, not just asserted.

Many philosophers, of course, have argued the contrary view—but not, I find, convincingly. To expound and then criticize in adequate detail the various arguments I reject would be tedious, even if I restricted myself to a few of the view's more prominent advocates. Kant, for example, is as obscure on this point as he has been influential. Fortunately, however, Kant's claim about existence and modern attempts to support it have been getting a good deal of critical attention in recent work on the philosophy of religion.[14] So I shall deal only with one argument, which is both typical and instructive.

William Alston, in his article, "The Ontological Argument Re-

13. Cf. R. Routley, "Some Things Do Not Exist," *Notre Dame Journal of Formal Logic*, 7 (1966), 251–276.
14. E.g., Alvin Plantinga, *God and Other Minds* (Ithaca, N.Y.: Cornell University Press, 1967); Jonathan Barnes, *The Ontological Argument* (London: Macmillan, 1972).

visited,"[15] maintains that we cannot understand why existence is not a property unless we are able to give some account of what is involved in predicating a property of a subject. He begins from the Strawsonian (ultimately, Fregean) position that one essential element in predication is a presupposition that the subject of the predication exists:

> The existence of the subject must be presupposed before we can set about attaching (withholding, wondering whether to attach) any predicate to (from) it. (p. 281)

Given any statement of subject-predicate form, say, "The pie in the oven is done," the question of its truth or falsity does not arise unless the subject term designates something that exists—in this case, unless there is a pie in the oven.

If we accept this principle of presupposition, there does seem to be good reason to deny that existence is a property. For if the principle is true, and if existence is a property, then any positive statement predicating existence of a subject, any statement having a singular term (proper name or definite description) as subject and "exists" as predicate, will be true, and trivially so, if it has any truth-value at all. If the singular term did not designate something that existed, the statement would be neither true nor false. Analogously, any negative statement denying existence of a subject, any statement having a singular term as subject and "does not exist" as predicate, will be false, if it has any truth-value at all. If it has a truth-value, then the singular term designates something that exists. The result would be that we could never make a false positive existential statement, or a true negative one. But this is absurd. We do sometimes make such statements. Hence, when we say that something exists, we cannot be attributing a property to a subject.

This does strike me as a helpful way of articulating an objection many critics have had to treating existence as a property. Gassendi, for example, argues that existence is not a perfection, but that in the absence of existence there is no perfection, that if a thing lacks

---

15. *Philosophical Review*, 69 (1960), 452–474. References are to the reprint in Doney. Barnes notes the "remarkable popularity" of this line of reasoning and cites numerous examples, *The Ontological Argument*, p. 42.

existence, it is not said to be imperfect but to be nothing. And this may be regarded as an implicit application of the principle of presupposition. No doubt the principle requires some qualification to deal with the difficulties raised by past and future tense statements. "The pie Ruth baked yesterday was delicious" does not lose its truth-value merely because the pie was so good it no longer exists. But I suppose the problem of formulating the fundamental intuition so as to avoid such counterexamples is merely a technical one, requiring a little ingenuity.

Alston does not think this argument by itself establishes that existence is not a property. He accepts the principle of presupposition only with qualifications that have a different motivation. We can, he thinks, make true-or-false predications of subjects which we do not presuppose to "really exist," provided we presuppose that they have some nonreal mode of existence. For example, we can say truly that King Arthur was the son of Uther Pendragon, if we presuppose that Arthur exists in legends. And he holds Anselm's version of the ontological argument to be superior to Descartes', because Anselm makes it plain that the being of whom he wishes to predicate real existence is already presupposed to exist "in the understanding."

Alston, however, does not think that even with this improvement the ontological argument is satisfactory. For he also holds a principle which we may call the principle of partition, namely, that no statement 'about' something which exists in a nonreal mode of existence can have implications with respect to real things, except insofar as it implies that there are legends, or stories, or dreams, or thoughts which have a certain content (p. 295). So if "God exists" is about something which exists "in the understanding" or in any other nonreal mode of existence, it cannot have the implications, the religious significance, it is usually thought to have.

Now clearly the principle of partition, as stated above, is too strong. King Arthur 'exists in legend' and many historians think he also really existed. But if we take the principle of partition strictly, a historian who thinks this will be barred from saying anything about Arthur which has implications about real things (except insofar as he might imply that there are legends). For any statement about Arthur will be a statement about something which

GOD

exists in a nonreal mode of existence (in addition to existing really).

Alston, of course, wants to allow that we *can* say of King Arthur both that he exists in legend and that he really existed in the sixth century. These statements are independent of one another; neither presupposes the other. But he does not explain how we can say such things without violating the doctrine I have called the principle of partition. Presumably we should reformulate that principle along the following lines: "No statement whose subject term designates something which the person making the statement presupposes to exist *only* in a nonreal mode of existence can have implications with respect to real things, except . . ." This has the merit of not being obviously false. Unfortunately, the principle no longer appears to be effective against the Anselmian version of the ontological argument which it is directed at. For what Anselm presupposes is that God exists *at least* in the understanding, not that he exists only in the understanding.

Whatever the outcome of the controversy between Alston and Anselm, the soundness of Descartes' argument does not stand or fall with that of Anselm's. Descartes' response to Alston would be quite different. He thinks we can make true statements about objects without presupposing that the objects exist—either 'in reality' or 'in the understanding.' This Cartesian doctrine is what is formulated by the first step of the argument:

> (1) I have ideas of things which, whether or not they exist, and whether or not I think of them, have true and immutable natures or essences.

The prime examples here are mathematical objects:

> When I imagine a triangle, even though perhaps no such figure exists outside my thought, nor ever did exist, nevertheless it certainly has a determinate nature, or essence, or form, which is eternal and immutable, not invented by me, nor dependent on my mind. This is evident from the fact that various properties can be demonstrated of that triangle . . . which I now clearly recognize, whether I wish to or not, even though I have not previously thought of these properties in any way. So I have not invented them. (AT VII, 64; HR I, 180)

The objects of mathematics have determinate, eternal (true and immutable) natures, even though those objects may not exist. We

147

can have knowledge of these objects, and a fortiori make true and false statements about them, without knowing whether or not they exist.

In fact, to say that mathematical objects *may* exist is to suggest more than Descartes is sometimes prepared to allow. He does not think we have evidence that anything properly described as a triangle does exist. When Gassendi objected that our knowledge of 'the ideal triangle' might be derived from observation of material ones, Descartes replied:

> Though, doubtless, there could be in the world such figures as the geometers consider, nevertheless I deny that there are any about us, unless, perhaps, they are so small that they do not affect our senses. (AT VII, 381; HR II, 227)

Every figure we observe turns out, on close examination, not to be composed of lines which are strictly straight, as the sides of a triangle are supposed to be.

What is the force of saying that these probably nonexistent mathematical objects have determinate, eternal natures, or true and immutable natures? Descartes contrasts true and immutable natures with fictitious ones, and, to judge by his examples, he has in mind, in speaking of things with fictitious natures, such things as legendary creatures: for example, the chimera, a monster supposed to have had a serpent's tail, a goat's body, and a lion's head. These fictional creatures differ from mathematical objects in two important respects.[16]

First, the natures of fictional creatures are indeterminate in that, if the legends do not have anything to say on some question we might ask about chimeras (as, Were they carnivorous?), then such questions simply have no answer. The statement that they were carnivorous will be no more true or false than is the statement that Hamlet wore size ten shoes.

Second, the natures of fictional creatures simply are what their creators say they are. The person who first told a story about a chimera could not misdescribe it by ascribing to it properties it did not have any more than Shakespeare could have been mistaken

16. Cf. Plantinga's discussion of creatures of fiction in *The Nature of Necessity* (Oxford: Clarendon Press, 1974), pp. 153–159.

about Hamlet's marital status. The natures of fictitious creatures contain all that their creators have put in them and only what their creators have put in them.

Mathematical objects, as Descartes conceives them, are not like that. Of course they must 'exist in my thought,' I must think of them, if *I* am to make true predications of them. But I can discover that they have properties no one ever thought of before; I can be mistaken in ascribing certain properties to them; and I can discover that I have been mistaken. These objects are not simply the creatures of my fancy. As Descartes says, they are not "invented by me or dependent on my mind."

In interpreting Descartes in this way I am agreeing with Kenny, who ascribes to Descartes something like a Meinongian theory of pure objects as subjects of predication. Perhaps the clearest passage in support of this interpretation occurs in the interview with Burman:

> All the demonstrations of mathematics are concerned with true beings and objects; and so the whole object of mathematics, and whatever mathematics considers in it, is a true and real being, and has a true and real nature, no less than the object of physics. The only difference is that physics considers its object not only as a true and real being but also as actual, and, as such, existing; whereas mathematics considers its object only as possible, not actually existing in space, but still being able to exist. (AT V, 160; Bridoux, 1374)

Of course a contemporary defender of Meinong might want to question the distinction Descartes draws here between mathematics and physics; he might argue that physics is just as much concerned with ideal objects (such as frictionless planes, perfectly elastic bodies, and so on) as is mathematics.[17] And the Cartesian doctrine is one which only *resembles* Meinong's. Descartes thinks, as Meinong did, that an object need not exist in order to be the subject of a true predication. But he also seems to think, as

17. For Meinong, see "The Theory of Objects," in *Realism and the Background of Phenomenology*, ed. R. Chisholm (Free Press of Glencoe, Ill., 1960). For contemporary defenses, see two articles by Richard and Valerie Routley, "Rehabilitating Meinong's Theory of Objects," *Revue Internationale de Philosophie* (1973), pp. 224–254, and "Exploring Meinong's Jungle: Items and Descriptions," *Notre Dame Journal of Formal Logic*, forthcoming.

Meinong did not, that an object must be able to exist to be the subject of a true predication.

This point of difference bothered Burman, who asked whether the argument Descartes uses to show that nonactual possibles have essences could not also be used to show that *impossibilia* have essences, namely, that we can demonstrate various properties of them.[18] Descartes replied that whatever is conceived clearly and distinctly in an impossible object has a true and immutable nature; but apparently the impossible object itself does not have one.

The rationale here seems to be that the idea of an impossible object is always a composite idea; its component ideas may have objects with true and immutable natures, but composite ideas themselves do not have objects with true and immutable natures. Certainly Descartes does seem to think that ideas of impossible objects are composite:

> All contradiction or impossibility occurs only in our conception, which improperly conjoins ideas which are opposed to one another, nor can it be posited in anything outside the intellect; for if something is outside the intellect, it is plain that it does not involve a contradiction, but is possible. (AT VII, 152; HR II, 46)

And he also thinks that composite ideas do not have objects with true and immutable natures.

> Those ideas which do not contain true and immutable natures, but only fictitious natures, composed by the intellect, can be divided by the same intellect, not merely by abstraction, but by a clear and distinct operation. So those ideas which the intellect cannot divide in this way, have certainly not been composed by it. For instance,

18. In ascribing this argument to Burman I take him to be using "chimera" (AT V, 160) in the sense of an impossible object, and not in the sense of the legendary monster with a serpent's tail, a goat's body, and a lion's head. That "chimera" does sometimes have the former sense in the seventeenth century is illustrated by Spinoza—"The term 'chimera,' here and in what follows, signifies something whose nature involves a plain contradiction," *Cogitata Metaphysica* I, 1.

Some of the things Descartes says in reply to Burman suggest that *he* took the question to be about the legendary monster, not the impossible object. But if he had, he would had a more direct answer, viz., that we cannot demonstrate various properties of the chimera. Cf. his remarks to Gassendi on the universals of the dialecticians, AT VII, 380; HR II, 226–227; and First Replies, AT VII, 117; HR II, 20.

GOD

when I think of a winged horse, or a lion actually existing, or a
triangle inscribed in a square, I easily understand that I can also
think of a horse which is not winged, or a lion which does not
exist, or a triangle without a square, and so they do not have true
and immutable natures. But if I think of a triangle . . . then certainly whatever I understand to be contained in the idea of a triangle, I shall affirm of it—for example, that its three angles equal two
right angles. For though I can understand a triangle in abstraction
from [that property], I cannot deny [that property] of it by a clear
and distinct operation, that is, understanding what I say. (AT VII,
117–118; HR II, 20)

It is clear that Descartes here anticipates one Russellian criticism of
Meinongian objects. Russell wanted to argue that on a Meinongian
view we could proliferate ontological arguments by analyzing concepts such as that of the existent golden mountain, whose nature
would entail that it was golden and a mountain and that it existed.

Descartes would reply that what we 'discover' from the analysis of a concept like that does not represent a genuine discovery,
that we get out of the analysis only what we have put in. It is no
surprise to learn that there is a contradiction involved in the
concept of an existent lion that does not exist. But it is a discovery
to learn that there is a contradiction in the concept of a supremely
perfect being who does not exist. So we can see the motivation for
denying that composite ideas have objects with 'true and immutable' natures.

If this is right, and if ideas of impossible objects are always
composite, then the only knowledge we would have of impossible
objects would be knowledge of 'trifling propositions,' like "the
square circle is square." Descartes' denial that they have true and
immutable natures may then seem reasonable.

Nevertheless, the distinction Descartes wants to draw between
fictitious essences and true and immutable ones is difficult, as his
vacillation over the triangle inscribed in the square illustrates. On
the face of it, the idea of this object is a composite one, since I can
conceive clearly and distinctly a triangle which is not inscribed in a
square, and a square which does not have a triangle inscribed in it.
So Descartes first says that it does not have a true and immutable
nature. Then reflecting that he can prove nontrivial truths about
such a figure, truths which do not follow simply from the nature of

151

a triangle as such, or from the nature of a triangle inscribed in a figure of any sort whatever, he says that, though the idea of a triangle inscribed in a square is composite, that object does have a true and immutable nature.

Now if Descartes' rationale for rejecting *impossibilia* as subjects of predication is what I have represented it as being—that their ideas are composite, and that composite ideas do not have objects with true and immutable natures—then it looks as though allowing an exception for composite ideas which give rise to nontrivial demonstrations will let in *impossibilia* as well. For surely some properties do follow from the nature of a square circle which do not follow either from the nature of a square alone or from the nature of a circle alone. Nonexistence, for example. And this will be true generally of *impossibilia*. So perhaps Descartes is left without any good reason for rejecting *impossibilia*. Perhaps his best course is to accept them and deal as well as he can with the objection that impossible objects violate the principle of noncontradiction.

Kenny, who thinks Descartes' rejection of *impossibilia* is sound, holds that there are insurmountable objections to admitting even *possibilia* as subjects of predication. First, he raises Quinean difficulties about the lack of identity conditions for such objects. If something is to be a subject of predication,

> it is essential that it shall be possible to tell in what circumstances two predications are made of *that same subject*. Otherwise we shall never be able to apply the principle that contradictory predications should not be made of the same subject. (p. 168)

But while we have criteria for deciding whether or not two statements are about the same actual man, we have no criteria for deciding whether or not two statements are about the same possible man. In support of this contention Kenny quotes a well-known series of rhetorical questions from W. V. Quine's essay "On What There Is":

> Take . . . the possible fat man in that doorway; and again, the possible bald man in that doorway. Are they the same possible man, or two possible men? How do we decide? How many possible men are there in that doorway? Are there more possible thin ones than fat ones? How many of them are alike? Are no *two* possible things alike? Is this the same as saying that it is impossible for two things

to be alike? Or . . . is the concept of identity simply inapplicable to unactualised possibles?

And so it goes. Kenny regards these questions as unanswerable and as presenting an insurmountable obstacle to positing pure objects as subjects of predication. Fortunately, he suggests, modern logic offers us an alternative method of dealing with the nonexistent. By this he evidently means that statements which Descartes would construe as categorical subject-predicate statements about unactualized possibles ought to be construed as conditional statements about the properties a triangle would have if it existed (Kenny, 169, 147).

Kenny also objects that when Descartes rejects the principle of presupposition in the ontological argument, he implicitly contradicts himself, since he requires the principle of presupposition for the *cogito* argument:

> If the ontological argument is not to be a great *petitio principii*, it is essential that it should be possible to prove properties of the problematically existent. It must be possible, at least in some cases, to be sure that X is F, without being sure that X exists. But if that is so, then what becomes of *cogito, ergo sum* . . . what right has Descartes to assume that the substance, of which his thought is an attribute, exists? (Kenny, 169–170)

If the inference "The triangle has its three angles equal to two right angles, so the triangle exists," is not valid, then the inference "I think, so I exist" cannot be valid. Conversely, if the inference from thought to existence is valid, then Descartes must admit the existence of anything which demonstrably has certain properties. Kenny concludes that the *cogito* and the ontological argument cannot both be valid. And he regards this as a major difficulty in the Cartesian system.

What are we to say to this? As for Kenny's first objection, I think the problem of the nonexistent is not to be dismissed as easily as he suggests. If Descartes is right in maintaining that geometry gives us knowledge of things which never actually exist, there is no great advantage to be gained by treating this as knowledge of conditional rather than categorical propositions. For the antecedents of these conditionals will be eternally unfulfilled, so that the conditionals will be counterfactual. And I suppose it is no easier to state truth-conditions for counterfactual conditionals than it is to state identity conditions for nonactual possibilities.

We might reject the demand for identity conditions. There are many types of object we are prepared to countenance for which we cannot (yet, at least) supply theoretically satisfactory identity conditions. Actual material objects are typically individuated by their spatiotemporal positions. But this, arguably, is satisfactory only if we possess a principle of individuation for spatiotemporal positions. If, as is typically the case, they are individuated by reference to the material objects which occupy them (or some of them), then our circle has a very small circumference.

Suppose we don't reject the demand for identity conditions. What then? It might be said on Descartes' behalf that we cannot answer Quine's questions because they are not properly framed. After all, we would be equally puzzled if we were asked whether the American president who was assassinated is identical with the one born in a log cabin. Neither description is sufficiently definite to pick out just one individual, even if we restrict ourselves to the actual. If we permit our descriptions to range over *possibilia*, then it is plausible to hold that a description will not be really definite (that is, refer to at most one individual) unless it gives a complete description of that individual—assigns one or the other of each pair of contradictory predicates to the individual. We would then say that *possibilia* are identical if and only if their complete descriptions are identical. This, I suppose, would be Leibniz' way out.

It may be that this is not, in the end, a satisfactory way out. Leibniz' doctrine of complete individual concepts may involve serious problems of its own. The apparent need to give a complete description to refer definitely to a nonactual possible might mean that we (unlike God) could never frame singular propositions about them. But Kenny's criticism on this point seems to me only to set a research problem for philosophical logicians, not to state an insurmountable objection.[19] It does seem that we can make true

19. For alternative approaches, cf. Nicholas Rescher, "The Concept of Non-existent Possibles," in *Essays in Philosophical Analysis* (Pittsburgh: University of Pittsburgh Press, 1969), and the Routleys' "Rehabilitating Meinong's Theory of Objects," cited above.

154

statements about things which might have existed but don't, for example, the identical twin I would have had if the cell from which I developed had divided in a certain way at a certain time. If so, logic must in some way accommodate such statements.

Kenny's second objection was that allowing true statements to be made about nonactual *possibilia*—or better, *possibilia* whose actuality is in doubt—would undercut the basis for the *cogito*. This raises a serious systematic problem for Descartes, and it is not clear what his answer would be. But the following reply suggests itself. Earlier (Chapter 4) I rejected what I regarded as overly formal or logical versions of the principle justifying the inference from thought to existence, such as:

> Whenever a predicate can be truly or falsely applied to a subject that subject exists,

in favor of a more metaphysical principle, like:

> Whenever there is a thought (or more generally, an activity), there is a thing that has the thought (an agent).

And certainly Descartes does sometimes express himself in this way (for example, at AT VII, 175–176; HR II, 64).

What difference does this make? Well, the point, I suppose, is that in the *cogito* we are inferring, not from the truth (or falsity) of a statement, but from the existence of a property or activity, from its instantiation at some point in time. The distinction between agents and their acts (or between substances and attributes) must cut across that between the possible and the actual. If there is a thought in this, the actual world, then there must be a thinker in this, the actual world. If thinking were instantiated only in some other possible world, and not in this one, then there would be a thinker in that world, but not in this.

Putting the inferential principle in this way implies that the *cogito* might be recast in the following terms:

> A thought exists.
> So, a thing that thinks exists.

And since this eliminates the term "I" from both the premise and the conclusion, anyone who imagines that the force of the *cogito* argument depends on logical peculiarities of the first-person pronoun will resist this formulation. But wrongly. As Descartes emphasizes immediately after the *cogito* argument in the Second Meditation, he does not at that stage know much about the nature of the thing whose existence he has just proved. The "I" of the conclusion is short for "that thing, whatever it is, of which the aforementioned thought is an activity."

It may be objected that if "A thought exists" means "Thinking is instantiated at some point in time," then the premise is equivalent to the conclusion, and that is a sign that something has gone wrong. But is it? I can imagine someone denying the equivalence. I suppose, for example, that a philosopher who believes that processes are the fundamental metaphysical category, and denies that processes presuppose things which undergo those processes, will not think the premise and the conclusion equivalent. So something is being said which some people might (wrongly) wish to reject.

I conclude, then, that the first step of Descartes' argument involves a commitment to doctrines about truth and predication which, although not without difficulty, are neither absurd nor inconsistent with other elements of his philosophy. The correctness of these doctrines is an open question. But if they are correct, there is no reason not to take the natural view that existence is a property. So I turn to the second step:

(2) Whatever property I perceive clearly and distinctly as belonging to the true and immutable nature of something I have an idea of, really does belong to that thing.

The following objection seems inevitable. This is merely a form of the principle:

(2') Whenever I perceive *p* clearly and distinctly, then *p* is true.

But the truth of our clear and distinct perceptions is supposed to be subject to reasonable doubt so long as the existence and veracity of God have not been proved. So if this step is essential to the ontological argument, that argument cannot constitute an independent proof of the existence of God. The "proof" will be a good one only if we already have a proof of God's existence (and veracity). Whatever persuasive value the argument might have for those who are unimpressed by the Cartesian program of radical doubt, in the end it has no philosophical value in itself, apart from the other Cartesian arguments for God's existence.

Now surely, if this objection could be established, it would be quite damaging to the ontological argument. That argument would be made to depend on arguments which are implausible in themselves, and in any case, arguably dependent on the ontological argument. We would be faced with a new Cartesian circle. So it is disconcerting to find distinguished Cartesian scholars contending not only that the objection is correct but also that Descartes would have conceded the points just made. Yet this is precisely what Gueroult has claimed.[20] On his reading of Descartes the ontological argument presupposes the arguments of the Third and Fourth Meditations.

Some of Gueroult's arguments for this interpretation are directly textual. He notes, for example, a number of passages in which Descartes characterizes the causal argument as the *principal* argument for God's existence (for instance AT VII, 14, 101; HR I, 141, II, 9) and stresses particularly a passage in the Fourth Replies:

> I think it is manifest to everyone that the consideration of the efficient cause is the first and principal means—not to say the only one—that we have to prove God's existence. (AT VII, 238; HR II, 109)

I do not find such passages as unambiguous as Gueroult does. To say that an argument is the principal argument for a certain conclusion is not to say that it is the only one but to imply that there are others. And when someone says "not to say the only one," he does *not* say it is the only one; he deliberately refrains from saying that.[21]

Other passages are more troublesome. For example, in the Fifth Meditation, in the paragraph preceding the one in which he enunciates (2), Descartes writes:

20. Initially, in *Descartes selon l'ordre des raisons*, I, chap. 8, but also in *Nouvelles réflexions sur la preuve ontologique de Descartes* (Paris: J. Vrin, 1955). Dismissed abruptly by Kenny (pp. 231–232), Gueroult's thesis has been accepted by Beck (*Metaphysics*, 231–237).

21. For other ways of dealing with this passage, see Alquié, *Oeuvres* II, 681, n1, or Henri Gouhier, "La preuve ontologique de Descartes (A propos d'un livre récent)," *Revue Internationale de Philosophie*, 8 (1954), 295–303.

I have already fully demonstrated that all those things which I clearly know are true. (AT VII, 65; HR I, 180)

And just after stating (2), he says:

I understand *no less clearly and distinctly* that it pertains to the nature [of a supremely perfect being] to exist always than I understand that a property which I demonstrate of some figure or number pertains to the nature of that figure or number; and consequently, even though not all of the things which I have contemplated these past few days were true, *the existence of God would have to be at least as certain to me as the truths of mathematics previously were.* (AT VII, 65; HR I, 180–181; my emphasis)

It cannot be less certain, according to Gueroult, because no natural doubt inhibits my spontaneous inclination to accept the proof.[22] But it also cannot be more certain, unless the proof is supplemented by an argument which would enable it to avoid the metaphysical doubt, an argument like that of the Third and Fourth Meditations.

Again, in the First Replies, immediately after having formulated a syllogism which has (2) as its major premise, Descartes remarks that this

major cannot be denied, because it has already been conceded that *whatever we understand clearly and distinctly is true.* (AT VII, 116; HR II, 19)

But if Caterus, the author of the First Objections, had not conceded this principle, it would have had to be demonstrated (cf. AT VII, 95, 112; HR II, 5, 17, Gueroult, *Réflexions*, 24–26).

Gueroult, however, does not argue solely from textual evidence of this sort. He also maintains that only by so interpreting Descartes can we understand why the ontological argument is placed in the Fifth Meditation, rather than in the Third. Descartes accords great importance to the order in which he presents his philosophy:

It is to be noted, in whatever I write, that I do not follow the order of subjects, but only the order of reasons—that is, I do not under-

22. Or so Gueroult implies, as it seems to me, in his comment on this passage in *Descartes selon l'ordre des raisons*, I, 335–6. But in the *Réflexions*, 112–115, Gueroult concedes to Gouhier that psychological prejudices do stand in the way of our acceptance of the ontological argument and contends that this is further confirmation of his interpretation.

take to say everything which pertains to a topic in one place, because it would be impossible for me to prove it properly, since
some reasons would have to be drawn from further afield than
others. But reasoning in an orderly fashion, from the simpler to the
more difficult, I deduce what I can from it, now on one subject,
now on another. In my opinion this is the right way to find and
explain the truth. (Letter to Mersenne, 24 December 1640 (?);
Alquié, *Oeuvres* II, 301; Kenny, *Philosophical Letters*, 87)

Gueroult draws from this a rule of interpretation—where one
thesis is stated before another, we must assume that it is a condition of the other and try to understand why it is a condition of the
other.

Taken strictly, Gueroult's rule of interpretation is too strong.
Descartes' statement that he follows the order of reasons may
imply that he could not have deduced God's existence from his
nature *before* the Fifth Meditation, and hence that it depends on
some thesis stated before it, but surely not that it depends on *every*
thesis stated before it. Still, this is sufficient to pose a problem. For
the only premise of the ontological argument which looks as
though it might have been demonstrated in preceding meditations
is (2).

Against this Henri Gouhier has pointed out that in texts like the
Geometrical Exposition and the *Principles*, Descartes makes the
ontological argument precede his causal arguments. If the causal
arguments are supposed to be a condition of the ontological argument, how can this be?

Gueroult replies that preference must be given to the *Meditations*, where Descartes proceeds according to the analytic order, the
order of discovery, not to the Geometrical Exposition and the
Principles, where he proceeds according to the synthetic order, the
order of exposition. The analytic order is the true order, the one in
which scientific rigor is placed above expository convenience (*Réflexions*, 17–19).

This, however, puts more weight on the distinction between
analysis and synthesis than it can bear. When Descartes distinguishes the analytic mode from the synthetic (AT VII, 155–157;
HR II, 48–50), he distinguishes them as two different ways of
demonstrating things geometrically. The analytic mode shows the

way in which the proposition demonstrated has been discovered; but it omits the synthetic mode's elaborate apparatus of definitions, postulates, axioms, theorems, and problems and so may fail to convince the hostile or the inattentive. But both are modes of demonstrating something "geometrically" and hence are bound to obey the requirements of order, that is, are bound to arrange matters so that each proposition is demonstrated solely from ones that precede it. The fact that the *Principles* and the Geometrical Exposition are written in the synthetic mode cannot explain the violation of order which, on Gueroult's interpretation, would be involved in placing the ontological argument first.[23]

To reject the contention that the ontological argument is dependent on the causal arguments does not require us to say that the order of presentation in the *Meditations* is fortuitous. It may well be that Descartes placed the arguments of the Third Meditation first because he thought that the most natural way to prove God's existence, the one most likely to occur first to someone attempting to reconstruct his beliefs on a firmer foundation, would be to proceed from common assumptions about the causality of our ideas. The ontological argument, relying on uncommon assumptions about mathematical truth, is much more difficult. It runs contrary to our empiricist instincts, as the interchange with Gassendi illustrates.

So I do not find Gueroult's argument from the order of presentation persuasive. But his more directly textual arguments are more difficult to deal with.

---

23. In the *Réflexions*, 99–102, Gueroult also argues that the doubt of the *Principles* is less radical than that of the *Meditations*, that it does not involve intuitions themselves, but only things we do not know well. But this seems to be an incorrect reading of *Principles* I, 5, according to which the principles of mathematics are called in question, as well as its demonstrations, and it is suggested that God may have chosen to make us such that we would always be deceived "even in the things we think we know best." In correspondence, Gueroult argued that the correct reading of article 5 is conditioned by subsequent articles like 6 and 13, where the suspense of judgment is limited to "things we do not know well" or "do not know distinctly." But article 6 is concerned only with our psychological ability to doubt. And though Descartes is talking about what we have reason to doubt in article 13, I do not find that he limits that to what we do not know well. His conclusion is that I cannot have *any* certain knowledge until I know him who created me.

Before stating (2), Descartes does profess to have demonstrated "fully . . . that all those things which I clearly know are true." (2) looks very much like a version of this principle, and, if it is, it requires the arguments of the Third and Fourth Meditations.

But is (2) in fact a version of (2′) as Gueroult takes it to be? If it is, then the key phrase in (2) is the reference to clear and distinct perception, and it would be very surprising to find Descartes presenting a form of the ontological argument in which the analogue of (2) made no reference to clear and distinct perception. Moreover, the apparent contrast in (2) between saying that a property belongs to the true and immutable nature of a thing and saying that it belongs to the thing would be inconsequential.

But Descartes does take the latter contrast to be important. When Mersenne objects to the syllogism in the First Replies:

(a) Whatever we clearly and distinctly understand to pertain to the true and immutable nature of something, can truly be affirmed of it.
(b) But we understand clearly and distinctly that existence pertains to the true and immutable nature of God.
(c) Therefore, we can affirm truly that God exists.

that the conclusion ought to be

(c′) Therefore we can affirm truly that existence pertains to God's nature. (AT VII, 127; HR II, 28)

Descartes replies that if so, the major premise would have to be:

(a′) Whatever we clearly understand to pertain to the nature of something can truly be affirmed to pertain to its nature. (AT VII, 149; HR II, 45)

This proposition Descartes dismisses as containing nothing more than a useless tautology. My major premise, he writes, was (a). And he goes on to offer instances of (a) in which the reference to clear and distinct perception is altogether omitted:

if being an animal pertains to the nature of man, it can be affirmed that man is an animal; if having three angles equal to two right angles pertains to the nature of a triangle, it can be affirmed that a triangle has three angles equal to two right angles; if existence pertains to the nature of God, it can be affirmed that God exists. (AT VII, 150; HR II, 45)

When he restates the ontological argument in the Geometrical Exposition, his analogue of (2)

> Def. 9. When we say that something [FV: some attribute] is contained in the nature or concept of something, that is the same as if we were to say that it is true of that thing, or can be affirmed of it. (AT VII, 162; HR II, 53)

also omits all reference to clear and distinct perception. Descartes does not think (2) is equivalent to (2′).

But if not, with what right does Descartes assert (2)? On Gueroult's interpretation we can at least suppose that Descartes has laid the groundwork for his assertion of (2) by the arguments of the Third and Fourth Meditations. When we give up the equation of (2) with (2′), we give up that rationale for (2). Yet surely (2) needs some defense.

The answer I suggest above (p. 142) is that Descartes sees (2) as following from (1). And though this claim may not seem particularly plausible so long as we understand (2) to be equivalent to (2′) and see it as establishing a connection between clear and distinct perception and truth, once we deny that equivalence, we can see why Descartes would say this.

Note that in the Geometrical Exposition, when Descartes is forced to declare whether (2) is a definition, postulate, axiom, or theorem, he treats it as a definition. "To say that something is contained in the nature or concept of something is the same as saying that it is true of that thing, or can be affirmed of it." I take it that, for Descartes, this equivalence provides an analysis of what it is to say that a property belongs to the (true and immutable) nature of a thing. So when I assert, in (1), that I have an idea of something which has a true and immutable nature, I imply that the properties I understand to be contained in that nature are true of the thing. The connection is between belonging to a true and immutable nature and being true of something, not between clear and distinct perception and truth. This connection is not one for which the arguments of the Third and Fourth Meditations are required. It is a connection which is supposed to be inescapable once we recognize that things have true and immutable natures whether they exist or not, that is, that truths about the nature of a triangle, for example, are not statements about existing triangles, but statements about possible objects which may or may not exist.

At this point Gueroult's objection may recur in a somewhat different form. Suppose he were to say: "Yes, I concede that step (2) of Descartes' argument is not in fact intended by him to be a form of the principle that whatever we perceive clearly and distinctly is true (though *you* must concede that Descartes sometimes expresses himself on this point in a most misleading way). Hence the ontological argument is not in that way dependent on the arguments of the Third and Fourth Meditations. Still, to rest everything on (1) is to permit the objection to come in again by a different door. (2) is supposed to be something we are committed to by accepting the doctrine that some things have true and immutable natures whether they exist or not. But why do we accept that doctrine? According to Descartes, what shows that the triangle has a true and immutable nature is the fact that I can demonstrate various properties of it. But when we say that we can demonstrate various properties of the triangle, do we not assume something which is in question so long as God's existence and veracity have not been proved? Do we not assume that we have geometrical knowledge?"

To this I reply that, when Descartes says that he can demonstrate various properties of the triangle, and that hence the triangle has a true and immutable nature, he is stating propositions which may be doubtful in the normative sense, but which he cannot but believe when he considers them:

> Even though I had not demonstrated this [that whatever I clearly know is true], the nature of my mind is certainly such that nevertheless I could not but assent to these [mathematical propositions], at least so long as I clearly perceive them. (AT VII, 65; HR I, 180)

In the preceding chapter I contended that Descartes is entitled to use propositions of this assent-compelling character provisionally, while he is considering whether or not there is a God who is a deceiver. I do not see how any Cartesian argument for the existence of God, ontological or otherwise, would be possible unless this much were granted. Certainly the Third Meditation arguments rely on general maxims about causality which are, at best, assent-compelling. One strength of the ontological argument is that its mathematical assumptions are more likely to compel assent in reflective readers than the causal maxims are.

I reject, then, Gueroult's thesis that the ontological argument in Descartes depends on the other Cartesian arguments for God's existence and veracity. Consideration of his thesis, however, leads to clarification of the status of (2) and to the conclusion that, properly understood, it provides no ground for objection which is not at the same time an objection to (1).

I turn now to (3). One classical objection to the ontological argument is that it proceeds from a definition of "God." And it may be held that, quite apart from any general difficulties there may be about defining singular terms, there are special difficulties about defining the term "God." So St. Thomas objected that Anselm's ontological argument was unsound because it presupposed a knowledge of God's essence which we do not have.

If this objection is to be applicable to Descartes' argument, it seems it must strike at (3), which is the closest thing to a definition of "God" this argument gives us. And indeed, in the Geometrical Exposition the analogue of (3) is presented as the eighth definition.

Nevertheless, I want to suggest that this is not the best view of (3) and that any objections we may have to defining "God" do not go to the heart of the matter. (3) may be regarded as combining two distinct claims:

(3a) I have an idea of a supremely perfect being.
(3b) Something is God if and only if it is supremely perfect.

Whether or not we regard (3b) as a definition, it certainly lays down plausible necessary and sufficient conditions for something's being God. A theological tradition of long standing would decline to call God anything which was not supremely perfect. So being supremely perfect is at least a necessary condition for being God. And arguably, being supremely perfect is also a sufficient condition for being God. There could not be two supremely perfect beings. Being supremely perfect entails being omnipotent, and there could not be two omnipotent beings (cf. AT VII, 68; HR I, 182; and the comment on this passage in the interview with Burman, AT V, 161; Bridoux, 1375).

In any case, (3b) is only necessary for the transition from

(5) A supremely perfect being exists.

to

(6) God exists.

It is not needed for the derivation of (5) itself, which follows from (2), (3a), and (4). So if the problem were only with (3b), we would have a sound conceptual argument for the existence of *some* supremely perfect being, and the only question would be whether we could identify that being with God. Most philosophers who reject Descartes' (or any other philosopher's) ontological argument will want to get off the train before they get to the fifth stop.

So any objection to (3) which goes to the heart of the matter had better be an objection to (3a). Yet it is difficult to see what that objection would be. (3) may be paraphrased as "I can conceive of a supremely perfect being." And isn't that true?

Perhaps not. But I think the best way to decide whether or not it is will be to consider yet another classical objection to 'the' ontological argument.

It is often said that the flaw in any ontological argument is the attempt to prove existence by a purely conceptual investigation, that we cannot discover what exists merely by examining our ideas, and that this is shown by the fact that we can produce arguments parallel to the ontological argument for a wide variety of things. For example, the notion of a supremely perfect island which does not exist involves a contradiction just as much as does the notion of a supremely perfect being which does not exist. The same holds for the notions of a supremely perfect tennis player, a supremely perfect strawberry, and so on. It is plainly absurd to suppose that all of these things exist. But since ontological arguments for their existence have as much force as the ontological argument for God's existence, the latter argument must be rejected.

To this criticism, two things must be said. First, it does not so much locate a flaw in the ontological argument as attempt to persuade us that there must be a flaw. Certainly if the parallel arguments are really parallel, and if their conclusions are absurd, then the ontological argument for God's existence must in some way be defective. But we would still want to be told which premise was false, or which inferential step was invalid.

Second, it is clear that Descartes would deny that the 'parallel' arguments are really parallel. In the Fifth Meditation he writes that

> No other thing can be conceived by me to whose essence existence belongs, except God alone. (AT VII, 68; HR I, 182)

In the Fifth Meditation, this is merely asserted without argument; but I think it is possible to construct from Cartesian doctrines an argument for the claim of uniqueness.

Suppose the 'parallel' argument is for the existence of a supremely perfect island. An island, Descartes might say, is a kind of body, that is, it is a necessary truth that whatever is an island is extended in three dimensions. But whatever is extended is divisible, and divisibility is an imperfection.[24] So when we speak of a supremely perfect island, we cannot take the term "supremely perfect" absolutely—we cannot mean a being in which *all* perfections are found. Some perfections are incompatible with being an island. Hence, the attempt to construct a parallel argument breaks down in the subargument for (4). Step (a) of that subargument,

> (a) All perfections belong to the true and immutable nature of a supremely perfect being,

will not be true if the term "being" is replaced by the term "island." This holds for all general terms designating some kind of body. Supremely perfect tennis players and supremely perfect strawberries are alike excluded. And any argument for the existence of something supremely perfect which is not a body (that is, for a supremely perfect mind) will be an argument for God's existence.

Now there are various grounds on which this defense might be challenged. Some may not share Descartes' intuition that divisibility is an imperfection. And perhaps Descartes might argue that it is by connecting divisibility with a liability to be destroyed. Others,

---

24. This argument is suggested by a passage in the Second Replies in which Descartes argues that the notion of a most perfect body involves a contradiction. AT VII, 138; HR II, 37.

for example, Spinoza, might argue that an extended substance is not divisible.

But it seems to me that the fundamental objection is this: there is more difficulty in the concept of a supremely perfect being than we might at first suspect. Note that when the idea of God was first introduced in the Third Meditation we were not given the formula "a supremely perfect being" but an enumeration of some of God's perfections. This may have been sufficient for the causal arguments of that meditation, but not for the ontological argument. For it would make the idea of God composite, and Descartes does not, as a rule, want to allow that composite ideas have objects with true and immutable natures. One way the Third Meditation has laid the groundwork for the Fifth was by its gradual transition from explicating the idea of God by an enumeration of his perfections to explicating it by a more general formula. This was essential, if the ontological argument for God was not to be as trifling as the ontological argument for the existent golden mountain.

But was this transition legitimate? *Can* we conceive of a supremely perfect being? Do we really understand what we mean when we use this language? "Perfect," on the face of it, is an evaluative term, like "good." If it is not used here as an evaluative term, then I cannot see that we have any grasp of its meaning. But if it is used here as an evaluative term, then (arguably) it must be used in conjunction with some general term which provides us with guidance as to the characteristics a thing must have to be a perfect thing of that kind. The characteristics which make something a good or perfect thing of one kind (say, strawberry) may be very different from those which make something a good or perfect thing of another kind (say, tennis player). Descartes' argument uses "perfect" in conjunction with that most general of general terms, "being." Do we really understand what it would be to be a good or perfect thing of *that* kind?

Descartes supposes that a supremely perfect being must possess *all* perfections. But is it possible for something to possess all perfections?

Suppose some perfections are incompatible with others. We have seen that according to Descartes possessing the perfection of indivisibility is incompatible with being extended. Suppose some other perfections presuppose that their possessor *is* extended. Descartes seems to allow that there are some specifically corporeal perfections (AT VII, 118; HR II, 21). Doesn't it follow that *nothing* could possess all perfections?

In at least one place, Descartes seems prepared to allow that some perfections are incompatible with one another:

> If we ask . . . of a thing, whatever it may be, which has *all those perfections which can exist together*, whether existence ought to be numbered among them, at first we will be in doubt. For our mind, which is finite, is only accustomed to considering them separately. So perhaps it will not immediately notice how necessarily they are conjoined with one another. (AT VII, 118–119; HR II, 21; my emphasis)

But when we replace the idea of a being possessing all perfections with the idea of a being possessing all compossible perfections (that is, all perfections which can exist together), we introduce a fatal weakness into the argument. The idea of a being possessing all compossible perfections is hopelessly indefinite. Suppose there were just three perfections, F, G, and H, that G and H are incompatible with one another, though each is compatible with F. Would a being who had all compossible perfections have F and G or F and H?

This worry about the coherence of the concept of a supremely perfect being is not an idle one, or dependent merely on admissions Descartes makes but perhaps shouldn't make. The theological tradition in which Descartes is working ascribes to God a number of characteristics of doubtful consistency with one another, for example, that he is a person who acts, and acts for the sake of an end, and loves his creatures; and that he needs nothing, does not change, and has no limits on his power. Perhaps our (Spinozistic) doubts about the coherence of the traditional concept of God can be resolved. But until they are, the right conclusion seems to be that we cannot conceive of a supremely perfect being—not clearly and distinctly, at any rate, if being supremely perfect is supposed to entail possessing all perfections.

So Descartes' ontological argument does, in the end, fail, though not, I think, for the reasons usually advanced against it. If I am correct, the reason it fails has implications for the whole theological tradition in which Descartes is working, and not merely for the ontological argument. But the problems raised here are not ones Descartes really addresses; so further consideration of them must be left for another day.[25]

25. I have given some consideration to this question in "Spinoza and Recent Philosophy of Religion," to appear in a special issue of the *Southwestern Journal of Philosophy* commemorating the tercentenary of Spinoza's death.

7

MIND

IF DESCARTES' arguments for the existence of God fail, then his system fails *as a system*. But to say this is not to deny philosophical interest to the doctrines Descartes held to be dependent on those arguments. A case in point is Descartes' philosophy of mind. That the mind is distinct from the body, and better known than the body, are among Descartes' central contentions in the *Meditations*. That is why they are singled out for attention by the titles of the Second and Sixth Meditations (cf. Alquié, *Oeuvres* II, 316). And Descartes certainly thinks that his argument for the former of these doctrines, at least, is dependent on his having established the existence of God. But Descartes' conception of the mind and its relation to the body has exercised an extraordinarily pervasive influence on subsequent philosophers, including many who have no use at all for the rational theology of the *Meditations*. So Ryle, setting out to demolish Cartesian dualism in *The Concept of Mind*, characterizes it as 'the official theory.' And one of Ryle's most recent critics has countered that what Ryle thus disparages is nothing more than "the commonsense view . . . Cartesian only inasmuch as it has found its clearest philosophical expression in Descartes' works."[1]

Clear Descartes may be. But we, I'm afraid, are not clear, even at this late date, about what the Cartesian theory of the mind is, what arguments Descartes uses to defend that theory, or the value of those arguments. I hope here to dispel some of the confusions

1. Z. Vendler, *Res Cogitans, an Essay in Rational Psychology* (Ithaca: Cornell University Press, 1972), p. 144.

which plague twentieth-century discussion of Descartes' philosophy of mind.

I

LET US take first the doctrine that the mind is better known than the body. Some scholars make this thesis definitive of Cartesian dualism.[2] And interpreted in a very special way, it plays a vital role in the Cartesian 'myth' which Ryle undertakes to refute in *The Concept of Mind*. But Ryle writes polemic, not a serious exercise in the history of philosophy. Like all strong medicines, it must be used only as directed and kept out of the reach of children.

Ryle ascribes to Descartes an extreme doctrine of privileged access, which makes the mind omniscient with respect to its own states, only partially and tenuously knowledgeable about the states of bodies, and totally and invincibly ignorant of the states of other minds. In particular, he ascribes to Descartes the following three theses:

(1) *Consciousness:* Mental states are, by their very nature, conscious states. This means that, necessarily, if a person is in a particular mental state, he knows that he is in that state. His knowledge is a direct, non-inferential awareness, which he has continuously, willy-nilly, not something he sometimes acquires by deliberately attending to his mental states.

(2) *Incorrigibility:* Our beliefs about our mental states are incorrigible, in the sense that, necessarily, if a person believes that he is in a particular mental state, he is in that state.

(3) *Privacy:* Our own mental states are private, in the sense that, necessarily, if a person is in a mental state, no other person [except, presumably, God] knows that he is in that state.

So whereas knowledge of other minds is quite impossible, knowledge of my own mind is not merely very easy, it is unavoidable.

For our purposes those are the most important features of Ryle's account of the Cartesian concept of mind. But it is worth noting in passing one complication. In Ryle's version of Cartesianism there are two paths to self-knowledge. In addition to the informa-

2. E.g., Kenny, "Cartesian Privacy," in *The Anatomy of the Soul* (Oxford: Basil Blackwell, 1973). I have commented on Kenny's essay in some detail in my review of this book in the *Australasian Journal of Philosophy*, 54 (1976), 80–86.

tion we have about our mental states because they are conscious, we are also able to gain information about them by exercising a special faculty of perception, independent of any sense organs. When we exercise this faculty, we are said to introspect. Introspection, unlike consciousness, is supposed to involve a deliberate act of attending to our mental states, a cognitive act distinct from its object[3] and only intermittent.

The puzzling thing here is that, if consciousness is as good a way of knowing one's own mind as it is supposed to be, it is difficult to see what contribution introspection could make. If I am omniscient with respect to my own states of mind, simply because they are *my* states of mind, what do I have to gain by attending to certain of those states? How could I acquire, from such an act of attention, information I don't already have? So far as I can see, Ryle offers no answer to these questions. And that suggests a certain incoherence, either in the theory he is expounding, or in his exposition of it.

Ryle allows that holders of the official, Cartesian theory of mind have lately been forced to make some qualifications in their doctrine. "Evidence adduced recently by Freud" has shown that people do have at least some mental states which they are not aware of—motives and desires they will sincerely disavow, thoughts they are able, somehow, to keep hidden even from themselves. Nevertheless, "holders of the official theory tend . . . to maintain that . . . in normal circumstances a person must be directly and authentically seized of the present state and workings of his own mind" (Ryle, 14).

The truth is at once more complicated and more interesting than Ryle's fiction. The first point to notice is that when Descartes argues that the mind is better known than the body, he is not the innovator he is sometimes made to appear.[4] He is, rather, writing in a long tradition. Earlier I had occasion to cite a passage from

3. Ryle does not always make this a point of difference between consciousness and introspection. Sometimes, as he expounds the official theory, consciousness is not a distinct cognitive operation (Ryle, 158–159); sometimes, it is (162–163). And as we shall see, Descartes is ambiguous on this point.

4. E.g., in Kenny, *The Anatomy of the Soul*, p. 113. In what follows I am very much indebted to G. (Rodis-) Lewis, *Le problème de l'inconscient et le cartésianisme* (Paris: PUF, 1950).

Montaigne in which he stresses that men should seek first to know "themselves and their own state, which is in them" (Montaigne, 481). But the notion that men have *some* kind of privileged access to their own mental states goes back much farther than that. So, for example, Augustine writes that "nothing can be more present to the mind than the mind itself," and asks, rhetorically, "what is so intimately known as the mind, which perceives that it itself exists and is that by which all other things are perceived?"[5]

But though both Montaigne and Augustine would agree with Descartes that the mind is better known than the body, and that knowledge of one's own mind is prior to knowledge of any body, both also stress the great difficulty of knowing oneself. Thus Montaigne writes that his mind's "principal *and most laborious* study is studying itself" (Montaigne, 621; cf. pp. 822–823). And Augustine, no more adverse than Montaigne to a good paradox, will ask:

What then does the mind love, when, being unknown to itself, it seeks ardently to know itself? (*De Trinitate X*, iii, 5)

This in the very same passage in which it is claimed that nothing can be more present to the mind than the mind itself.

Sometimes in Augustine the difficulties of self-knowledge are connected with difficulties about knowledge of other minds. For example, in the *Soliloquies*, a dialogue which opens with a prayer to God, summed up by Augustine in the formula: "To know God and myself—that is my desire," Reason asks:

The friend you have said you do not know—do you wish to know him by the senses or by the intellect?

5. *De Trinitate X*, iii, 5, and VIII, vi, 9, respectively. The latter passage is only one of many in Augustine which are apt to make one think of Descartes. So there is an extensive literature on the relation between the two. See, e.g., E. Gilson, *Etudes sur le rôle de la pensée médiévale dans la formation du système cartésien* (Paris: J. Vrin, 1951); A. Koyré, *Descartes und die Scholastik* (Bonn: F. Cohen, 1923); G. Matthews, "Si Fallor, Sum," and "The Inner Man," both in *Augustine, A Collection of Critical Essays*, ed. R. A. Markus (Garden City, N.Y.: Doubleday, 1972). Translations from St. Augustine are mine and are made from the Latin texts given in Aurelius Augustinus, *Oeuvres*, ed. F. Cayré et al. (Paris: Desclée, 1941).

And the following interchange ensues:

> Augustine: What I know of him by the senses—if indeed I do know anything of him by the senses—is not worth much. . . . But that part of him in virtue of which he is my friend, his mind, I wish to grasp by the intellect.
> Reason: Can it be known in any other way?
> Augustine: In no other way.
> Reason: Do you dare, then, to say that your friend, who is so close to you, is nonetheless unknown to you?
> Augustine: Why not? I think most just that law of friendship which prescribes that everyone should love his friend neither more nor less than himself. Since I do not know myself, how can I wrong him by saying that I do not know him—especially when, as I believe, even he does not know himself. (*Soliloquies* I, 8)

Some of Augustine's ignorance about himself is ignorance of what we might call metaphysical properties of the self. He does not know whether he is a simple or a complex being, or whether or not he is immortal (*Soliloquies* II,1). But some is ignorance of things a recent French editor of Augustine plausibly calls his moral dispositions. So Augustine is at least initially uncertain whether he loves anything other than knowledge of God and himself:

> Augustine: I could reply, according to the frame of mind that I am now in, that I love nothing else. But it is safer to answer that I do not know. For it has often happened to me that, when I thought I would not be affected by anything else, nevertheless something came to mind which disturbed me much more than I would have thought. (*Soliloquies* II, 16)

A similar uncertainty about his moral dispositions is prominent in the *Confessions*. In the well-known passage in which he agonizes over his youthful theft of pears, one of the things which most troubles him is the difficulty of understanding why he sinned as he did:

> What kind of mental disposition [*affectus animi*] was that then? Surely it was very shameful, and I am most miserable that I had it. But still, what was it? Who understands his crimes? (*Confessions* II, 9)

And again, discussing the sin of pride:

> I cannot easily tell how far I am cleansed of that pollution, and
> I greatly fear my secret sins, which are known to your eyes,
> God, though not to mine. In other kinds of temptation I have some
> sort of ability to explore myself, but in this one, hardly any at all.
> (*Confessions* X, 36)

Passages of this sort are characteristic of Augustine, and illustrate
a realistic appreciation of the difficulties of self-knowledge.

Indeed, it would be extremely surprising not to find such an
appreciation in philosophers as much under the influence of Plato
as both Augustine and Montaigne were (cf. the *Phaedrus* 230a, or
the *Republic* 571–572b). I should add, however, that we need not
look only to Plato as a possible source of the psychological realism
to be found in Augustine and Montaigne. The passages I have
cited from the *Confessions* echo the Psalm:

> Who understands his crimes? Cleanse me of my secret sins. (Vulg.
> Ps. 18:13 [= RSV 19:12])

And there are similar passages in the New Testament (for instance,
I Cor. 4:4–5).

Ryle writes that when the 'official' doctrine of consciousness first
became popular

> it seems to have been in part a transformed application of the
> Protestant notion of conscience. The Protestants *had to hold* that a
> man could know the moral state of his soul and the wishes of God
> without the aid of confessors and scholars. (Ryle, 159, my em-
> phasis)

A priori historians are not required to footnote their claims, so it is
hard to know whom Ryle has in mind here. But presumably not the
Luther who wrote that

> many more and far greater evils are there within man than any that
> he feels . . . when God in his mercy chastens us, He reveals to
> us . . . only the lighter evils; for if he were to lead us to a full
> knowledge of our evil, we should straightaway perish.[6]

6. *Works*, ed. H. E. Jacobs et al. (Philadelphia: A. J. Holman, 1915), vol. I,
p. 115.

Nor the Calvin who wrote,

> it is evident that man never attains to a true self-knowledge until
> he have previously contemplated the face of God and come down
> after such contemplation to look into himself. For (such is our
> innate pride) we always seem to ourselves just, and upright, and
> wise, and holy.[7]

Both Luther and Calvin did object to confession as it was conceived
by the Roman Catholic Church—but not on the ground that a man
could know the state of his soul without the aid of a confessor. On
the contrary, one of their main objections to the Roman Confession
was that it required an exhaustive enumeration of the penitent's
sins, which man's ignorance of his soul rendered impossible.[8]

Two points emerge from this excursion into the history of doctrines of self-knowledge. First, philosophers nowadays often
ascribe to Freud an entirely unwarranted degree of originality. Not
only is he credited with having 'discovered' the unconscious, it is
often said that in talking about unconscious desires and motives,
he was engaging in a major piece of conceptual revision, extending
the use of terms like "desire" and "motive" by dropping what in
ordinary language is a necessary condition of the correct use of
those terms.[9] These philosophers represent it as a conceptual truth
that desires, motives, and so forth are conscious in that they are
necessarily known to the person who has them. Freud claimed no
such originality:

> The poets and philosophers before me discovered the unconscious.
> What I discovered was the scientific method by which the uncon-
> scious can be studied.[10]

Whatever we may think about the merits of psychoanalysis as a
scientific method, surely Freud is right to deny having discovered

7. *Institutes of the Christian Religion* I, i, 2; trans. H. Beveridge (London:
James Clarke, 1957).
8. Cf. Luther, *Works*, pp. 76–77; Calvin, *Institutes* III, iv, 15–18.
9. Thomas W. Smythe cites a number of examples—B. McGuinness, A. Mac-
Intyre, R. Peters, and A. Goldman—in his interesting article "Unconscious
Desires and the Meaning of 'Desire,'" *Monist*, 56 (1972), 413–425.
10. Cited in Ilham Dilman, "The Unconscious: A Theoretical Construct?"
Monist, 56 (1972), 316.

the unconscious. A little history should clear us of any illusions about the way these mental concepts have been used.

Second, Augustine and Montaigne anticipated Descartes in his doctrine that the mind is better known than the body; they are like Descartes in so many other respects, we are frequently tempted to cite them as probable influences on Descartes. If, in such authors as these, one finds also a strong emphasis on the great difficulty of knowing one's own mind, it would be surprising *not* to find some recognition of that difficulty in Descartes. This is not to say that Ryle's ascription to Descartes of an extreme doctrine of privileged access is entirely without foundation. We shall shortly look at passages which support that ascription. The point is simply that we ought not to expect to find that Descartes is unequivocally a Cartesian.

Let us begin with a brief selection of passages in which most uncartesian thoughts are expressed. First a pair of passages on belief. In the *Discourse on Method*, noting his resolution to pay more attention to people's actions than to their words, Descartes remarks that this is necessary

> not only because, in our state of moral corruption, few wish to say all that they believe, but also because some don't themselves know what they believe. For since the act of thought by which one believes a thing is different from that by which one knows that he believes it, the one often occurs without the other. (AT VI, 23; HR I, 95)

This text is particularly interesting in the reason it assigns for our ignorance of our beliefs, namely, that knowledge of a mental act is a distinct act of thought from the mental act which is its object.

In a parallel passage in a letter to Huygens (10 October 1642) Descartes, claiming to know clearly that the soul lasts longer than the body, writes that

> although religion teaches us a great many things on this topic, I must nevertheless confess to a weakness in myself, which is, it seems to me, common to most men—namely, although we wish to believe, and even think we do believe quite firmly all that religion teaches us, all the same we are usually not so much affected by it as we are by those things of which we are persuaded by very evident natural reasons. (Alquié, *Oeuvres* II, 937–938)

At the very least this implies that we may be mistaken about the firmness of our beliefs; but how could we be mistaken about the firmness of our belief and not be mistaken about our having the belief?

Again, according to *The Passions of the Soul*, if a person is subject to some very strong emotion, this may interfere with his self-awareness:

> Experience teaches us that those who are the most agitated by their passions are not those who know them best. (AT XI, 349–350; HR I, 344)

Descartes does not elaborate on this proposition here, but perhaps the view is that where we have conflicting emotions (for example, the case described at AT XI, 441; HR I, 398), one emotion interferes with adequate recognition of the other.

Against such passages as these we might set the following one, also from *The Passions of the Soul*. Descartes notes that sometimes experiences which are generated internally—by chance movements of the animal spirits—can be so like those produced by the action of external objects on our nerves that we are deceived in our beliefs about the external world. But the same mechanism is not available to produce error regarding our passions:

> They are so close and interior to our soul that it is impossible for the soul to feel them without their really being as the soul feels them. So . . . one cannot feel sad, or moved by any other passion, unless the soul really has this passion in itself. (AT XI, 348; HR I, 343–344)

This gives us at least incorrigibility regarding our passions. And in the Sixth Replies Descartes makes quite a strong and general claim when he says that we cannot but be conscious of our own thought. Indeed, the French version, which Descartes *may* be responsible for, speaks of "one's own thought, which one cannot not know in oneself by a continual and infallible experience" (AT VII, 427, IX, 229; HR II, 245).

So far I have deliberately not mentioned the most familiar passages which can be adduced in support of a Rylean construction of Descartes—deliberately, because it seems to me that they are not so unequivocal as they are usually taken to be. For example, in the Second Replies Descartes *defines* thought as "whatever is in us in such a way that we are immediately conscious of it."[11]

Now this certainly can be read as excluding, say, unconscious desires. But I think Descartes' intent is different, and that his concern is not to deny the existence of a certain kind of thought, but to justify the inclusion under that heading of something which would not normally be counted as thoughts, namely, sensations. At any rate, this seems to me to be the import of the parallel passage in the *Principles* (I, 9):

> By the term *thought* I understand all those things which, we being conscious, occur in us, insofar as the consciousness of them is in us. So not only understanding, willing and imagining, but also sensing, are the same thing here as thinking. (AT VIII–1, 7–8, IX–2, 28; HR I, 222)

We then get a brief résumé of an argument in the Second Meditation which is designed to show that, strictly speaking, sensation is nothing other than thinking. If I say that I see a table—and mean by that that I am aware, through my sense organs, of some body external to me—then what I say is not absolutely certain. It may be that I am asleep and dreaming. But even if I am asleep and dreaming, it is nonetheless true that *it seems to me* that I see a table. This state, which is what is properly called sensing, is nothing but thinking and is something which we are directly aware of in ourselves (AT VII, 29; HR I, 153).

Another interesting, but, in the end, equivocal passage is provided in the Third Meditation, where Descartes is considering whether or not he has the power of bringing it about that he, who now exists, should continue to exist in the future. He remarks that

11. The Latin is: "Cogitationis nomine complector illud omne quod sic in nobis est, ut ejus immediate conscii simus" (AT VII, 160; HR II, 52). The French: "Par le nom de *pensée*, je comprends tout ce qui est tellement en nous, que nous en sommes immédiatement connaissants" (AT IX, 124). This raises an interesting linguistic point. Alquié remarks that "Au lieu de *connaissants*, nour dirions mieux : *conscients*" (*Oeuvres* II, 586). Apparently prior to Descartes, *conscience* and its cognates were not used in the psychological sense they can have in modern French, but only in a moral sense. See Lewis, *Le problème de l'inconscient*, p. 39.

since I am nothing but a thinking thing—or at least since I am now dealing only with that part of me which is a thinking thing—if such a power were in me, I would be conscious of it. But I do not experience any power of that sort. (AT VII, 49; HR I, 169)

But when he comments on this argument in the First Replies, the doctrine is stated less strongly:

I can affirm with certainty that there is nothing in me, of which I am *not in any way* conscious. (AT VII, 107; HR II, 13; my emphasis)

Or as the French version has it, "nothing of which I do not have *some* knowledge" (AT IX, 85).

The topic comes up again in the Fourth Objections, when Arnauld asks:

Who does not see that there can be many things in the mind of which the mind is not conscious? The mind of an infant in its mother's womb has the power of thinking, but is not conscious of it. I pass over a great many similar things in silence. (AT VII, 214; HR II, 92–93)

Two points are of interest here. First, though Arnauld does not deny that fetuses think, he considers it obvious that there are a great many things in the mind that the mind does not know.

Second, one of Arnauld's themes in the Fourth Objections is the similarity between Augustine's thought and Descartes'. It is interesting in this connection that Arnauld should choose to illustrate the unconscious by appealing to an infant's alleged lack of consciousness. For the question "What sort of knowledge of itself can an infant have?" is one Augustine wrestles with (*De Trinitate* XIV, iv, 7-v, 8) and gives up as unanswerable.

In reply, Descartes makes what looks to be an important distinction. He reaffirms that there is nothing in the mind, insofar as it is a thinking thing, of which the mind is not conscious, claims that this doctrine is known per se, and accepts its implications for infants:

I do not doubt but what the mind, as soon as it is infused into the body of an infant, begins to think, and at the same time is conscious of its thought, though it may not afterward remember what it thought, because traces of those thoughts are not preserved in the memory.

180

But he adds,

> it must be noted that the mind is indeed always actually conscious of its acts or operations, but not always actually conscious of its faculties or powers; of them it is sometimes only potentially conscious. (AT VII, 246; HR II, 115)

One function this distinction can serve is to enable Descartes to hold, for example, that we have an innate idea of God, even though we may not, for many years, be aware of having that idea. So in the *Notes against a Program* he says that he calls certain ideas innate in the same sense in which an illness may be innate in someone—not that infants are afflicted by the illness in their mothers' wombs, but that they are born with a certain disposition or faculty of contracting them (AT VIII-2, 358; HR I, 442; Alquié, *Oeuvres* III, 807). Presumably the innate idea of God is a disposition or faculty of conceiving of a supremely perfect being. And as Descartes says to Hyperaspistes, he does not suppose that infants in the womb meditate on things metaphysical (Alquié, *Oeuvres* II, 361; *Philosophical Letters*, III).

Arnauld was not satisfied with this answer, and returned to the problem of infantile self-knowledge in later correspondence with Descartes. In doing so, he prompted Descartes to introduce a further distinction, between first and simple thoughts—such as feelings of pleasure or pain which he thinks an infant can have—and reflective thoughts—such as the thought that a man may have when he senses something new, and at the same time is aware that he has not sensed anything of this sort before (29 July 1648, AT V, 220–221; Alquié, *Oeuvres* III, 862; *Philosophical Letters*, 234). This latter kind of thought, which involves a "pure intellection," is something which Descartes thinks infants are incapable of (4 June 1648 (?), AT V, 192; Alquié, *Oeuvres* III, 855; *Philosophical Letters*, 231). If we held that consciousness must evolve reflective thought, then it would become very obscure just what the sense is in which an infant might be said to be conscious of its pleasures and pains.

The topic of consciousness is certainly not one on which Descartes can be accused of a foolish consistency. Earlier we saw a passage in which Descartes maintained that believing something and knowing that you believe it are distinct acts of thought. Belief is supposed to involve an act of the will. But in the *Passions of the Soul* (Alquié, *Oeuvres* III, 967–968; HR I, 340–341), Descartes maintains that when we will something, the perception by which we are invariably aware that we will it is one and the same as the volition.

In the Third Objections Hobbes raised the problem of consciousness in the following way:

> I do not infer that I think by another thought; for though someone can think that he *has* thought—which thought is nothing but memory—nevertheless it is quite impossible to think that one is thinking, just as it is impossible to know that one knows. For there would be an infinite series of questions: How do you know that you know that you know that you know? (AT VII, 173; HR II, 62)

This is quite reminiscent of Ryle, not only in its attempt to generate difficulties about infinite regresses but also in its suggestion that memory and retrospection are genuine processes, which can account for whatever phenomena consciousness and introspection are supposed, in a Cartesian philosophy of mind, to account for (cf. Ryle, 159–160, 166).

Descartes clearly had a low opinion of Hobbes' philosophical abilities, and he treats this objection with characteristic contempt:

> What this philosopher says here—that one thought cannot be the subject of another thought—is irrelevant. For who, besides himself, ever supposed this? (AT VII, 175)

Descartes' meaning here is obscure. Does "this" refer to the proposition Hobbes is asserting, or the proposition he is denying? The claim that what Hobbes says is irrelevant naturally suggests the latter, that no one, including Descartes, has ever asserted what Hobbes is denying, and so the passage is typically translated (HR II, 64; AG, 131).

But it just isn't true that no one has ever said that one thought can be the subject of another. Descartes himself is a counterexample. Augustine provides an even more interesting case. In one of his *cogito*-like passages (*De Trinitate* X, xii, 21), he contends that someone who says "I know that I live" claims to know one thing;

if he says that he knows that he knows that he lives, this is another thing he knows. Indeed Augustine is apparently prepared to embrace the paradox that the "I know that . . ." operator could, in principle, be iterated indefinitely, even though an infinite iteration could neither be grasped nor uttered. This is used as an argument *contra academicos,* to show that we know, not merely a few things, but innumerably many. In any case, Descartes' reply to Hobbes would be more consonant with other Cartesian passages if we supposed him to mean that only Hobbes would think that one thought could *not* be the subject of another.

Fortunately, when Burman raised essentially the same difficulty, Descartes was more forthcoming. Burman's question was directed at the claim in the Fourth Replies, that there is nothing in the mind of which the mind is not conscious.

> But how can the mind be conscious, since being conscious is thinking? When you think that you are conscious you already pass to another thought, and so no longer think about what you were thinking about before; so you are not conscious that you are thinking, but that you have been thinking. (AT V, 149; Bridoux, 1359)

The view that thought is too quick to be caught in the act (or not quick enough to catch itself) seems to have a natural appeal. Descartes replies by identifying consciousness with reflective thought, and claiming that consciousness can be contemporary with the thought which is its subject:

> Being conscious is indeed thinking and reflecting on one's thought; but it is false that this cannot occur while the prior thought remains. As we have already seen, the soul can think of several things at once [a reference back to AT V, 148], persevere in its thought, reflect on its thought as often as it pleases, and so be conscious of its thought. (ibid.)

In what follows Descartes goes on to say that it is improbable that the minds of infants have any thoughts which they do not derive from some affect of the body. So infants have no "pure intellections," and hence no reflective thoughts. Though infants think, they are not "conscious" in the sense in which this term is used in the *Entretien avec Burman*. Of course, that work is not an actual publication of Descartes, only Burman's record of the answers

Descartes gave to his questions. Still, these remarks, as reported, fit in well with what Descartes wrote to Arnauld three months later. One common feature of both discussions—and of the much earlier letter to Hyperaspistes as well—is that Descartes is prepared to extend his qualifications of the doctrine of consciousness beyond infants to sleepers and to people suffering from various mental disorders, such as apoplexy.

So far I have argued that Descartes does not, and should not be expected to, consistently adhere to the doctrines Ryle ascribes to him. Can Descartes' various statements be made consistent with one another by introducing distinctions, or by understanding some statements to be tacitly qualified in some way? Or did Descartes simply change his mind over a period of time?

Neither of these ways of reconciling his statements seems very promising. First, the dates of the passages which speak for and against a Rylean construction of Descartes will not permit them to be arranged in any simple chronological pattern. Passages on both sides came from all periods of Descartes' published work. Nor does it seem possible to use such distinctions as Descartes acknowledges to reconcile his various statements.

The most hopeful distinction is that between acts and dispositional properties. It is much more plausible to claim privileged access to mental occurrences than to dispositions. This point is well illustrated by the prominence given to moral dispositions in our historical survey of doctrines about self-knowledge. And it is interesting to see Descartes apparently recognize this in his Reply to the Fourth Objections. Nevertheless, when Descartes claims in the *Discourse* that we often do not know what we believe, he characterizes both belief and knowledge of one's belief as *acts* of thought. And although it might seem to a twentieth-century philosopher that this analysis of belief could, and should, be jettisoned in favor of a dispositional analysis, it is far from clear that such an analysis can be successfully carried through or that Descartes could accept it if it were.

It is important to Descartes' whole project in the *Meditations* to treat belief not merely as a mental occurrence, but as an occurrence which is, frequently at least, an act in that full sense of the term which implies something done voluntarily. Both the initial methodological doubt, and the ultimate resolution to assent only to clear and distinct ideas, conceive of belief as something we can either do, or not do, as we choose.

Reconciling projects are not, in this instance, very promising. But given that Descartes does contradict himself extensively on this topic, we can nevertheless ask whether he *needs* to hold so extreme a doctrine of privileged access as he sometimes subscribes to.

There is a good deal in some current interpretations of Descartes which makes it appear that he does. Kenny, for example, writes:

> Descartes . . . *makes it true by definition* that if I think, I know that I think. It is here that the indubitability of the premise of *"cogito ergo sum"* is to be found. (Kenny, 49, my emphasis; cf. pp. 70–71)

On the face of it, this makes what we have called the consciousness thesis an essential step in Descartes' argument for his own existence. It is, moreover, not merely the general proposition "I think" which is defended in this fashion:

> Thoughts cannot occur without our knowing that they occur, and we cannot think that a thought is occurring unless that thought actually is occurring. Perhaps I only think I see; but that I think I see cannot be doubted . . . it is not just the occurrence of *thought* that cannot be doubted, but the occurrence of the particular thought in question. (Kenny, 72–73)

Here we have both the consciousness thesis and the incorrigibility thesis invoked to provide a rationale for claiming that there are many synthetic propositions besides "I exist" which are quite certain. And although it may not be necessary for Descartes to establish the certainty of such propositions in order to be certain that he exists (as I have argued in Chapter 4), it is necessary for him to establish their certainty in order to justify his claim that the mind is better known than the body.

In Chapter 4 I argued that it does not help the *cogito* argument to assume the principle "If I think, then I know that I think." If we are genuinely puzzled about Descartes' entitlement to assert "I think," our puzzlement should not be removed by the invocation of a conditional whose consequent can only be detached if we are already entitled to assert "I think." Nor are we likely to be satisfied with a justification which rests its case on an apparently stipulative definition.

Fortunately, Descartes does not need to invoke the consciousness-thesis in the *cogito* argument. The status of "I think" is not that of a premise in a proof, whose premises must be known to be true. Its status is that of a necessary element in any skeptical hypothesis which purports to provide a ground for doubting "I exist." Descartes does not offer an Aristotelian demonstration of his existence; he shows that it is implied by any serious attempt to doubt it.

Something similar is true of the other propositions Descartes claims to be certain of in the Second Meditation. Descartes' procedure is essentially a negative one. He wants to know what he is, not in the sense of knowing his essence, but simply in the sense of knowing some properties of himself other than the property of existence. He will enumerate various properties which he formerly believed himself to have, then eliminate those which are rendered at all improbable by the skeptical hypotheses which still govern his discussion.

The kinds of property which might figure prominently in a traditional Aristotelian account of his essence get very short shrift. He has believed himself to be a man, but he neither accepts nor rejects that property, on the ground that he does not have an answer to the question "What is a man?" To say that a man is a rational animal will lead only to more difficult questions about what being an animal and being rational involve. So he prefers to remain on the level of common sense, among the properties which would naturally occur to someone innocent of philosophy (AT VII, 25; HR I, 150).

He has believed himself to have a body, with all that that involves—having a face, hands, arms—and he has believed himself to have various other properties which only living bodies have—of nourishing himself, moving, sensing, and thinking. These latter properties he ascribed to something he called a soul, without being very clear about what the soul was. Insofar as he thought about the matter at all, he thought of the soul as something corporeal. But he finds no difficulty with the question "What is a body?" A body is something which can be bounded by a shape and contained within a place, so that it fills space and excludes other bodies from that space; it is something which can be perceived by the various senses.

How many of these former beliefs about himself can survive the hypothesis of a supremely powerful deceiver (AT VII, 26; HR I, 151)? Not many. Certainly none of those which involve ascribing to himself any property of bodies, nor any which ascribe to himself a property of the soul which presupposes the having of a body— such as nourishing himself, moving, or sensing.

But thinking survives the elimination. For it is implied by the hypothesis of a deceiver. If he deceives me, I think. So Descartes knows at least one property which he has in addition to the property of existing. He is a thinking thing. But he does not, at this stage, know any other properties that he has, and is unwilling to either affirm or deny of himself any properties which he does not know himself to have (AT VII, 27; HR I, 151–152).

So he explores the property of thought and asks what it involves. What is a thinking thing? "It is one which doubts, understands, affirms, denies, wills, rejects, and also which imagines and senses" (AT VII, 28; HR I, 153). Now the inclusion of imagination and sensation in this list is, and is meant to be, surprising. Only a page earlier Descartes had distinguished sensation from thought and rejected it as requiring a body. But this list of properties of a thinking thing is only a tentative one. *If* he knew that he had all of these properties, he would know a good deal about himself. But does he?

This crucial question is answered, in effect, by two rhetorical questions. The first serves to particularize the very general properties of the preceding list:

> Am I not the very one who now doubts almost everything, who nevertheless understands some things, affirms this one to be true, denies the rest, wants to know more, wants not to be deceived, imagines many things, sometimes unwillingly, and is also aware of many things, which are as if they came from the senses? (AT VII, 29; HR I, 153)

The second asks why these various properties do not survive the skeptical hypotheses of the First Meditation:

Which of these things is not as true as the proposition that I exist, even though I may be dreaming all the time, and even though he who created me uses all his power to deceive me? (AT VII, 28; HR I, 153)

It is not obvious why this question should get the answer it is plainly intended to get. But I would suggest that Descartes is confident here because it is not just coincidental that these propositions are common ground between Descartes, the would-be dogmatist, and his skeptical alter ego.

Classical skepticism *in fact* questioned whether things were as they seemed, and did not question the appearances. But it *had* to leave the mental element unchallenged. The aim of the skeptic is to get his opponent, the dogmatist, to suspend judgment. This project is intelligible only if the skeptic assumes that the dogmatist makes judgments. But to make a judgment is to understand a proposition and to affirm it. We are told this explicitly only in the Fourth Meditation. But the structure of Descartes' list in the Second Meditation foreshadows the later analysis of judgment as a joint function of the intellect and the will. So the skeptic's project requires him to ascribe to the dogmatist both understanding and volition. And that accounts for a number of the items on Descartes' list (cf. AT VII, 28–29; HR I, 153).

Not all of them, however. If the skeptic is to succeed in his project, he must convince the dogmatist that there is some likelihood of his beliefs being mistaken. The standard way of doing this—and the only way in which one *could* do this—is to say to the dogmatist something of the form "Perhaps you are mistaken in believing *p;* perhaps it only seems to you that *p* because . . ." And this is how such things as imagination and sensation get on the list. They are part of the skeptic's conjectural explanation of the dogmatist's possible error. It is a presupposition of the dialogue between skeptic and dogmatist that the skeptic will offer at least conjectural explanations of the errors he claims the dogmatist may be making. Statements of the form "Perhaps it only seems to you that *p*" are necessary in any such explanation. And anything the skeptic must concede, Descartes is entitled to claim as knowledge.

So far we seem to be able to account for the Second Meditation's claims to self-knowledge in terms of the requirements of the dialogue between skeptic and dogmatist. We have not found it necessary to invoke any of the privileged access doctrines enumerated at the beginning of this chapter. That is all to the good, for those doctrines are neither very plausible in themselves nor consistently adhered to by Descartes. And it seems particularly desirable not to have to invoke the consciousness-thesis. To rest important knowledge claims on a stipulative definition would be to seek by stealth what should be got by honest labor.

But things may not be as easy as they seem. Kenny makes the following objection to the certainty of propositions like "It seems to me that I see a light." Descartes, he says, never really faced up to the possibility that the evil genius might "be deceiving him into thinking that he seems to see a light when in fact he seems to smell a rose" (Kenny, 60–61). And so far as I know, Descartes does not consider any objection which takes that form. What would, or could, he say to it?

To put things in as concrete a form as possible, let us imagine the following dialogue between a skeptic and a dogmatist:

> Skeptic: What do you know?
> Dogmatist: Well, one thing I know is that there is a light shining over there.
> Skeptic: How do you know that?
> Dogmatist: Because I see it.
> Skeptic: But perhaps you don't see a light at all; perhaps it only seems to you that you see a light; perhaps some very powerful being is deceiving you—a god, or a devil, or a clever scientist who knows which part of your brain to stimulate.
> Dogmatist: All right, I suppose it's true that, strictly speaking, I don't know that there is a light shining over there. Perhaps I do only seem to see a light. But at least you must grant me this—I *do* seem to see a light—that is certain.
> Skeptic: Not at all, I only said "Perhaps." Precisely the same sort of question can be raised about your pretention to know that it seems to you that you see a light. Perhaps it only seems to you that it seems to you that you see a light; perhaps the truth really is that it seems to you that you smell a rose. Perhaps God or a devil . . .

And here we break off, because it is unclear what the dogmatist should respond.

Descartes' argument requires, apparently, the reduction principle.

(i) If it seems to me that it seems to me that p, then it seems to me that p.

Before we can make any judgment about the truth of that principle, we need to be clearer than we are about what we mean here when we say "It seems to me that . . ."

One use the English phrase "It seems to me that p" (and the Latin and French phrases it is supposed to translate) can have is to express, cautiously, a belief in p. But the phrase does not mean that here. In this kind of context Descartes will say that it seems to him that he sees a light even though he abstains from judging that he sees a light. He will also want to be able to say that it seems to him that he sees a light, even though he abstains from judging that he does not see a light. So "It seems to me that p" is neutral as far as belief in p is concerned.

Descartes' use of "seems"-language is closely connected with one way in which he uses the term "idea." For example, in the Third Meditation he speaks of

> the two different ideas of the sun which I find in myself, one of which is as if it were drawn from the senses . . . through it the sun appears very small to me; the other is taken from astronomical reasoning . . . and through it the sun is presented to me [LV: *exhibetur*, FV: *me paraît*] as several times larger than the earth.[12]

As Descartes *sometimes* uses the term "idea," it appears correct to gloss having an idea of a as having an idea that a has some property, and to identify the latter with being in a state in which it seems that a has that property.

Two points emerge from the passage about the two ideas of the sun. First, two different sources can give rise to two different, conflicting ideas. It can seem to me (at one and the same time) both that the sun is a very small object and that it is not a very small object. "It seems to me that p" is compatible with "It seems to me

---

12. AT VII, 39; AT IX, 31; HR I, 161. I have discussed this passage in connection with Descartes' theory of judgment in "Descartes, Spinoza, and the Ethics of Belief," in *Spinoza, Essays in Interpretation*, ed. M. Mandelbaum and E. Freeman (LaSalle, Ill.: Open Court, 1975), pp. 163–173.

that not-p." Second, being in a state in which something seems to me to be the case, neither is, nor is necessarily accompanied by, having a sense impression. I may or may not have a sense impression of the sun as a very small object. But I certainly do not have a sense impression of the sun as a very large object.

Finally, though "It seems to me that p" does not entail "I believe that p," the converse entailment does hold. "I believe that p" entails "It seems to me that p." Being in a state in which it seems to me that p is being in a state closely related to, though not identical with, believing that p. Call it a tendency or inclination to believe that p—a tendency which, if not opposed by a conflicting tendency, that is if I am not at the same time also inclined to believe that not-p, will naturally lead me to believe p. I may believe p in spite of a conflicting tendency. Having studied astronomy, I believe the sun to be a very large body, in spite of the fact that sensation still inclines me to believe the contrary. That I have this much freedom in judgment is the doctrine of the Fourth Meditation. But if the teachings of astronomy were unopposed, I could not but believe the sun to be a large body. The will is not entirely free in forming its judgments.

There is, then, a close analogy between its seeming to me that p and my believing p. Does this shed any light on the "reduction principle" cited above? Hintikka, in his work in epistemic logic,[13] considers two possible reduction principles for belief statements:

(ii) If someone believes that he believes that p, then he believes that p;

and

(iii) If I believe that I believe that p, then I believe that p.

These two principles, he argues, have a very different standing. (ii) is unacceptable. We may well wish to say of someone else that he believes (mistakenly) that he believes p. (It's interesting to note, in passing, that Hintikka cites a passage from Montaigne to support this claim.) But the first person analogue of (ii) *is* acceptable. Though someone else may say of me that I believe (mistakenly)

13. *Knowledge and Belief, an Introduction to the Logic of the Two Notions* (Ithaca: Cornell University Press, 1962), pp. 123–125.

that I believe p, I cannot (sincerely) say this of myself. I cannot sincerely say anything of the form: "I believe (mistakenly) that . . ."

Can the reduction principle Descartes apparently needs, namely,

(i) If it seems to me that it seems to me that p, then it seems to me that p,

trade on the acceptability of (iii)? At one stage I thought so. Its-seeming-to-me-that-p and my-believing-that-p are, after all, very closely related. And there is *something* uncomfortable about saying "It seems to me that it seems to me that p, but it doesn't in fact seem to me that p."

Now I think not. Its-seeming-to-me-that-p and my-believing-that-p are, after all, not the same thing. And their disanalogies are perhaps more important than their analogies. The acceptability of (iii) depends on the indefensibility of saying "I believe p, but p is false." But on the account given above of "It seems to me that p," there is nothing indefensible about "It seems to me that p, but p is false." This form of words may simply record the fact that, faced with conflicting inclinations to believe, I opt for one proposition rather than the other.

So far, then, we have a negative result. If Descartes' argument requires (i), it is in trouble, since (i) is not generally true. But does Descartes' argument require (i)? Not if what I argued in Chapter 4 is correct. The skeptic wants me to suspend my judgment that I see a light, and to that end offers me grounds for doubt. This project makes no sense at all unless I do judge that I see a light. So the skeptic must concede that I believe I see a light. But that does (on the account given above) entail that it seems to me that I see a light.

I conclude, then, that Descartes is entitled to claim certainty for statements like "It seems to me that I see a light" without committing himself even to the modified version of the incorrigibility thesis encapsulated in (i), much less the consciousness thesis. If so, the way is clear for him to maintain that the mind is better known than the body. Whenever he believes himself to have knowledge of some body, this must be on the ground of some 'sensation'—that is, in the revised conception of sensation which Descartes adopts in the Second Meditation, on the ground of some state of its-seeming-to-me-that-p which is taken to be caused by that body. It will be certain both that he exists and that he has that sensation. It will not be certain—or at least, not certain without a great deal more argument—that the body exists and has the properties it seems to have. This part of Descartes' philosophy of mind strikes me as being fundamentally correct.

I might add that, though Descartes does not seem to *need* either the consciousness thesis or the incorrigibility thesis he does not seem even to *state* the privacy thesis. At any rate, the evidence on which that thesis is typically ascribed to him is very unsatisfactory. But that is a topic I have dealt with elsewhere,[14] and I shall not attempt to recapitulate the discussion here.

II

I TURN now to Descartes' second main claim about mind and body, the doctrine that the mind is distinct from the body. Central though this conclusion may be, the argument for it is no less problematic than any other in the *Meditations*. As with the circle and the ontological argument, so also here: a certain criticism has regularly been leveled at Descartes, from his time to ours, and though that line of criticism was forcefully presented to Descartes himself by his contemporaries, he always maintained that it rested on a misunderstanding.

At the very least we have an intellectual puzzle: What is Descartes' argument? Is it open to certain plausible criticisms? But here, of all places, the puzzle is not prompted merely by historical curiosity. Perhaps few people are drawn to theism by the ontological argument. But Cartesian dualism is very much a live option in the philosophy of mind, partly because of a persistent feeling that there may be something in Descartes' argument for dualism. So it should be worthwhile to try to find out just what his argument is.

Let us begin with Descartes' earliest statement of the argument for a distinction between mind and body. In the *Discourse on Method*, immediately after he has established the existence of the

14. In my review of Kenny's *The Anatomy of the Soul, Australasian Journal of Philosophy*, 54 (1967), 80–86.

self as a first principle, Descartes goes on to argue in the following way.

> examining attentively what I was, I saw that I could feign that I had no body, and that there was no world, nor any place where I was, but that I could not feign, for all that, that I did not exist. On the contrary, I saw that from the very fact that I thought of doubting the truth of other things, it followed very evidently and very certainly that I existed, whereas if I had only ceased to think— even though all the rest of what I had always imagined was true— I had no reason to think that I existed. (AT VI, 32–33; HR I, 101)

These are Descartes' premises. From them, he says,

> I knew that I was a substance whose whole essence or nature is only thinking, and which, in order to exist, has no need of any place, and does not depend on any material thing. So that this I, that is, the soul by which I am what I am, is entirely distinct from the body. (AT VI, 33; HR I, 101)

By the time Descartes wrote the *Meditations*, he appears to have been persuaded that he had not made himself sufficiently clear in the *Discourse*. He remarks in the Preface to the Reader of the *Meditations* that his earlier work had encountered only two objections worth mentioning. Of these, the first was that

> it does not follow from the fact that the human mind, reflecting on itself, does not know itself to be anything other than a thing that thinks, that its nature or essence is *only* to think.[15]

The criticism, then, is that the argument of the *Discourse* is an argument from ignorance, that it infers that the mind is not essentially extended from the fact that the mind is not known to be extended. Thinking may be part of the mind's nature. But it has not been shown that it is the whole of the mind's nature.

To this Descartes replies that it was not his intention in the *Discourse* to exclude other things from the soul's nature,

> according to the order of the truth of the matter (which I was not treating of then), but only according to the order of my thought. What I meant was that I was aware of nothing else which I knew to pertain to my essence except that I was a thinking thing.

15. AT VII, 8; HR I, 137; cf. the letter to Mersenne, 27 Feb. 1637, Alquié, *Oeuvres* I, 522.

As Malcolm notes,[16] Descartes seems here to be retreating in the face of criticism. The conclusion in the *Discourse* certainly seems to be that (i) I know that only thinking pertains to my essence, and not merely that (ii) I do not know that anything other than thinking pertains to my essence.

However, this apparent retreat is immediately followed by a claim that the argument from ignorance alleged by his critics is really valid. For he writes:

I shall show subsequently how, from the fact that I know nothing else to pertain to my mind, it follows also that nothing else really does pertain to it. (AT VII, 8; HR I, 138)

The suggestion, then, is that the *Meditations* will have something to add to the argument of the *Discourse*, something that will overcome the objection about arguing from ignorance.

But it is not easy to see that the *Meditations* do add anything material. The authors of the *Objections* to the *Meditations* repeatedly raise the same point against Descartes. And Descartes repeatedly insists that the criticism rests on a misunderstanding. The objectors fail to see that, though the argument of the Second Meditation does not even purport to establish the real distinction of mind from body, the argument of the Sixth Meditation does establish it successfully.[17]

To see whether or not Descartes' reply is valid, we need to consider how the argument of the Sixth Meditation proceeds and what new elements, if any, it contains. Translating a bit freely, the argument runs:

Since I know that [1] whatever I clearly and distinctly understand can be made by God as I understand it, [2] if I can understand one thing clearly and distinctly without the other, I may be certain that the one is distinct from the other. For [1.1] they can be made to exist apart by the power of God at least, and [1.2] it does not matter by what power things are made to exist separately—if there is any power by which that can be done, they must be regarded as distinct. Therefore, from the fact that [3] I know that I exist, and that in the meantime [4] I notice nothing else to pertain to my nature or

16. See "Descartes' Proof That His Essence Is Thinking," *Philosophical Review*, 74 (1965), 315–338. Reprinted in Doney.
17. See, e.g., AT VII, 129–133, 219–231; HR II, 30–33, 96–104.

essence except this, that I am a thinking thing, I rightly conclude that [5] my essence consists in this one thing, that I am a thinking thing. And . . . because on the one hand [6] I have a clear and distinct idea of myself, insofar as I am only a thinking thing, not an extended one, and on the other [7] I have a distinct idea of the body, insofar as it is only an extended thing, not a thinking one, it is certain that [8] I am really distinct from my body and can exist without it. (AT VII, 78; HR I, 190)

I find a number of curious things in this argument. First, the heart of the argument, prima facie, lies in the claims I have numbered [3]–[5]. [5] seems to state quite a strong conclusion, the conclusion, in fact, that the critics of the *Discourse* objected to. If [5] has really been established, why could we not infer [8] from it directly? Why are [6] and [7] necessary? [5] is presented as following from [3] and [4], though apparently our entitlement to infer [5] from [3] and [4] depends in some not very clear way on [2].

The move from [3] and [4] to [5] is open to the following objection. It is supposed to be a reprise of the Second Meditation (cf. Alquié, *Oeuvres* II, 488, n1). But [4], in the Latin version, at least, is ambiguous. *Nihil plane aliud ad naturam sive essentiam meam pertinere animadvertam praeter hoc . . .* might mean

> [4a] I notice that nothing else pertains to my nature or essence except this . . .

or

> [4b] I do not notice that anything else pertains to my nature or essence except this . . .

Perhaps [4a] represents what the Latin ought to mean; but in the authorized French translation (AT IX, 62) it comes out as equivalent to [4b].[18] And however we take it, there is trouble. If we read [4] as [4a], there is no difficulty in getting from [4] to [5]. The move is trivial. But then there is difficulty in seeing that the Second Meditation has really established [4]. On the other hand, if we read [4] as [4b], there is no difficulty in seeing that [4] has been established by the Second Meditation, but there is a problem about getting from [4] to [5]. Having [1] through [3] available does not

18. There is a similar problem about Descartes' definition of free will in the Fourth Meditation. Cf. AT VII, 57, with AT IX, 46.

seem to be any help. What we have is still patently an argument from ignorance.

Perhaps none of this matters. For another curious thing about the argument is that when Descartes restates it in the Geometrical Exposition, [3]–[5] seem to disappear. The argument runs:

(1′) Whatever we conceive clearly can be made by God as we conceive it. [= 1]

(2′) We conceive clearly the mind (a substance which thinks) without the body (without an extended substance) [= 6] and we also conceive clearly the body without the mind [= 7].

(3′) Therefore, at least by God's omnipotence, the mind can exist without the body and the body without the mind.

(4′) Substances which can exist one without the other are really distinct. [= 1.2]

(5′) Mind and body are substances (by definition) which can exist without one another.

(6′) Therefore, they are really distinct.

I said above that [3]–[5] seem to disappear in this argument. They are there in the background. For (2′) is justified by an appeal to Postulate II:

[I ask my readers] to consider their own mind, and all those attributes of it which they find they cannot doubt, even though they suppose that whatever they have received by the senses is entirely false. (AT VII, 162; HR II, 54)

So I think the best view of the Second Meditation is that it is supposed to provide us, not with conclusions we can later use as premises in further arguments, but with clear and distinct ideas. If I practice the methodical doubt properly, I will find myself compelled to assent to the propositions that I exist and that I think, but not to any other propositions about myself (except those which specify how and what I think). In particular, I will find that I am not compelled to ascribe to myself any properties which involve extension. And this, I take it, is having a clear and distinct idea of myself as a thinking, nonextended thing. My idea of myself becomes clear when I recognize that there are some properties I *must* ascribe to myself. It becomes distinct when I recognize that I *need not* ascribe to myself those other properties I used to (cf. *Principles* I, 45).

The next point to note about this argument is the role which the concepts of God and clarity and distinctness play in it. Some commentators[19] have emphasized that what distinguishes the Sixth Meditation argument from that in the Second Meditation is that in the interim Descartes has established that God, being veracious, guarantees the truth of our clear and distinct ideas. Perhaps so. But this is only partly true, at best. The only property of God that Descartes *mentions*, either in the Sixth Meditation or in the Geometrical Exposition, is his omnipotence (cf. Alquié, *Oeuvres* II, 658, n2). And it is not easy to see how God's veracity would be helpful. Having a clear and distinct idea of myself as thinking, but not extended, involves being compelled to ascribe thought to myself, but does not involve being compelled to deny extension to myself, just a recognition that I am not compelled to ascribe extension to myself. Indeed, it seems that it would be awkward if I were compelled to deny extension of myself, since Descartes wants, in the end, to insist that he has a body very closely joined to him (AT VII, 78; HR I, 190). We do not want to prove too much. What the appeal to clear and distinct ideas is primarily supposed to show here is that at least an omnipotent being could cause mind and body to exist apart, that is (or so I take it), it is logically possible for mind and body to exist apart (cf. AT VII, 227; HR II, 102).

Of course, if we were to invoke the doctrine of the creation of eternal truths, we might say that a really omnipotent being could cause the mind and the body to exist apart even if that were not logically possible. But in the *Meditations* Descartes is careful not to invoke that extravagant conception of omnipotence, and we would do him no service by bringing it in.

I propose to understand Descartes' argument in the following way:

(1″) If I can clearly and distinctly conceive a thing as being complete as an F without its being a G, and if I can clearly and distinctly conceive a thing as being complete as a G without its being an F, then it is logically possible that an F exists without being a G and that a G exists without being an F.

(2″) If it is logically possible that an F exists without being a G and

19. E.g., Kenny (p. 89) and Margaret Wilson, "Descartes: The Epistemological Argument for Mind-Body Distinctness," *Nous*, 10 (1976), 5–6, 13.

that a G exists without being an F, and if there is an omnipotent being, then there is a power that can cause any F to exist without any G and any G to exist without any F.

(3″) If there is a power that can cause any F to exist without any G and any G to exist without any F, then no F is identical with any G.

(4″) I can clearly and distinctly conceive myself as being complete as a thinking thing without my being extended, and I can clearly and distinctly conceive a body as being complete as an extended thing without its thinking.

(5″) There is an omnipotent being.

(1″) and (4″) entail

(6″) It is logically possible that a thinking thing exists without being extended and that a body exists without thinking.

(2″), (5″), and (6″) entail

(7″) There is a power that can cause any thinking thing to exist without any extended thing and any extended thing to exist without any thinking thing.

(7″) in conjunction with (3″) entails

(8″) No thinking thing is identical with any body.

So in particular,

(9″) I (the thing I am compelled to ascribe thought to) am not identical with any body.

This way of stating the argument has, I submit, the advantage of bringing into prominence what Descartes thought was at least a main reason why his argument could not be stated as early as the Second Meditation. If, in the preceding chapter, I have correctly assessed the merits of Descartes' arguments for an omnipotent being, the apparent need for (5″) may be unfortunate. But apart from that the argument seems to have a certain plausibility. And perhaps (5″) is eliminable, in spite of what Descartes thought.

(1″) is problematic. Arnauld objected (AT VII, 201–202; HR II, 83) that even if I conceived a thing (say, a triangle) clearly and distinctly as having one property (say, right-angledness) without another (say, having the square of the hypotenuse equal to the sum of the squares of the other two sides), those properties might, nevertheless, be necessarily connected. Even if God is not a deceiver, my failure to perceive a necessary connection cannot guarantee that there is no necessary connection.

But (1″) is stated in a way calculated to avoid this objection.[20] If I am compelled to conceive something as being complete as an F, that is, as being a substance (= a thing that needs nothing else in order to exist) in virtue of its having that property, then God will be a deceiver if it needs some other property. I do not conceive the triangle as being complete as a triangle in virtue of its being right-angled. Being right-angled or, for that matter, being a triangle, presupposes being extended. But I do conceive a body as complete in virtue of its being extended.

I doubt that many people will think this much of an improvement. If we really need to know that there is a God who is not a deceiver to get the argument going, then the defects of Cartesian theism are rather critical. But perhaps the argument can be so reconstructed as to avoid this assumption.

After all, we want (1″) and (4″) only in order to be able to establish (6″); and it might be argued that (6″) is plausible enough on its own. Surely it is at least *logically possible* that some thinking thing exists without being extended. Surely the traditional concept of God, for example, is not inconsistent just because it conceives God as a disembodied mind. And surely it is not merely logically possible, but true, that some extended thing exists without thinking. Who could deny this?

I suppose a certain kind of behaviorist *will* deny the logical possibility of there being something that thinks but is not extended. If you hold that sentences ascribing mental properties to someone must be analyzed in terms of sentences describing how his body would behave in certain circumstances, then it *will* be logically necessary that anything that thinks has a body. But behaviorist analyses of mental concepts do not, in fact, seem very promising,[21] and I think the most interesting question is "What

20. Here I adopt a suggestion from the article by Margaret Wilson cited above (though she cannot be held responsible for the peculiar way I use the idea).

21. See, e.g., the discussion of behaviorism in David Armstrong's *A Materialist Theory of the Mind* (New York: Humanities Press, 1968), pp. 54–72; or my "Dreaming and Conceptual Revision," *Australasian Journal of Philosophy*, 53 (1975), 119–141.

follows if we grant Descartes his very minimal claim that it is logically possible for mind and body to exist one without the other?"

One way of defending Descartes' argument would be the following. A good many current systems of modal logic[22] contain the thesis:

(LI) If x = y, then L(x = y),

that is, if x is identical with y, then it is necessary that x is identical with y. And this is equivalent to saying that if it's logically possible that x and y have different properties, then x and y are distinct. So in particular, if it's logically possible that the mind and the body differ as regards the property of existence, then they are not identical. On this view, Descartes' central contention (that mind and body are distinct) would follow just from the very weak claim we granted in the preceding paragraph, without there being any need for a further premise asserting the existence of an omnipotent being. And one leading defender of the modal principle has recognized and insisted on its applicability to the defense of Descartes. So Saul Kripke writes:

> Descartes . . . argued that a person or mind is distinct from his body, since the mind could exist without the body. He might equally well have argued the same conclusion from the premise that the body could have existed without the mind. Now the one response which I regard as plainly inadmissible is the response which cheerfully accepts the Cartesian premise while denying the Cartesian conclusion.[23]

If mind and body are identical, their identity must be necessary. Modal logic here offers to take over the role of theology in Descartes' philosophy. Is the offer one Descartes could or should accept?

One reservation I have about this way of defending Descartes is that it is perhaps too economical in its premises. Consider the

22. See, e.g., George Hughes and Max Cresswell, *An Introduction to Modal Logic* (London: Methuen, 1972), pp. 189–192.

23. "Naming and Necessity," in *Semantics of Natural Language*, ed. D. Davidson and G. Harman (Dordrecht: Reidel, 1972), p. 334. For an earlier version, cf. his "Identity and Necessity," in *Identity and Individuation*, ed. M. Munitz (New York: New York University Press, 1971).

second sentence in the passage just quoted. Kripke clearly hadn't looked at the Sixth Meditation very recently when he wrote that, or he would not have put it in counterfactual form. Descartes does appeal to the fact that the body can exist without the mind. But he does not (as Kripke does) treat that fact as another premise which—like the fact that the mind could exist without the body— would have been sufficient in itself to establish the distinctness of mind and body. He seems to regard neither of these facts as sufficient by itself. Only their conjunction is sufficient. So (besides God's omnipotence) something else Descartes thought important is being treated as nonessential.

Moreover, Kripke's approach does make things very easy. I have been supposing it to be an essential step in Descartes' argument that it is logically possible that the mind exist without the body. And though I have little doubt that this is true, it is at least fairly controversial. Behaviorism is tempting, even if false. Kripke offers us an argument which could equally well proceed from the far less controversial assumption that it is logically possible for the body to exist without the mind. I suppose a certain kind of idealist will deny this. But if we may disregard such extravagances, Kripke's argument promises a high return from a very small investment.

Perhaps we should simply be grateful that such modest assumptions can be made to yield Descartes' conclusion. More probably, we should examine closely the magician's hat. The modal principle Kripke relies on seems to have many counterexamples, as modern materialists have emphasized.[24] The morning star is identical with the evening star, but this identity statement is a contingent one, whose truth had to be learned by empirical investigation. And of course Kripke agrees that this identity is contingent. The modal principle

(LI) If $x = y$, then $L(x = y)$

is valid only if we restrict the possible substitutions for the variables to 'rigid designators,' and definite descriptions are not (generally) rigid designators. Proper names, however, are rigid designators. So "Hesperus is Phosphorus," if true, is necessarily true.

24. The classic article, of course, being J. J. C. Smart's "Sensations and Brain Processes," *Philosophical Review*, 68 (1959), 141–156.

What, then, is a rigid designator? Is that technical term just a synonym for "proper name"? No. A rigid designator is a term which designates the same object in all possible worlds in which that object exists. Proper names are rigid designators because, when we use them to talk about counterfactual situations, we are talking about the same individual we would be talking about if we were making a statement about this world. For example, when we make conjectures about what Nixon's fate would have been if he had handled the Watergate situation differently, we are speaking about the same individual 'in another possible world,' not a numerically different individual who merely shares important properties with Nixon. By contrast, a definite description like "The president of the United States in 1972" is not a rigid designator. We can consistently describe counterfactual situations in which Humphrey won the election in 1968. In talking about such possible worlds we might use that definite description to refer to Humphrey. (But not all definite descriptions are nonrigid designators. "The square of three" designates the same number in all possible worlds. Cf. "Naming and Necessity," pp. 264–271.)

One reason people have thought that even identity statements involving proper names must be contingent is that they are, sometimes at least, empirical discoveries.[25] They are not, at any rate, truths we can learn by analysis of the meanings of the terms involved. But Kripke argues that this reasoning rests on a confusion of the necessary with the a priori and the analytic. When we find out that Hesperus is Phosphorus, this may be the result of a laborious empirical investigation; when we learn that Tully was Cicero, this is commonly something we accept on the authority of someone who tells us so—probably Quine, for most of us these days. But it does not follow that these are not necessary truths, any more than it follows from our having learned a mathematical truth by induction or on authority that it is contingent. When we say of Hesperus that it is Phosphorus, we are saying of an object that it is identical with itself. And self-identity is a property all objects necessarily have.

Kripke's defense of the necessity of a large class of identity

25. For example, Quine, in his "Reply to Professor Marcus," *The Ways of Paradox* (New York: Random House, 1966), pp. 179–180.

statements is not merely an ad hoc device for rescuing an otherwise dubious thesis in modal logic. It is motivated partly by an ingenious and complex theory of the meaning of proper names, and partly by intuitions about identity which I find congenial. If Hesperus really *is* Phosphorus, it does not seem right to say that it would be possible for Hesperus to exist and Phosphorus not exist. Attempts to shake this conviction by appealing to counterexamples involving definite descriptions look like sophistry.

But there do seem to be severe difficulties about applying the principle thus qualified to the defense of the historical Descartes. The passage from Kripke quoted above continues:

> Let "Descartes" be a name, or rigid designator, of a certain person and let "B" be a rigid designator of his body. Then if Descartes were indeed identical to B, the supposed identity, being an identity between two rigid designators, would be necessary, and Descartes could not exist without B and B could not exist without Descartes. ("Naming and Necessity," p. 334)

The first thing that must strike the student of Descartes about this is its third-person character. The referring expressions Descartes uses are "I" and "my body." Perhaps the certainty which attaches to "Possibly I exist and my body does not" will not transfer to "Possibly Descartes exists and B (his body) does not." So it is natural to ask whether we should class "I" and "my body" as rigid designators.

Neither expression, of course, is a proper name. "I" doesn't always designate the same individual even in this world, let alone all possible worlds. But then proper names often have more than one referent (for example, "John Wisdom"). And it does seem that whenever *I* use the term "I," even in referring to counterfactual situations, I refer to the same individual. Perhaps "I" is a rigid designator.

Perhaps "my body" is too, though this is hardly clear. Even if "I" is a rigid designator, it won't be true in general that expressions of the form "my F" will be rigid designators. It seems unduly fatalistic to suppose that "my car" designates the same object in every possible world in which I own a car.

Kripke argues as if none of this mattered. We simply introduce rigid designators for myself and my body by stipulation. "Let

'Descartes' be a name, or rigid designator, of a certain person, and let 'B' be a rigid designator of his body." On his (very plausible) view, all names get introduced by a kind of baptismal ceremony in which the reference is fixed either by ostension or by a description ("Naming and Necessity," pp. 302–303). Such meaning as they subsequently have depends on the existence of communication chains going back to the "baptismal ceremony." So all Descartes needs, to introduce rigid designators for himself and his body, is some way of fixing the reference of those designators. This will be easy enough. He can say: "By 'I' I mean that thinking substance whose existence was established in the Second Meditation. By 'my body' I mean that extended substance which seems to be related to me in the peculiarly intimate way described in the Sixth Meditation; for example, when it is injured, I feel pain, and so forth."

But couldn't we use different descriptions to fix the reference of two rigid designators and then discover that in fact they both named the same thing? Of course. "Hesperus" and "Phosphorus" were, let us suppose, introduced by different descriptions (say, "the morning star" and "the evening star"). What would block an argument to their distinctness would have to be that we could not, in their case, justifiably assert the possibility of the one's existing and the other's not existing. Before their identity was discovered, of course, someone could conceive that the one existed and the other did not. He could even conceive this clearly and distinctly. For the descriptions by which the names were introduced were logically independent of one another. But the clear and distant conceivability of this will be no guarantee of its possibility.

So, in the case of "I" and "my body," the logical independence of the descriptions by which these rigid designators were introduced (or the fact that statements ascribing mental properties cannot be analyzed into statements ascribing behavior to bodies) will be no guarantee of the possibility of my existing and my body's not existing.

I conclude that the attempt to make modal logic do the work of theology does not lead to any very real vindication of Descartes' argument. Perhaps Kripke's articulation of certain intuitions about identity makes it easier to understand why the argument seemed plausible to Descartes. But the refinements that articulation requires only serve, in the end, to call in question the one thing in the argument that seemed solid—its claim that possibly I exist and my body does not.

This side of Descartes' philosophy of mind, then, does not seem to me as well argued as that we considered in the first half of this chapter. If 'Cartesian dualism' is the thesis that mind and body are distinct, Descartes' arguments leave its truth open to question.

8

BODY

On the twenty-eighth of January, 1641, Descartes, in the midst of replying to the objections of those learned men who had been given the privilege of seeing the *Meditations* in proof, wrote ruefully to Mersenne:

> I see that people pay more attention to the titles of books than they do to their contents . . . these [the titles he wished to have attached to the various Meditations] are the things I want them to pay the most attention to.

But, he continued,

> I think I have put in them a great many other things. Between you and me, I shall tell you that these six Meditations contain all the foundations of my physics. But please, one must not say this; for those who favor Aristotle would perhaps make more difficulty about approving them. I hope that my readers will imperceptibly become accustomed to my principles, and will recognize their truth before they realize that they destroy Aristotle's principles. (Alquié, *Oeuvres* II, 316; *Philosophical Letters*, 94)

In this final chapter I want to consider how Descartes has contrived to smuggle the foundations of his physics into this treatise on first philosophy.

There is, of course, a certain sense in which it is obvious how the *Meditations* lay the foundations of physics: by providing a validation of our clear and distinct ideas, they license us to trust that our clear and distinct ideas are true. So to the extent that physics rests on clear and distinct ideas, the *Meditations* give it an epistemological foundation. But Descartes clearly has something more in mind than that. Giving physics an epistemological foundation in our creation by a veracious God does not say anything concrete about the content of physics, or anything that would necessarily bring Descartes into conflict with Aristotle. How do the *Meditations* accomplish that?

I

THE PROCESS begins as early as the First Meditation. Immediately after the dream argument, and before Descartes introduces the argument from God's omnipotence, there is a transitional passage (AT VII, 19–20; HR I, 146–147) in which Descartes reflects on the nature of thought. He has resolved, on the strength of the dream argument, to give up all particular experiential beliefs—that his eyes are open, that he is moving his head, even that he has eyes and a head. But he finds himself compelled to believe (*fatendum est*) that even if his experiences are dream experiences, they are in some way representative of reality. "The things seen in sleep are *like* certain painted images, which can only be invented in the likeness of true things." The point of the comparison here seems to be this: even if a painter wishes to create a picture of a fantastic being, which never did and never will exist, he must use certain pigments; in the same way, whether our thoughts about the world are true or false, they must be constructed out of certain elements, certain very general and simple properties; whatever particular properties we believe things to have, we must ascribe these more general properties to them:

> corporeal nature in general and its extension, the shape of extended things, quantity (their size and number), the place where they exist, the time through which they endure and so on. (AT VII, 20; HR I, 146)

These simple and universal properties are all ones Locke was later to call primary qualities of bodies, and they are all among the properties Descartes took as fundamental in his physics (cf, AT XI, 26), properties which (in conjunction with motion, not mentioned in this list), he used to explain the "secondary qualities." None of the secondary qualities—color, taste, smell, sound, weight, etc.—appear in the list.

This last point must be emphasized, since it can easily be missed. The mention of color earlier in the passage has misled some scholars (for one, Gueroult, *Ordre* I, 34) into thinking that "sensible qualities" *are* among the simple and universal qualities. But color is mentioned only by way of analogy. The simple and universal things are *like* the colors the painter must use in creating his picture. We may mix the 'colors' as we will, but we must think of things as having *some* size, *some* shape, *some* place, and so on. Descartes neither affirms nor denies that things must be thought of as having some color.

The reference to color also seems to be among Frankfurt's reasons (Frankfurt, 56–60) for holding that the theory of imagination suggested here is not Descartes' own, but merely one his hypothetical beginner in philosophy is naturally inclined to. There is a good deal of truth in Frankfurt's interpretation, but the differences between Descartes and his hypothetical inquirer are not those Frankfurt suggests. Even the hypothetical inquirer does not think color is among the more simple and universal things. Nor is he, it seems to me, really proposing a theory of imagination. It is, rather, a theory of thought, namely, the theory that our thoughts about things, whether true or false, are *like* images. He begins by saying that the "things seen in sleep" (in the language of the Third Meritation, things insofar as they exist objectively in our intellect) are "like certain painted images." This is a theory about the nature of our ideas, and so far forth it is an anticipation of the theory Descartes will assert in his own person in the Third Meditation. The hypothetical inquirer does not say that these ideas must be derived from prior experience of the simples in reality. They must be "invented in the likeness of true things," but all this means is that they must represent bodies as having certain general characteristics which bodies must indeed have if they exist at all. Where the hypothetical inquirer goes astray is in sliding from saying, at the beginning of the passage, that ideas are like images to speaking, at the end of the passage, as if what are invented in our thought *are* images of things. Ideas are not images, and the simple and universal things are not known by the imagination. But these errors of the hypothetical inquirer will be corrected later, in the Second and Sixth Meditations.

In the First Meditation nothing very much is done with the list of simple and universal properties of things. Descartes takes the mention of extension and number as an opportunity to raise the question whether the propositions of mathematics can reasonably be doubted, and the rest of the Meditation is concerned with the hypothesis of an omnipotent deceiver. But it would not have suited Descartes' purposes to elaborate very much on this theme here. His aim was to accustom people imperceptibly to the principles of his physics.

II

THIS PROCESS is continued in the Second Meditation. We naturally think of this Meditation as the one in which Descartes finally achieves certainty regarding *something*, namely, his own existence. But though that is surely an important result, and one emphasized in Descartes' synopsis of the *Meditations*, it occupies very little actual space (one and one-half pages out of nine in Adam and Tannery) and is not among the themes picked out for attention in the title. According to the title of the Second Meditation, the principal topics treated there are the nature of the human mind and that it is better known than the body. But as we shall see the Second Meditation has a good deal to say about the nature of body.

Immediately after having assured himself of his own existence (AT VII, 25; HR I, 150), Descartes raises the question "What am I?" and proceeds, characteristically, to review his past opinions about himself. This not only conforms to the requirements of the method but provides a convenient device for indirect criticism of scholastic views. The first answer he considers is that he is a man, a rational animal. This traditional Aristotelian answer does not get much attention. Descartes pretty quickly dismisses it as unhelpful. The questions it raises—"What is an animal?" "What is it to be rational?"—are more difficult than the one it seeks to answer. We have an implicit application of the rule of method which says that we should try to reduce difficult questions to those which are more simple.

So Descartes resolves to attend not to Aristotelian subtleties but to the things which would occur spontaneously to the thought of someone who is led by nature. And here we get an enumeration of my properties. I suppose myself to have some things—a face, hands, arms—which I have in common with corpses; having these is having corporeal properties. I also engage in certain activities which I do not ascribe to corpses: nourishing myself, walking, sensing, thinking. The list is obviously constructed with one eye cocked on the Aristotelians, but the natural man is not an Aristotelian. "I referred these activities to the soul"—not nourishing myself to the nutritive soul, walking to a motive soul, sensing to a sensitive soul, and so forth—but all of these activities to *one* soul.

The natural man has a strong tendency to Cartesian dualism; but he is, at the beginning of his reflections, rather confused both about the nature of the soul and about the nature of body. Insofar as he has any idea of the soul at all, he tends to think of it as corporeal. And his idea of body involves a mixture of properties acceptable to Descartes with properties whose status is going to be called in question:

> By body I understand all that is apt to be bounded by some shape and circumscribed in a place, that fills space so that it excludes every other body, that is perceived by touch, sight, hearing, taste or smell, and that moves in various ways—not indeed by itself, but by something else which touches it. (AT VII, 26; HR I, 151)

The capacity to move oneself—like capacities to sense and to think—does not "pertain to the nature of body," for it is not common to all bodies. It is a capacity we are surprised to find in some bodies. And we are being set up for the Cartesian explanation of the fact that some bodies do have this capacity.

At this stage Descartes begins to consider how much of what he has formerly believed about himself can survive the hypothesis of an omnipotent deceiver, and this leads him, for a time, away from reflections on the nature of body. But he returns to that topic toward the end of the Second Meditation in the well-known passage in which he considers the piece of wax. This passage has, I think, a number of functions. It serves, for example, to illustrate the thesis that the mind is better known than the body. Any claim to knowledge I want to make about this particular body, insofar as it is based on experience, must presuppose some genuine knowledge of the mind, of how things seem to me. The passage serves also to introduce the notions of clarity and distinctness. It is characteristic of the analytic mode of presentation (as opposed to the synthetic mode) that it does not offer us formal definitions of key terms, but introduces them informally, by way of examples.[1]

But it also serves to purify the natural man's concept of body, just as earlier sections of the Second Meditation had purified his concept of mind. Our idea of the mind becomes clear and distinct as we recognize that some properties must, and others need not, be ascribed to it. And a similar thing happens to our idea of body. We find ourselves compelled to ascribe some properties to it and not others.

We are invited to consider a particular piece of wax, only recently taken from the hive:

> It has not yet lost all the taste of its honey; it retains something of the fragrance of the flowers from which it was gathered; its color, shape and size are evident; it is hard, it is cold, one can touch it easily, and if you rap it, it will give out a sound—all those things are present which seem to be required for a body to be known as distinctly as possible. (AT VII, 31; HR I, 154)

But then we are to imagine that circumstances change. The wax is brought near the fire and

> the traces of taste are removed, the fragrance vanishes, the color is changed, the shape is taken away, the size increases, it becomes liquid, it becomes hot, one can hardly touch it, and now if you strike it, it will not give out a sound.

And the question is: Does the wax survive all of these changes?

---

1. So I argue, at any rate, in "Spinoza as an Expositor of Descartes," in *Speculum Spinozanum*, ed. Siegfried Hessing (London: Routledge & Kegan Paul), forthcoming.

Does the same wax still remain? It must be confessed that it does remain; no one denies this, no one thinks otherwise.

This is, or should be, very surprising, for a number of reasons. First, and least interestingly, Descartes has still not proved the existence of *any* body yet. We are still, it seems, operating under the hypothesis of an omnipotent deceiver. So it is surprising to be told that one *must* confess that the body is there at all, much less *still* there. The solution to this puzzle is easy, however. The analysis of the piece of wax has been introduced by a dialectical maneuver which allows Descartes temporarily to suspend the deceiver hypothesis. In spite of all his arguments Descartes has found that:

> I cannot abstain from thinking that corporeal things, whose images are formed in thought, and which the senses ascertain, are much more distinctly known than that I whose nature I do not know [*istud nescio quid mei*] which does not come under the imagination. (AT VII, 29; HR I, 153)

So he will give the mind free rein for a while,[2] and see what follows even if we allow the assumption that there are bodies.

What is more surprising is that some of the things we "must" confess when we relax the reins are things that will not be vindicated by the subsequent argument of the *Meditations*. That the wax might remain numerically one thing while its shape changes seems to be contradicted, for example, by the Synopsis of the *Meditations* (AT IX, 10; HR I, 141). And as Alquié observes (*Oeuvres* II, 425, n2), in Cartesian physics when a body seems to expand, its size does not really change. When its volume apparently increases, we must assume that there are various intervals between its parts which come to be filled by other, much smaller bodies (*Principles* II, 6). The identification of body with extension will require that, strictly speaking, one and the same body cannot occupy more space at one time than at another. And the solution here seems to be that in the piece of wax passage Descartes is not

---

2. *Adhuc semel laxissimas habenas ei permittamus.* AT VII, 30; HR I, 154. I am much indebted to Alquié's excellent annotation of this passage, *Oeuvres* II, 422–428. It will be seen, however, that I do not accept all of his conclusions. He appears to think, e.g., that some of the difficulties of this passage are due to the French translator. But I find the Latin equally problematic.

yet giving a correct account of what happens according to his physical principles; he is merely responding as his hypothetical natural man would respond.

What, then, does the natural man infer from the wax's retention of its identity through change? First, that if he understood anything distinctly in the wax, it was not any of the things he became aware of through the senses. The identity of the wax does not depend on the identity of any of its "sensible" qualities, for they have all changed and it has not. Second, that there are some very general properties that the wax does retain in spite of the changes in its "sensible" qualities: it is extended, flexible (capable of changing its shape), and mutable (capable of change in general).[3]

Now what is the purpose of this distinction between the properties the wax does retain and those it does not? In particular, is Descartes here distinguishing between primary and secondary ("sensible") qualities? It is easy to understand why someone would think so (cf. Beck, *Metaphysics*, 101). Secondary qualities are prominent in the list of those that change and primary qualities are prominent in the list of those that don't change. But if Descartes intends to draw that distinction here, he manifestly does not succeed. For certainly the list of qualities that change contains some we will want to class as primary (as, size and shape). And if it should be said, "Yes, the wax no longer has this particular size and this particular shape, but it still has *a* size and *a* shape," it may be replied that this seems to be equally true of some of the secondary qualities. Perhaps the wax no longer has any taste, or smell, or capacity to produce sound, but it still has (and is recognized as having) some color and some temperature, even if it does not have the particular color and temperature it originally had.

All of this must be admitted. Descartes does not, in this passage, succeed in distinguishing primary qualities from secondary ones. At most he softens us up for that distinction. But probably he is not even trying to make the distinction in this passage. His primary purpose seems to be rather to eliminate from the natural

3. So I understand *mutabile* (FV: *muable*). Veitch, Kemp Smith, and Haldane and Ross all have "movable," but not for any reason that I can see. Beck (*Metaphysics*, 100) renders it as "changeable," as do Anscombe and Geach.

man's concept of body the idea that a body is essentially something we can know by the senses or even form images of in thought. This comes out in the continuation of our passage. He does not see anything else that "pertains" to the wax except that it is something extended and flexible or changeable. And the question is what these properties consist in. In particular, Are they properties I am aware of by my faculty of imagination? No. For to be flexible, say, is not just to be able to change from one shape to another, but to be capable of infinitely many changes, and I cannot grasp an infinity by my imagination. The imagination is too closely tied to perception for that. Anything I can sense or imagine is finite. Similarly with extension. To be extended is to be endowed with one of an infinite variety of shapes and sizes, and I cannot grasp that infinite variety by imagining it. To be aware of what extension and changeability are I must perceive these properties by the mind alone; I must exercise my faculty of judgment, inferring these quite general properties from the more specific properties I believe myself to perceive via the senses. But even my awareness of the more specific properties involves an exercise of judgment. When I say that I see this wax as having its particular color and shape, I make an inference from the way it seems to me, which itself is a quasi judgment.

Now if all of this is correct it may seem that the analysis of the piece of wax is primarily of interest for what it says about Descartes' theory of perception, placing him with those who want to analyze perception in terms of beliefs or inclinations to believe[4] (as opposed to those who bring in acquaintance with or possession of a private object, a sense datum). But that would be a mistake. The passage does have two important implications for physical theory.

First, the infinite variety of shapes and sizes extended objects can have is going to be very important to Descartes later on. He will be trying to carry out a reductionist program, explaining all the phenomena of nature in terms of variations in primary qualities like size, shape, and motion. One reason this project seems a

4. E.g., George Pitcher, *A Theory of Perception* (Princeton: Princeton University Press, 1971), or David Armstrong, *Perception and the Physical World* (New York: Humanities Press, 1961).

feasible one to him, one reason he thinks he will not need to invoke any other primitive properties of extended objects, is that there is infinite variety in his favored explanatory factors (cf. *Principles* II, 64).

The other point is this. To explain some phenomena, such as rarefaction and condensation, Descartes' physics will want to deploy the concept of bodies so small as to be imperceptible. We are so used to such explanations that we take them for granted. Descartes cannot. So he writes in the *Principles* that we should not object to his account of rarefaction that it speaks of bodies we do not perceive by our senses. "There is no reason which obliges us to believe that we must perceive by our senses all the bodies around us" (*Principles* II, 7). Indeed, for some phenomena, like motion, to occur at all, Descartes thinks that matter must be not merely indefinitely divisible but actually divided into indefinitely small parts (*Principles* II, 34). For this purpose it is essential to rid the natural man of his prejudice that a body is something essentially perceptible by the senses. And this is one of the several things the analysis of the wax does.

Before we leave the Second Meditation, we might note that there is, toward the end of the wax passage, a brief hint of that most notorious of Cartesian doctrines, the claim that animals are mere machines. What, Descartes asks, was there that was distinct in his first perception of the wax?

> What was there which does not seem as though it could have been had by any animal whatever? But when I distinguish the wax from its external forms, and consider it bare, as if its clothes had been stripped from it, then though there may still be some error in my judgment, I cannot really perceive it in this way without a human mind. (AT VII, 32; HR I, 156)

So among the animals only a human can rise to the level of true perception; for only the human has the faculty of judgment (as evidenced by his possession of language). This, of course, is quite gratuitous. Nothing has been said to prepare us for this; it is not adequately explained, and there does not seem to be any real need to offer such an inviting target to the enemy. But there it is, nonetheless.

III

THE THIRD MEDITATION has as its main theme the demonstration of God's existence. Nevertheless, it is a peculiarly rich store of grist for our mill.

One important subsidiary theme is the relation of our ideas to external reality. Very early in the meditation (AT VII, 35; HR I, 158) Descartes reports having believed—and because the belief was familiar and customary, having thought he perceived clearly— that there were things outside him from which his ideas proceeded and which his ideas were altogether like. This is very reminiscent of the opening paragraph of Le monde (AT XI, 3), where a similar common belief is described. A bit later it is asserted—without any sign of an argument—that the chief and most frequent error we make consists in judging that the ideas which are in us are like certain things outside us. Our former belief quickly reasserts itself (AT VII, 38; HR I, 160). I seem to be taught by nature that my ideas come from external things which are like them, as, that my idea of heat comes to me from something different from me, namely, from the heat of the fire by which I sit. "Nothing is more obvious than that I should judge that that thing sends its likeness to me, rather than something else."

But this is not allowed to stand for very long (any more than it was in Le monde). Even if my ideas do proceed from things external to me, they cannot all be like those things. For sometimes I have two quite different ideas of the same thing (AT VII, 39; HR I, 161); for example, I have two ideas of the sun, one of which represents it as very small, the other of which represents it as very large. And I trust less the one that seems to come more directly from the sun.

It is important not to misunderstand the contrast which is being drawn here. The first (and less trustworthy) idea is one that is "as if drawn from the senses." The other is "taken from reasonings of astronomy, that is, elicited from certain notions innate in me, or made by me in some other way" (my emphasis). But Descartes is under no illusions about the need for empirical data as an ingredient in the astronomical reasoning which constructs the latter idea. We do not discover in a wholly a priori manner that the sun is many times larger than the earth. The point is simply that the empirical data are not sufficient to decide the matter. The situation is like that discussed in the Sixth Replies (AT IX, 238; HR II, 252–253), where my visual idea of a stick partially immersed in water conflicts with my tactual idea of the same stick. I must exercise my faculty of judgment and choose between conflicting appearances on nonempirical grounds—like the simplicity and comprehensiveness of the alternative theories. The contrast is not between perception and pure reason, but between a naive, instinctual use of perception and a more sophisticated use of perception.[5]

This example provides grounds for skepticism of a different order than any Descartes considered in the First Meditation. It appeals to the distinction between the world of science and the world of naive perception. But although that distinction is often associated with the distinction between primary and secondary qualities, and although ideas of secondary qualities like heat figure prominently in the Third Meditation, the two distinctions are not the same. The contrast between the way things are to science and the way they are to naive perception can be drawn within the realm of primary qualities; in fact, Descartes' example is drawn from that realm. The size of the sun is a primary quality, not a secondary one. Descartes' distinction between primary and secondary qualities does not involve the belief that all and only ideas of primary qualities are true. We may easily be mistaken in our judgments about them too.[6]

If the distinction between primary and secondary qualities does not rest on that kind of belief in the veridicality of our ideas of primary qualities, what does it rest on? The Third Meditation does, for the first time in the *Meditations*, draw a sharp distinction

5. This is hardly a full or adequate treatment of Descartes' view of the role of experience in scientific reasoning. But the question is, I find, well discussed by R. M. Blake's "The Role of Experience in Descartes' Theory of Method," in Blake, Ducasse, and Madden. See also Alan Gewirth, "Experience and the Non-mathematical in the Cartesian Method," *Journal of the History of Ideas,* 2 (1941), 183–210.

6. It is appalling that one should have to say, of any seventeenth-century philosopher, that he was not such a fool as to be unaware of this elementary fact. But unfortunately we do, as I have argued in "Locke, Boyle and the Distinction Between Primary and Secondary Qualities," *Philosophical Review,* 81 (1972), 438–464.

between primary and secondary qualities, and does provide some rationale for that distinction, though possibly not a very helpful one.

Finding it clear that his ideas are not invariably caused by objects which are as our ideas represent them to be, Descartes asks which of his ideas he might have formed from his own resources, consistently with his general beliefs about causality. This leads him naturally to classify the various kinds of ideas he has, and naturally ideas of corporeal things figure prominently among these. What is not so natural, indeed somewhat gratuitous, is that Descartes takes this opportunity to consider his ideas of corporeal things "more thoroughly" and examine each of them "as yesterday I examined the idea of the wax." What follows is not a close examination of our ideas of other particular bodies, but an enumeration of the various properties of bodies—a rather hasty generalization, it seems, from the discussion of the wax. The properties are divided into two categories, of which the first are those we perceive clearly and distinctly:

> Size, or extension in length, breadth and depth; shape, which arises from the boundary of the extension; the position which the variously shaped bodies maintain among themselves; and motion, or the change of that position. (AT VII, 43; HR I, 164)

These are all familiar primary qualities, and there is some plausibility in claiming that the analysis of the wax has led us to a clear perception of them. Extension was the only first-order property which the analysis of the Second Meditation found to be unchanging in the wax. (The only other property which it seemed had to be ascribed to the wax was the second-order property of changeability.) But here, by a bit of sleight of hand, extension is made to let in a whole series of other properties. First, the sleight of hand: extension, the only unchanging first-order property of the wax, is here identified with size, which was not an unchanging property of the wax. That move having been made, it follows that a body must have a shape, for whatever has a size has a shape. (Or at least it seems to follow. If we can conceive an unlimited extension, and are prepared to say that it has a size, then perhaps having a size does not entail having a shape.) Once we have both size and shape, we

219

may add two other properties: position (the body's relation to other shapes) and motion (its change of position).

There is, at least, some discernible argument for adding shape, position, and motion to extension. None is offered for the next three items: "To these can be added substance, duration and number." These were not explicitly mentioned in the analysis of the wax, though arguably the description of the wax's change presupposed that there was *one* thing (or *substance*) which endured through the various changes. But these are not peculiar to bodies. As Descartes notes, they are common to both bodies and minds (AT VII, 44; HR I, 165; cf. *Principles* I, 51–59).

Then we get a list of "the rest": light and colors, sounds, smells, tastes, heat and cold, and other tactile qualities. These familiar secondary qualities are all ones we think quite confusedly and obscurely. So the distinction between the primary and the secondary corresponds to that between those properties of bodies we perceive clearly and distinctly and those we don't.

Now if all our ideas of primary qualities are clear and distinct, and if (as we learn later) all clear and distinct ideas are true, doesn't this entail that our perception of primary qualities is invariably veridical? That would follow, I think, but I do not think Descartes means to say that all our ideas of primary qualities are clear and distinct. First, there is the distinction, already suggested earlier, between our idea of the extension of this particular object and our idea of extension in general. The latter may, I suppose, be clear and distinct without the former being clear and distinct (though I conjecture that the converse would not be true). But even at the level where they are not ideas of a primary quality of a particular object, our ideas of primary qualities are not always clear and distinct.

Some people imagine that they can distinguish between a body and its extension or size, and so imagine that there must be something more to body than extension, such as hardness or resistance (cf. *Principles* II, 4) or that one and the same body may have a different size at one time than at another. Descartes does not expose these misconceptions here, but he lays the groundwork for correcting them. They arise from a failure to realize the implications of the doctrine of substance. Extension (as we learn at AT VII, 45;

HR I, 165) is nothing but a mode of substance. So wherever there is extension, there must be a substance that is extended, a something which is not nothing. A void is impossible; nothing has no attributes.

Again, Descartes will want to distinguish in the *Principles* between "motion" as the term is commonly understood, where it signifies the action by which a body passes from one place to another (*Principles* II, 24; cf. *Le monde*, chapter VII, AT XI, 39), and "motion" in the proper sense of the term, where it signifies the transfer of one body from the vicinity of those immediately touching it to the vicinity of others (*Principles* II, 25). The common concept of motion is confused and the Third Meditation, not so incidentally, insinuates a clearer concept of motion by defining it in terms of change of position, and defining position as a relation to surrounding bodies.

The most we can say, even of our general ideas of primary qualities, is that they are capable of becoming clear and distinct, not that they invariably are clear and distinct. And this in itself is enough to cast some doubt on the way Descartes distinguished between primary and secondary qualities in the Third Meditation. Further doubt is cast by what Descartes says about ideas which are not clear and distinct:

> The ideas I have of cold and heat are so little clear and distinct that I cannot learn from them whether cold is only the privation of heat or heat the privation of cold, whether both are real qualities or neither is. (AT VII, 43–44; HR I, 164)

But this obscurity does not hold generally for the ideas of secondary qualities in the Third Meditation. Light is a secondary quality, motion a primary one; but my idea of light is clear enough for me to recognize that darkness is the negation of light, just as my idea of motion indicates to me that rest is the negation of motion (AT VII, 45; HR I, 166).

Insofar as laying the foundations of physics involves leading us to have clearer and more distinct concepts of body and other fundamental notions of physics (like place and motion), the Third Meditation goes a long way toward laying the foundations of physics, even if it does not provide an adequate basis for the distinction between primary and secondary qualities. By the end of his discussion of our ideas of bodies, Descartes is able to say that he conceives body as a substance both extended *and* nonthinking (AT VII, 44; HR I, 165). The negative part of this conception is important, as we have seen above, in excluding certain kinds of explanation in physics, namely, explanations which involve ascribing mental attributes to physical things. But the contribution of the Third Meditation does not lie only in its digressions into what is fairly obviously the territory of physics. Its more directly theological passages also contribute.

For example, in the *Principles of Philosophy* (II, 36), having discussed at some length the nature of body and of motion, Descartes goes on to discuss the cause of motion. He distinguishes two kinds of cause of motion: the first and most universal, which produces, in general, all motion in the world, and the second, the laws of nature, which produce particular motions in things not previously in motion. We must acknowledge God as the universal cause of motion in general because he continuously creates the world. But because we know it to be one of God's perfections that he is immutable, we must suppose that the total quantity of motion in matter remains constant from one moment to the next. To suppose otherwise would be to ascribe the imperfection of inconstancy to God.

Here we have two theological doctrines—that God creates the world continuously, and that he is, because perfect, immutable—deployed to establish a fundamental law of Cartesian physics, the conservation of motion. And both of these theological doctrines are stated in the Third Meditation. Continuous creation is woven into the second of the causal proofs of God's existence (AT VII, 48–49; HR I, 168); God's perfection is repeatedly emphasized (for instance, at AT VII, 46, 48; HR I, 166, 167); that this entails his immutability is not made explicit in the Latin version of the *Meditations* (cf. the enumerations of attributes at AT VII, 40, 45; HR I, 162, 165), but this defect is consistently remedied in the French version (AT IX, 32, 36).

Other properties ascribed to God in the Third Meditation have a somewhat different importance for physics. The doctrine of continuous creation is justified, in part, on the ground that every period of time can be divided into countless parts,[7] each of which is independent of the others. And this possibility of division is one Descartes will wish to ascribe to extension as well as time (cf. the Sixth Meditation, AT VII, 85–86; HR I, 196; and *Principles* II, 20). But Descartes is careful not to say either that time and space can be divided to infinity or that they can be extended to infinity. What he will say, in the *Principles*, is that the extension of the world, for example, is indefinite rather than infinite (II, 21), where this means merely that we are incapable of finding limits in it, not that we know positively that it has no limits (I, 27). We should reserve the term "infinite" for God.

This is the kind of passage in which Descartes' intentions may easily be questioned. Perhaps he merely wishes to avoid offending the theologians, as he might, if he called any created thing infinite. But Descartes did employ the distinction between the infinite and the indefinite in his earlier, unpublished, and less cautious *Le monde* (AT XI, 32), as well as in private correspondence.[8] More- over, there are paradoxes involved in the notion of infinity which may well have given Descartes a philosophical reason for avoiding use of the term outside of the theological contexts. We should never become

> entangled in the disputes concerning the infinite, especially as it would be ridiculous for us, who are finite, to try to determine any- thing about it and, in trying to grasp it, to suppose it finite. That is why we should not concern ourselves to answer those who ask whether the half of an infinite line is infinite, and if the infinite number is even or odd and other things like that. (*Principles* I, 26)

These puzzles were a cause of some concern to any seventeenth century philosopher who thought seriously about the alleged in- finity of the world. If there is an infinite line, surely it can be divided in half. If the two halves are finite, then we have an infinite quantity arising from two finite quantities. If they are infinite, then

---

7. AT VII, 48–49; HR I, 160; AT IX, 39. Haldane and Ross translate the French (*une infinité de parties*) rather than the Latin (*partes innumeras*), but this seems to me a case where the Latin is to be preferred as more cautious.

8. Cf. the letter to Clerselier, 23 April 1649, Alquié, *Oeuvres* III, 923. It is not, however, clear that his way of drawing the distinction in this letter is equivalent to that in the *Principles*.

we have one infinite quantity which is twice as large as another. Spinoza worried about this (*Ethics* I, P12, P15S) and responded by saying that extension was indivisible. Descartes' solution is no more artificial than Spinoza's.

However we resolve the question of Descartes' sincerity in distinguishing between the infinite and the indefinite, we can at least agree that one purpose the Third Meditation serves is to introduce that distinction, which will play a large role in his public physics. God's infinity is one of the most prominent of the divine attributes (AT VII, 40, 45; HR I, 162, 165). But it is of the nature of the infinite that I, who am finite, should not grasp it (AT VII, 46; HR I, 166). And though I find that a finite thing (such as my knowledge) may be gradually increased, and though I do not see anything to prevent my knowledge from being increased "to infinity," I still recognize a difference between the merely potential infinity of my knowledge and the actual infinity of God's (AT VII, 47; HR I, 167). And by the end of the Third Meditation this distinction between the potentially and the actually infinite has been identified with the distinction between the indefinite and the infinite (AT VII, 51; HR I, 170).

IV

THE FOURTH MEDITATION may be dealt with more briefly. It does not contribute a great deal to insinuating Descartes' physical theory, but it does lay the groundwork for one important negative result. The discussion of infinity has paved the way for making an interesting addition to the list of God's attributes: because God is infinite, he is incomprehensible to a finite intellect like my own. From this I can infer that

> he is capable of innumerable things whose causes I do not know, and this is sufficient to convince me that that whole species of causes customarily drawn from purpose are useless in matters of physics; for I do not think I can, without being rash, inquire into God's [FV: *impénétrables*] purposes. (AT VII, 55; HR I, 173)

Here one of God's properties is made to yield, not a physical law, but the exclusion of a whole kind of explanation.

224

V

THE TITLE of the Fifth Meditation, "Of the essence of material things; and again, of God, that he exists," suggests that it will be much concerned with founding physics. The contents are apt to be disappointing. What the title makes seem a merely secondary concern the actual course of the meditation makes seem primary. For most readers the Fifth Meditation is the one where Descartes offers his ontological argument for God's existence, not one where he says anything very helpful about the nature of material things. Nevertheless, if we look at its contribution in the light of what has preceded it, we shall see that it does more than might at first appear.

The meditation begins by asking "Whether we can know anything certain regarding material things?" The first step toward answering this question is to consider which of our ideas of material things are clear and distinct. Here Descartes can draw on the results of the Third Meditation, but those results are subtly modified:

> I imagine distinctly that quantity which the philosophers commonly call continuous, or the extension of this quantity in length, breadth and depth—or rather, the extension of the thing to which quantity is attributed; I number various parts in it; I assign any sizes, shapes, positions and local motions that I like to those parts, and I assign any durations I like to those motions. (AT VII, 63; HR I, 179)

Note that extension, though identified with continuous quantity, is not identified with size. Size and shape are assigned to *parts of the thing to which quantity is attributed*. We have thus a hint—no more than that—of the doctrines that, strictly speaking, there is only one extended substance, and that particular corporeal things are not substances, doctrines which will be stated explicitly in the Synopsis of the *Meditations*. Explaining there why he has argued only for the distinctness of mind from body, and not for the immortality of the soul, Descartes maintains that to prove the latter would require an explanation of "the whole of physics." First, one must know that generally all substances, that is, all things which cannot exist without being created by God, are by their nature incorruptible, and can never cease to exist unless they are reduced to nothing by the same God, who denies them his concurrence. (AT VII, 14; HR I, 141)

This, to say the least, is startling. The Second and Third Meditations have clearly suggested that particular corporeal things like a piece of wax or a stone are corporeal substances.[9] But surely it would not require a miraculous change in the will of the immutable God to cause these things to cease existing.

The answer seems to be that we must not regard finite extended things as corporeal substances:

> Body, taken in general, is a substance, that is why it also [like the soul] does not perish. But the human body, insofar as it differs from other bodies, is only formed and composed of a certain configuration of members and other similar accidents . . . [it] is no longer the same if even the shape of some of its parts is changed. (AT VII, 14; HR I, 141)

"Body taken in general" is to be identified, I presume, with "the thing to which continuous quantity is attributed" in the Fifth Meditation. This object of our geometrical knowledge, this indefinitely extended thing, this physical world, is the only true corporeal substance (cf. *Principles* II, 1). If we were to add that everything is either a substance or a mode, we would quickly have the Spinozistic view that all finite extended things are only modes of one extended substance.

The Fifth Meditation (by implication) and the Synopsis (quite explicitly) show a shift in the denotation of the term "substance" away from traditional scholastic usage. Arguably this shift comes only from taking seriously the implications of traditional scholastic definitions. When the Third Meditation introduced the term "substance," it offered the following gloss: "A thing which of itself is able to exist" (*rem quae per se apta est existere;* AT VII, 44; HR I, 165). As Alquié notes (*Oeuvres* II, 663, n1) regarding a similar formula in the Fourth Replies, this follows scholastic definitions

---

9. The wax is never *called* a substance, but the passage in AT VII, 32, very strongly suggests that it is thought of as a substance. The stone is called a substance (AT VII, 44).

which can be found in Saint Thomas and Eustachius of St. Paul. But even when this is qualified as it will be in *Principles* I, 51–"a thing which needs only the ordinary concurrence of God in order to exist"—it does not leave room for many corporeal substances.

Body taken in general is not, of course, the only object of our geometrical knowledge. I know countless particulars "concerning shapes, number, motion and the like" (AT VII, 63; HR I, 179). Note the inclusion of general propositions about motion here along with mathematical truths. Together they form a class of propositions which compel my assent (AT VII, 65; HR I, 180). Insofar as physics consists of such more or less general propositions, it receives its epistemological foundation in the Fifth Meditation.

V I

THE TITLE of the Sixth Meditation announces that it will be concerned to show that material things exist and that mind and body are distinct. And so it is. But the argument for the latter thesis is compressed into one paragraph, and the argument for the existence of bodies occupies less than half of a long meditation. Descartes clearly has other fish to fry here.

One illustration of this is the curiously roundabout way Descartes approaches the solution of his main question. We know that material things *can* exist, since we perceive them clearly and distinctly insofar as we ascribe mathematical properties to them, and we know that God, being omnipotent, is capable of producing whatever we perceive in this way. But Descartes' first assault on the question "Whether material things *do* exist?" is unsuccessful:

> From the faculty of imagining which I find I use when I apply myself to those material things, it seems to follow that they exist. (AT VII, 71; HR I, 185)

Descartes will later (AT VII, 73; HR I, 187) decide that this does not in fact follow, and it is not easy to see why it should even seem to. Descartes, however, defines imagination as "a certain application of the cognitive faculty to a body which is intimately present to it" (AT VII, 72; HR I, 185), a body to which the mind is "so conjoined that it can apply itself to it whenever it pleases" (AT VII, 73; HR I, 186). This definition incorporates a certain theory of what causes the phenomenological difference between my idea of a triangle (which I can imagine) and my idea of a chiliagon (which I cannot imagine at all distinctly, though I have an idea of it sufficiently clear and distinct for me to know some of its properties). If that causal theory is correct, then there must be at least one body. But Descartes does not pretend that his explanation of our ability to imagine things is more than merely probable, and he seems to want certainty.

So Descartes' first start is a false one. Nevertheless it does offer him the opportunity to accustom his readers to the idea that if there are any bodies at all, there is probably one body to which the mind is peculiarly closely united. Moreover the distinction between intellection and imagination is quickly associated with that between primary and secondary qualities (AT VII, 74; HR I, 187). The primary qualities, which a body has insofar as it is an object of pure mathematics, are ones we can understand, whether we imagine them or not. But secondary qualities, like colors, sounds, tastes, are ones we imagine or sense, rather than understand. The implication is that our ideas of secondary qualities are ones we have only because we are united peculiarly closely to a particular body (cf. *Principles* I, 48).

Descartes' next attempt to prove the existence of bodies is more natural, appealing to sensation rather than imagination. Descartes begins (AT VII, 74; HR I, 187) by reviewing the things he had previously believed on the evidence of the senses and his grounds for doubting those beliefs. But the review is not just a reprise of the First Meditation.

New classes of belief are mentioned: he has sensed not only that he had a body with various parts but that his body was situated among other bodies which were either beneficial or harmful to it; he has measured these advantages and disadvantages by a certain sense of pleasure or pain; in addition to pleasure and pain, he has sensed various appetites (hunger, thirst) and inclinations to various affects (cheerfulness, anger). This interest in bodily sensations was suppressed prior to the Sixth Meditation, but now it is emphasized that these sensations are what give Descartes some reason to call this body *his* body (AT VII, 76; HR I, 188). And when Descartes turns to his beliefs about other bodies, the now familiar distinction between primary and secondary qualities is further amplified. A new and contentious (cf. *Principles* II, 4) secondary quality, hardness, is mentioned for the first time (AT VII, 75; HR I, 187), and the point is made that variations in the secondary qualities are what enable us to distinguish different bodies from one another.

Again, the grounds of doubt reviewed are not just the First Meditation's dream argument from God's omnipotence. Previously Descartes had passed very quickly over the classical examples of perceptual illusion—like the tower which looks round at a distance and square when we are close to it, or the statue which looks small at a distance and very large from close up (N.B.: these illusions, characteristically, involve primary qualities)—probably because they would not have yielded a sufficiently radical conclusion. Now (AT VII, 76; HR I, 189) they are mentioned, along with errors in judgment we can make even regarding bodily sensations, as when it seems to an amputee that he feels pain in a limb he no longer has.

The question, then, is "How much of what he has previously thought he sensed can survive these grounds of doubt?" This is clearly a much broader question than "Are there bodies?" though the latter question is the one Descartes undertakes to answer first. Among the various faculties I find in myself (AT VII, 79; HR I, 191) is a passive faculty of receiving the ideas of sensible things. This faculty would be useless to me unless something had an active faculty of producing those ideas. That something cannot be me, the thing whose nature it is to think, because it does not presuppose any intellection and the ideas are often produced against my will. So it must be some other substance. That substance must have either as much reality as our ideas represent it as having, or more reality. But if it had more reality, then since God has not given me any faculty for recognizing this and has given me a strong inclination to believe the contrary, he would be a deceiver if my ideas were not caused by bodies. So corporeal things exist.

Few readers have been satisfied with this argument, and I shall make no attempt to defend it here. In the Fourth Meditation Descartes had maintained that God would be a deceiver only if what we falsely believed were something we could not but believe.

If we gave our assent wrongly to a proposition we were merely inclined to believe (albeit very strongly), the fault would be ours for misusing our will, not God's. By the Sixth Meditation Descartes' ethic of belief is considerably less Pelagian. But quite apart from these questions of consistency, it is clear that the argument requires as well the same doubtful principle about the causality of our ideas as the first theistic argument of the Third Meditation.

Sometimes Descartes himself does not claim very much for his argument. In the Synopsis of the *Meditations*, for example, he writes that he does not judge his arguments for the existence of material things to be

> very useful for proving what they prove—that there is a world, that men have bodies, and the like—which have never been doubted by any man of good sense. (AT VII, 15–16; HR I, 142–143)

He offers them, he says, only because

> in considering them closely, one comes to see that they are neither so strong nor so evident as those which lead us to the knowledge of God and our soul.

Some may find in this concession a confirmation of their suspicion that the whole project of grounding certainty in the existence of a veracious God was never seriously intended.

The best view, however, seems to me to be that Descartes is careless of his proof of the existence of corporeal things because he knows it to be the least contentious of his major conclusions and he is really more interested in the broader question: "How much of what I previously thought I sensed was true?" He is certainly most anxious to emphasize that establishing the existence of material things does not entail establishing the existence of things which are, in every respect, as our ideas represent them (AT VII, 80; HR I, 191). They must have, of course, those general primary qualities which are essential to their being bodies: extension, size, shape. But they need not have the particular primary qualities we seem to perceive them as having—the sun need not have the size and shape we seem to see. Nor need they have those qualities which are not so clearly understood: light, sound, pain, and the like.

Note that here (for the first time in the meditation) bodily sensations and secondary qualities are linked together. In the Sixth

Meditation Descartes wants to assimilate secondary qualities to bodily sensations. Our perceptions of secondary qualities and our perceptions of the various states of our own bodies are alike in that both are "confused modes of thinking arising from the union, and as it were, mixture of mind with body" (AT VII, 81; HR I, 192).

When I feel pain, I am aware of a particular state of my body, namely, a state in which it is damaged in some way. But I am not aware of it merely as a damaged state of the body. "I am not only present to my body as a sailor is present to his ship." If I were, my awareness of damage to the body would be like the sailor's knowledge of damage to his ship. I would not be so deeply affected by it. As D. M. Armstrong says, "It is of the essence of physical pain that we have an *immediate* and *interested* desire that it should stop."[10] Similarly with other bodily sensations like hunger and thirst. In part they are awarenesses of particular bodily states, namely, the body's needs for food and drink. But they are not merely intellectual phenomena. They engage the will as well as the intellect.

Something similar is true of our perceptions of secondary qualities. They involve an awareness of a state of an external body. If God is not a deceiver, there must be some variations in external bodies corresponding to the variations I perceive in their colors, tastes, smells. If one thing is blue and another is yellow, there must be a further difference between them (say in the texture of their surface, and hence in the way they reflect light rays). But I do not perceive this difference simply as what it is, a difference in primary qualities. My perceptions of secondary qualities are confused by the fact that I find some of them agreeable and others unwelcome. They too engage the affective as well as the intellectual side of the mind.

Bodily sensations and perceptions of secondary qualities are part of an order instituted by God to inform me of the needs of my body and the opportunities and dangers presented to it by other bodies. Agreeable perceptions of secondary qualities are a sign that the bodies inducing them are to be sought; disagreeable ones, that they are to be avoided. So though the world of science is quite

10. D. M. Armstrong, *Bodily Sensations* (London: Routledge & Kegan Paul, 1962), p. 93.

different from the world of naive perception, there is still a foundation for my sensations.

Sometimes, however, the emphasis is on the difference between the two worlds. For example, if I judge that a space is empty because there is nothing in it which affects my senses (AT VII, 82; HR I, 193), that will be a rash error. The consideration of how much truth there is in our sensations here provides another opportunity for removing a prejudice which might stand in the way of accepting a Cartesian account of nature.

The account Descartes has given of the function of our perception of secondary qualities inevitably raises once again problems about God's goodness (AT VII, 83; HR I, 194). Though a pleasant taste and odor may be a sign that some substance will be beneficial to my body, it is not invariably so. Similarly my awareness of a bodily appetite may be quite misleading about the body's true needs, as when a man with dropsy feels thirsty. But if these bodily sensations and perceptions of secondary qualities are part of an order instituted by God, how can this be?

Descartes first considers and rejects a pseudo-explanation of the sort which would have appealed to the scholastics of his time (AT VII, 84; HR I, 194). It will not do to say that our nature is corrupt. The human body may be regarded as a kind of machine, constructed of bones, nerves, muscles, just as a clock is constructed of wheels and weights. The clock obeys the laws of nature just as much when it keeps time badly as when it keeps time well. In the same way, when the throat is dry and the body seeks drink, it obeys the laws of nature as much when it does not need drink as when it does.

Descartes is concerned with two things here. First, he wants to plant in us the idea that the human body can be conceived as a machine, capable (like a clock) of complex, regular, and precise movements even without the direction of a mind. But more importantly he wants to contrast two ways of explaining things (AT VII, 85; HR I, 195). One would explain the drinking of water by appeal to what is natural for a thing of a certain kind. Faced with a thing of that kind which drinks water when it does not need to, when, indeed, water would be harmful to it, this style of explanation will

232

speak of a nature that is corrupt. Descartes regards this as purely verbal. Both beneficial and harmful drinking are "natural" in the only clear and useful sense of the term: they exemplify laws of nature saying how a thing will act under certain conditions. Explaining things by appeal to the laws of nature is more instructive. When we are confronted with anomalous behavior, this style of explanation requires us to look for differences in the construction of things which, in conjunction with known laws, will regularly produce the anomalous result, not merely to compare it with our general idea of the kind of thing in question. So the *Principles* (II, 37), after having designated God as the first cause of motion, will characterize the laws of nature as the second cause, and will go into considerable detail regarding the laws of motion Descartes thought had to govern the world.

Having rejected scholastic explanations of self-damaging behavior, Descartes proceeds to sketch his own (AT VII, 85; HR I, 196). Roughly, it runs as follows. Mind and body are radically different substances, insofar as the one is essentially nonextended (and hence, indivisible) and the other essentially extended (and hence, divisible). Perhaps as a consequence of this, the mind cannot be directly united with the whole of the body, but only with one part of it. Physiology suggests that the locus of union is the brain, or more probably, a small part of the brain, rather than any other organ (cf. *The Passions of the Soul*, §31). But it is of the nature of body that no part of it can be moved except by a part which is in contact with it. So if one part of the body is damaged, or has a need, this can only be communicated to the mind via the brain and a complex chain of motions. But the complexity of this causal sequence inevitably means that it can be initiated at one point rather than another, and hence that the same final result (say, a sensation of thirst) can be produced in a variety of ways. Given the nature of man, as composed of mind and body, and the nature of the perceptual process, man's sensations *could* not always be indicative of the true nature of things. So the fact that they sometimes are not does nothing to impugn God's goodness.

With the soundness of this exercise in theodicy I am not concerned. What does interest me is the amount of Cartesian science that is packed into it: the divisibility of body, an outline of a mechanistic physiology of perception, and a denial of the possibility of action at a distance, with all that that implies.

The *Meditations* are indeed a good deal more than a treatise on first philosophy. The reader who has some familiarity with Descartes' physics and is alert to the possible significance of apparent digressions can find, woven into discussions of the work's main themes, much of what was to be presented more openly in the *Principles:* that body exists, that it may be identified with extension, that it is essentially divisible but not essentially perceptible to the senses, that particular bodies have certain primary qualities as a consequence of their being extended, that those qualities are capable of infinite variation, that our perception of secondary qualities depends on the union of mind and body, that variations in secondary qualities depend on variations in primary qualities, that bodies do not, of their own nature, have the capacity to move themselves, though they can respond in complex ways to external stimuli, and that they cannot move other bodies except by contact. All of this may be put under the heading of "making our concept of body clearer and more distinct." Apart from this we have a hint of the denial of the void, improved definitions of place and motion, theological doctrines which will be used to establish certain fundamental laws of motion, a rejection of final and formal causes, and an introduction to the preferred mode of explanation: laws of nature and mechanical, efficient causes. The *Meditations* are a very artfully constructed work.

POSTSCRIPT

Years ago I was asked, by a British philosopher with a keen interest in Descartes, about the then very recent book of another British philosopher with a keen interest in Descartes: "Is it *another* book on the *Meditations?*" I felt bound to answer "Yes," though I felt, as he did, that this was a criticism of a work which, in other respects, I liked very much.

This book, perhaps, is open to the same criticism. Certainly I have concentrated my attention on the *Meditations*. Perhaps one should not be too apologetic about that. A good book on the *Meditations*, a book which really improved our understanding of that difficult and fascinating classic, would not be nothing.

Nevertheless, I hope this is more than just a book on the *Meditations*. I have tried to give some sense of the larger context in which Descartes wrote his master work, of the philosophical concerns which led up to it, of the way in which it was instrumental to his later work. There is more in the *Meditations* than meets the eye.

But there is a side of Descartes which I have not even hinted at. His later writings were not concerned exclusively with answering objections and working out the details of the program sketched in the *Discourse* and the *Meditations*. Toward the end of his life he became very much interested in psychological and moral problems. This is the Descartes of *The Passions of the Soul* and the letters to Elizabeth and Christine of Sweden. He has been neglected in the English-speaking world, partly because not all the relevant materials have been translated, partly because his influence was not so enduring as that of the other Descartes. But he did have a strong influence on his contemporaries, and particularly on Spinoza. There is a story to be told about him, too. But it will have to wait for another day.

INDEX

INDEX

INDEX

Veitch, 214n

Vendler, Z., 170n

Walsh, W. H., 49n

Wax, piece of, 211–216, 219, 226

Weber, 35n

Will, 182, 231

Williams, B., 76n, 80, 81, 91–92

Wilson, M., 198n, 200n

Wittgenstein, L., 47

Wolpert, E., 54